"**A must-read. We need books like this to help us understand the world in which we live.**"

> —Nassim Nicholas Taleb, author of the *New York Times* bestseller *The Black Swan*

"**Valuable**. . . . We are a country built on self-sufficiency, Ripley writes, but we refuse to give ordinary people the information that, when delivered in factual and nonthreatening terms, can save their lives. Perhaps **it's time for the rest of us, the potential victims, to signal a Code Red. We need to know. Now.**"

> —*New York Daily News*

"**A sometimes stunning, sometimes sobering journey through disaster**, using great stories and respected science to show why some prevail and others do not. *The Unthinkable* **isn't merely a book about disaster; it's a book about survival—maybe yours.**"

> —Gavin de Becker, author of the *New York Times* bestseller *The Gift of Fear*

"Part study of the science of reaction to extreme fear, part indictment of the US government's response to the terrorist threat, part call to arms . . . **Despite its title and its subject matter, *The Unthinkable* is an optimistic book.**"

> —*The Times* (UK)

"**Entertaining** . . . the intellectual side of what could make the most instinctual difference in a moment of life-or-death odds."

> —*The Oregonian*

"Amazing tales . . . [Ripley's] **insights are absolutely fascinating,** and they could come in handy one day."

—WALTER ISAACSON, author of the *New York Times* bestseller
Einstein: His Life And Universe and vice-chairman of the Louisiana
Recovery Authority

"[Shows that] **the most important people in a pinch are the everyday ones.** . . . Ripley is a clear writer, good with an analogy, better with an anecdote."

—*Cleveland Plain Dealer*

"The most important lesson learned in this book is that **when the chips are down and the worst happens, it is most likely not the 'pros' who will save us.** It is the common, ordinary citizen—the yous and mes of the world, who will have to act and react in smart and admirable ways."

—*Knoxville News-Sentinel*

"The most magnificent account of a survivor's mind that I have ever read. It has helped me know and accept some of my reactions during my seventy-two-day ordeal in the Andes. **This book will help those who've never faced disaster to understand their own behavior and be prepared should their luck run out one day."**

—NANDO PARRADO, author of the *New York Times* bestseller *Miracle in the Andes*

"Makes sense of life today in an entirely entertaining and accessible way—all with a brimming dollop of optimism. **If you ever wondered, 'What would I do if the unthinkable happened to *me*,' you hold the answer in your hands."**

—DOUG STANTON, author of the *New York Times* bestseller
In Harm's Way: The Sinking of The USS Indianapolis *and the Extraordinary Story of Its Survivors*

"**Compelling** . . . Ripley's in-depth look at the psychology of disaster response, alongside survivors' accounts, makes for gripping reading, **sure to raise debate as well as our awareness of a life-and-death issue.**"

—*Publishers Weekly*

"Reveals why, under the same circumstances, some people caught up in a disaster survive and others do not. . . . **In her well-crafted prose, Amanda Ripley shows us all how to prepare to meet danger and increase our chances of surviving the unthinkable.**"

—BRUCE HENDERSON, author of the *New York Times* bestseller
Down to the Sea

"When a disaster occurs, we invariably learn the 'what' of the event—how many died, how many survived. . . . *The Unthinkable* **provides genuine insight into the 'why' behind the numbers. This remarkable book will not only change your life, it could very well save it.**"

—GREGG OLSEN, author of the *New York Times* bestseller *The Deep Dark: Disaster and Redemption in America's Richest Silver Mine*

"**Irresistible** . . . [Ripley] covers, with great clarity and accuracy, the science of how the body and mind respond to crisis . . . These tales leave your viscera enflamed."

—ROBERT M. SAPOLSKY, professor of biological sciences and neurology at Stanford University, and author of *Why Zebras Don't Get Ulcers*

"**Reading *The Unthinkable* will be life-changing.** While our politicians and media have been keen to exploit and fan our worst fears, **Amanda Ripley makes clear that individually and collectively we can meet head-on the hazards that periodically befall us.** We need not be afraid!"

—STEPHEN FLYNN, Senior Fellow for National Security Studies, Council on Foreign Relations, and author of *The Edge of Disaster*

The Unthinkable

Who Survives When Disaster Strikes—and Why

AMANDA RIPLEY

THREE RIVERS PRESS
NEW YORK

To John

Library of Congress Cataloging-in-Publication Data

Ripley, Amanda.
   The Unthinkable: who survives when disaster strikes and why / Amanda Ripley.
   Includes bibliographical references.
  1. Resilience (Personality trait)   2. Disasters—Psychological aspects.
3. Disaster relief.   4. Preparedness.   5. Risk management.   6. Emergency
management.   7. Crisis intervention (Mental health services)   8. Disaster
victims—Mental health.   9. Disasters—Risk assessment.   I. Title.
   BF698.35.R47R57 2008
   155.9'35—dc22   2007040315

ISBN 978-0-307-35290-3

Printed in the United States of America

Design by Lauren Dong

30 29 28 27 26 25

First Paperback Edition

Contents

Introduction

"Life Becomes Like Molten Metal"

ON THE MORNING of December 6, 1917, a bright, windless day, a French freighter called the *Mont Blanc* began to slowly pull out of the Halifax harbor in Nova Scotia. At the time, Halifax was one of the busiest ports in the British Empire. There was a war on in Europe, and the harbor groaned with the churn of ships, men, and weapons. The *Mont Blanc* was headed for France that day, carrying over twenty-five hundred tons of explosives, including TNT. While passing through a narrow channel in the harbor, a larger ship, the *Imo* from Belgium, accidentally rammed the bow of the *Mont Blanc*.

The collision itself was not catastrophic. The *Imo* sailed on, in fact. But the crew of the *Mont Blanc* knew that their ship was a floating time bomb. They tried to put out the fire, but not for very long. Then they scrambled into lifeboats and paddled for shore. For a few heartbreaking moments, the *Mont Blanc* drifted in the harbor. It brushed up against the pier, setting it on fire. Children gathered to watch the spectacle.

Many of the worst disasters in history started quite modestly. One accident led to another, until a fault line opened up in a civilization. About twenty minutes after the collision, the *Mont Blanc* exploded, sending black rain, iron, fire, and wind whipsawing through the city. It was the largest bomb explosion on record. The blast shattered windows sixty miles away. Glass blinded some one thousand people. Next, a tidal wave caused by the explosion swamped the shore. Then fire began to creep across the city. In the harbor, a black column of fire and smoke turned into a hovering white mushroom cloud. Survivors fell to their knees, convinced that they had seen a German zeppelin in the sky.

At the moment of the explosion, an Anglican priest and scholar named Samuel Henry Prince happened to be eating breakfast at a restaurant near the port. He ran to help, opening up his church as a triage station. It was, strangely enough, Prince's second disaster in five years. He had responded to another local cataclysm in 1912, when a luxury cruise liner called the *Titanic* had sunk some five hundred miles off the coast of Halifax. Back then, Prince had performed burials at sea in the frigid waters.

Prince was the kind of man who marveled at things others preferred not to think about. On the awful day of the explosion, he was astounded by what he saw. Prince watched men and women endure crude sidewalk operations without obvious pain. How was one young soldier able to work the entire day with one of his eyes knocked out? Some people experienced hallucinations. Why did parents fail to recognize their own children at the hospital—and, especially, at the morgue? Small details nagged at Prince. On the morning of the explosion, why was the very first relief station set up by a troupe of actors, of all people?

That night, a blizzard hit Halifax, the epic's final act. By the time the catastrophe had rippled out across the land, 1,963 people would be dead. In silent film footage taken after the blast, Halifax looks like it was hit by a nuclear weapon. Houses, train terminals, and churches lie like pick-up sticks on the snow-covered ground. Sleighs are piled high with corpses. "Here were to be found in one dread assembling the combined horrors of war, earthquake, fire, flood, famine and storm—a combination for the first time in the records of human disaster," Prince would write. Later, scientists developing the atomic bomb would study the Halifax explosion to see how such a blast travels across land and sea.

After helping rebuild Halifax, Prince moved to New York City to study sociology. For his PhD dissertation at Columbia University, he deconstructed the Halifax explosion. "Catastrophe and Social Change," published in 1920, was the first systematic analysis of human behavior in a disaster. "Life becomes like molten metal," he wrote. "Old customs crumble, and instability rules."

What makes Prince's work so engaging is his optimism. Despite his funereal obsessions, he saw disasters as opportunities—not just, as he put it, "a series of vicissitudes mercifully ending one day in final cataclysm." He was a minister, but he was clearly enchanted by industry. The horrific explosion had, in the end, "blown Halifax into the 20th century," forcing many changes that were for the better. His thesis opened with a quote from St. Augustine: "This awful catastrophe is not the end but the beginning. History does not end so. It is the way its chapters open."

After Prince's death, the field of human behavior in disasters would languish. Then with the onset of the cold war and a new host of anxieties about how the masses might respond to nuclear attacks, it would come back to life. After the fall of communism, it would stagnate again—until the terrorist attacks of September 11, 2001. Prince seemed to anticipate the temptation for people to avert their eyes. "This little volume on Halifax is offered as a beginning," he wrote. Don't let it be the end, he pleaded. "Knowledge will grow scientific only after the most faithful examination of many catastrophes." The remainder of the century would prove rich with material.

Most of us have imagined what it might be like to experience a plane crash or a fire or an earthquake. We have ideas about what we might do or fail to do, how it might feel for our hearts to pound in our chests, whom we might call in the final moments, and whether we might be suddenly compelled to seize the hand of the businessman sitting in the window seat. We have fears that we admit to openly and ones that we never discuss. We carry around this half-completed sentence, filling in different scenarios depending on the anxiety of the times: I wonder what I would do if . . .

Think for a moment about the narratives we know by heart. When I say the word *disaster*, many of us think of panic, hysterical crowds, and a kind of every-man-for-himself brutality; an orgy of destruction interrupted only by the civilizing influence of professional rescuers. Yet all evidence from Prince until today belies this script. Reality is a lot more interesting—and hopeful.

What Prince discovered in Halifax was that our disaster personalities can be quite different from the ones we expect to meet. But that doesn't mean they are unknowable. It just means we haven't been looking in the right places.

The Things Survivors Wish You Knew

This book came about unexpectedly. In 2004, as a reporter working on *Time* magazine's coverage of the third anniversary of 9/11, I decided to check in with some of the people who had survived the attacks. I wondered how they were doing. Unlike many of the families of the victims, the survivors had kept to themselves, for the most part. They felt so lucky—or guilty or scarred—that they hadn't wanted to make too much noise. But there were tens of thousands of these survivors out there, people who had gone to work in a skyscraper one morning and then spent hours fighting to get out of it. I was curious to hear what had happened to their lives.

I got in touch with the World Trade Center Survivors' Network, one of the first and largest support groups, and they invited me to sit in on one of their regular meetings. They met in a fluorescent-lit office space, high above the racket of Times Square. As I rode up in the elevator one evening, I prepared myself for an exchange of grief. After 9/11, I had heard so many stories. Every widow, firefighter, and victim had a unique tragedy to tell, and I can still recite those interviews almost word for word. The city's pain seemed to have no bottom.

But this meeting was not what I had expected. These people had an agenda. They had things they wanted to tell other people before the next terrorist attack, and there was urgency in the room. The survivors were from all different neighborhoods, professions, and ethnicities, but they said very similar, surprising things. They had learned so much that morning, and they wondered why no one had prepared them. One man even proposed starting a lecture circuit to educate people about how it feels to escape a skyscraper. "We were the first responders," one woman said. A sign-up sheet was passed around to start planning speaking engagements at churches and offices.

Watching them, I realized these people had glimpsed a part of the human condition that most of us never see. We worry about horrible things happening to us, but we don't know much about what it actually feels like. I wondered what they had learned.

I started to research the stories of survivors from other disasters. The overlaps were startling. People in shipwrecks, plane crashes, and floodwaters all seemed to undergo a mysterious metamorphosis. They performed better than they ever would have expected in some ways and much worse in others. I wanted to know why. What was happening to our brains to make us do so many unexpected things? Were we culturally conditioned to risk our lives for strangers in shipwrecks? Were we evolutionarily programmed to freeze in emergencies? My search for answers led me across the world, to England for its long history of studying fire behavior, to Israel for its trauma psychologists and counterterrorism experience, and back to the States to participate in simulated plane crashes and fires, as well as military research into the brain.

Writing a book about disasters may sound voyeuristic or dark, and there are times when it was. But the truth is, I was mesmerized by this subject because it gave me hope. You spend enough time covering tragedies and you start to look for a foothold. I knew there was no way to prevent all catastrophes from happening. I knew it made sense to prepare for them and work to minimize the losses. We should install smoke detectors, buy insurance, and pack "go bags." But none of those things ever felt very satisfying.

Listening to survivors, I realized we'd been holding dress rehearsals for a play without knowing any of our lines. Our government had warned us to be prepared, but it hadn't told us why. In New Orleans, after Hurricane Katrina, I learned more from regular people on street corners than I learned covering any homeland security conference.

In firehouses and brain research labs, I learned that if we get to know our disaster personalities before the disaster, we might have a slightly better chance of surviving. At the very least, we'll expunge some of the unknowns from our imaginations, and we'll uncover secrets about ourselves.

I never expected to use what I had learned anytime soon. I usually show up at disaster sites after they happen, in time for the regrets and recriminations, but not the shaking or the burning. But I was wrong, in a way. From a physiological perspective, everyday life is full of tiny disaster drills. Ironically, after writing a book about disasters, I feel less anxious overall, not more. I am a much better judge of risk now that I understand my own warped equation for dread. Having studied dozens of plane crashes, I'm more relaxed when I'm flying. And no matter how many Code-Orange-be-afraid-be-very-afraid alerts I see on the evening news, I feel some amount of peace having already glimpsed the worst-case scenario. The truth, it turns out, is usually better than the nightmare.

The Problem with Rescue Dogs

Conversations about disasters have always been colored by fear and superstition. The word *disaster,* from the Latin *dis* (away) and *astrum* (stars), can be translated as "ill-starred." After Hurricane Katrina in 2005, New Orleans mayor Ray Nagin said that God was clearly "mad at America" for invading Iraq—and at black people for "not taking care of ourselves." Inchoate as these plot lines may be, Nagin's impulse—to inject meaning into chaos—was understandable. Narrative is the beginning of recovery.

But narrative can miss important subplots. In books and official reports, the tragedy of Katrina was blamed on politicians, poverty, and poor engineering, as it should have been. But there was another conversation that should have happened—not about blame, but about understanding. What did regular people do before, during, and after the storm? Why? And what could they have done better?

These days, we tend to think of disasters as acts of God and government. Regular people only feature into the equation as victims, which is a shame. Because regular people are the most important people at a disaster scene, every time.

In 1992, a series of sewer explosions caused by a gas leak ripped through Guadalajara, Mexico's second-largest city. The violence came from below, rupturing neighborhoods block by block. Starting at 10:30 A.M., at least nine separate explosions ripped open a jagged trench more than a mile long. About three hundred people died. Some five thousand houses were razed. The Mexican Army was called in. Rescuers from California raced to help. Search-and-rescue dogs were ordered up.

But first, before anyone else, regular people were on the scene saving one another. They did incredible things, these regular people. They lifted rubble off survivors with car jacks. They used garden hoses to force air into voids where people were trapped. In fact, as in most disasters, the vast majority of rescues were done by ordinary folks. After the first two hours, very few people came out of the debris alive. The search-and-rescue dogs did not arrive until twenty-six hours after the explosion.

It's only once disaster strikes that ordinary citizens realize how important they are. For example, did you know that most serious plane accidents are survivable? On this point, the statistics are quite clear. Of all passengers involved in serious accidents between 1983 and 2000, 56 percent survived. ("Serious" is defined by the National Transportation Safety Board as accidents involving fire, severe injury, *and* substantial aircraft damage.) Moreover, survival often depends on the behavior of the passenger. These facts have been well known in the aviation industry for a long time. But unless people have been in a plane crash, most individuals have no idea.

Since 9/11 the U.S. government has sent over $23 billion to states and cities in the name of homeland security. Almost none of that money has gone toward intelligently enrolling regular people like you and me in the cause. Why don't we tell people what to do when the nation is on Orange Alert against a terrorist attack—instead of just telling them to be afraid? Why does every firefighter in Casper, Wyoming (pop. 50,632), have an eighteen-hundred-dollar HAZMAT suit—but we don't each have a statistically derived ranking of the hazards we actually face, and a smart, creative plan for dealing with them?

All across the nation we have snapped plates of armor onto our professional lifesavers. In return, we have very high expectations for these brave men and women. Only after everything goes wrong do we realize we're on our own. And the bigger the disaster, the longer we will be on our own. No fire department can be everywhere at once, no matter how good their gear.

The July 7, 2005, terrorist attacks on London buses and subway trains killed fifty-two people. The city's extensive surveillance camera system was widely praised for its help during the ensuing investigation. Less well known is how unhelpful the technology was to regular people on the trains. The official report on the response would find one "overarching, fundamental lesson": emergency plans had been designed to meet the needs of emergency *officials,* not regular people. On that day, the passengers had no way to let the train drivers know that there had been an explosion. They also had trouble getting out; the train doors were not designed to be opened by passengers. Finally, passengers couldn't find first aid kits to treat the wounded. It turned out that supplies were kept in subway supervisors' offices, not on the trains.

Luck Is Unreliable

Here's the central conundrum addressed by this book: we flirt shamelessly with risk today, constructing city skylines in hurricane alleys and neighborhoods on top of fault lines. Largely because of where we live, disasters have become more frequent and more expensive. But as we build ever more impressive buildings and airplanes, we do less and less to build better survivors.

How did we get this way? The more I learned, the more I wondered how much of our survival behaviors—and misbehaviors—could be explained by evolution. After all, we evolved to escape predators, not buildings that reach a quarter mile into the sky. Has technology simply outpaced our survival mechanisms?

But there are two kinds of evolution: the genetic kind and the cultural kind. Both shape our behavior, and the cultural kind has gotten a lot faster. We now have many ways to create "instincts": we can learn to do better or worse. We can pass on traditions about how to deal with modern risks, just as we pass on language.

So then the question became, why weren't we doing a better job instilling survival skills through our culture? *Globalization* is one of those words that gets hijacked so often it loses its meaning. That's partly because the word encompasses so much, including opposing ideas. In the past two centuries, we have become far less connected to our families and communities. At the same time, we have become more dependent upon one another and technology. We are isolated in our codependence, paradoxically.

More than 80 percent of Americans now live in or near cities and rely upon a sprawling network of public and private entities to get food, water, electricity, transportation, and medicine. We make almost nothing for ourselves. So a disaster that strikes one group of people is more likely than ever to affect others. But just as we have become more interdependent, we have become more detached—from our neighborhoods and traditions. This is a break from our evolutionary history. Humans and our evolutionary ancestors spent most of the past several million years living in small groups of relatives. We evolved through passing on our genes—and our wisdom—from generation to generation. But today, the kinds of social ties that used to protect us from threats get neglected. In their place, we have substituted new technology, which only works some of the time.

In May of 1960, the largest earthquake ever measured occurred off the coast of Chile, killing a thousand people. Luckily, Hawaii's automated alert system kicked in, and tsunami sirens went off ten hours before the island was hit. The technology worked exactly as planned. But it turned out that most of the people who heard the siren did not evacuate. They weren't sure what the noise meant. Some thought it signaled that they should be alert for more information. The technology was there but the traditions weren't. A total of sixty-one people died in Hawaii that day.

It's hard to trace a single cause for why we do what we do under extreme duress. The chapters that follow allow us to test several hypotheses against real disasters. I've tried to resist the urge to concoct one grand narrative. But even in that complexity, simple truths emerge. The more disaster survivors I met, the more convinced I became that the solutions to our problems were not necessarily complicated. They were more social than technological. Some were old-fashioned. But we need to understand how our brain works in disasters before we can save ourselves.

Before we go any further, it's probably wise to acknowledge that the vast majority of Westerners do not die in disasters; they die of diseases that attack from within, not violence that comes from outside. Alzheimer's disease kills many more people than fire. Even if you do make a particularly dramatic exit, it probably won't be in a disaster. You are more likely to die of food poisoning than you are of drowning.

It is, however, quite likely that you will be *affected* by a disaster. In an August 2006 *Time* magazine poll of one thousand Americans, about half of those surveyed said they had personally experienced a disaster or public emergency. In fact, about 91 percent of Americans live in places at a moderate-to-high risk of earthquakes, volcanoes, tornadoes, wildfires, hurricanes, flooding, high-wind damage, or terrorism, according to an estimate calculated in 2006 for *Time* by the Hazards and Vulnerability Research Institute at the University of South Carolina.

Traditionally, the word *disaster* refers to any sudden calamity causing great loss of life or property. You'll notice that in this book I veer off into misfortunes that don't technically fit: car accidents and shootings, for example. But I want to include these everyday tragedies for two reasons. First, because human behavior is the same, whether we are in a cruise ship or a Honda. We can, strange as it may sound, learn how we will behave in earthquakes from studying how we behave in a holdup, and vice versa. Car accidents and shooting rampages are, like airplane crashes, modern calamities that we did not evolve to survive.

The other reason to define disasters broadly is that small tragedies add up to megadisasters. Cumulatively, car accidents kill forty thousand people in the United States each year. Everyone reading this book knows someone who died in a car accident. Guns kill another thirty thousand Americans every year. For the rippling circles of friends and families that the victims leave behind, a gunshot feels exactly like a disaster, without the national recognition. So I define the word broadly to include all kinds of accidents that kill too many people.

One last caveat: disasters are predictable, but surviving them is not. No one can promise you a plan of escape. If life—and death—were that simple, this book would already have been written. But that doesn't mean we should live in willful ignorance, either. As Hunter S. Thompson said, "Call on God, but row away from the rocks."

We need to get to know our oldest personality, the one that takes over in a crisis and even makes fleeting appearances in our daily lives. It is at the core of who we are. "If an engineer wants to know about what he's designing, he puts it under great amounts of stress," says Peter Hancock, who has been studying human performance for more than twenty years for the U.S. military. "It's the same with human beings. If you want to find out how things operate under normal conditions, it's very interesting to find out how we operate under stress." Without too much trouble, we can teach our brains to work more quickly, maybe even more wisely, under great stress. We have more control over our fates than we think. But we need to stop underestimating ourselves.

The knowledge is out there. In laboratories and on shooting ranges, there are people who know what happens to our bodies and minds under extreme duress. Scientists who study the brain's fear response can now see which parts of our brains light up under stress. Military researchers conduct elaborate experiments to try to predict who will melt down in a crisis and who will thrive. Police, soldiers, race car drivers, and helicopter pilots train to anticipate the strange behaviors they will encounter at the worst of times. They know that it's too late to learn those lessons in the midst of a crisis.

Then there are the survivors of disasters, the witnesses who channel the voices of the victims. They were there, sitting next to them, seeing what they saw. And afterward, the survivors spend some portion of their lives thinking about why they lived when so many did not. They were lucky, all of them. Luck is unreliable. But almost all of the survivors I have met say there are things they wish they had known, things they want you to know.

Unfortunately, all of these good people rarely talk to one another. Airplane safety experts don't trade stories with neuroscientists. Special Forces instructors don't spend a lot of time with hurricane victims. And none of these people have much opportunity to share what they know with regular people. So their wisdom remains stashed away in a sort of black box of the human experience.

This book goes inside the black box and stays there. *The Unthinkable* is not a book about disaster recovery; it's about what happens in the midst—before the police and firefighters arrive, before reporters show up in their rain slickers, before a structure is imposed on the loss. This is a book about the survival arc we all must travel to get from danger to safety.

The Survival Arc

In every kind of disaster, we start in about the same place and travel through three phases. We'll call the first phase denial. Except in extremely dire cases, we tend to display a surprisingly creative and willful brand of denial. This denial can take the form of delay, which can be fatal, as it was for some on 9/11. But why do we do it, if it is so dangerous? What other functions does denial serve?

How long the delay lasts depends in large part on how we calculate risk. Our risk analysis depends less upon facts than upon a shadowy sense of dread, as Chapter 2 details through the story of a man waiting for Hurricane Katrina in New Orleans.

Once we get through the initial shock of the denial phase, we move into deliberation, the second phase of the survival arc. We know something is terribly wrong, but we don't know what to do about it. How do we decide? The first thing to understand is that nothing is normal. We think and perceive differently. We become superheroes with learning disabilities. Chapter 3 explores the anatomy of fear through the story of a diplomat taken hostage at a cocktail party. "There are times when fear is good," Aeschylus said. "It must keep its watchful place at the heart's controls." But for every gift the body gives us in a disaster, it takes at least one away—sometimes bladder control, other times vision.

We all share a basic fear response. So why do some people get out of a burning building while others do not? Chapter 4 investigates resilience, that elixir of survival. Who has it? Does gender matter? What about personality or race? But almost no one goes through a disaster alone. Chapter 5 is about groupthink, the effect of the crowd on our deliberation. How well our group functions depends largely on who is in the group. Whom we live and work with matters.

Finally, we reach the third phase of the survival arc: the decisive moment. We've accepted that we are in danger; we've deliberated our options. Now we take action. We'll start with the exception. Chapter 6 is about panic, the most misunderstood behavior in the disaster repertoire. What does it take to spark a panic? And what does it feel like to be caught in one?

Many—if not most—people tend to shut down entirely in a disaster, quite the opposite of panicking. They go slack and seem to lose all awareness. But their paralysis can be strategic. Chapter 7 will take us into the horrific Virginia Tech shooting rampage, the deadliest in U.S. history, through the eyes of a fortunate student who did nothing.

Next, we will consider the opposite of nothing. Chapter 8 investigates the hero. What possible evolutionary explanation could there be for a man who jumps into a frozen river to save strangers?

Finally, we think bigger: how can we turn ourselves into better survivors? We'll meet revolutionaries who have trained regular people to survive, according to how our brains actually work—individuals who have taught entire towns to escape tsunami and major corporations to flee a skyscraper.

The three chronological phases—denial, deliberation, and the decisive moment—make up the structure of this book. Real life doesn't usually follow a linear arc, of course. Sometimes the path to survival is more like a looping roller coaster, doubling up and back upon itself as we struggle to find true north. So within each section you will notice that we often glimpse the other stages. There is, unfortunately, no single script in these situations. But it's rare that anyone survives a disaster without pushing—or being pushed—through each of these three main stages at least once.

On our tour of the black box, I will take you down a stairwell in the World Trade Center, onto a sinking ship in the Baltic Sea, and out of a burning airplane that forever changed the way safety experts thought about passengers. The point of all of this is to answer two simple questions: What happens to us in the midst of a disaster? And why do some of us do so much better than others? Our disaster personalities are more complex and ancient than we think. But they are also more malleable.

Part One
Denial

1

Delay

Procrastinating in
Tower 1

ON FEBRUARY 26, 1993, when terrorists attacked the World Trade Center for the first time, Elia Zedeño was in an express elevator carrying a slice of Sbarro's pizza. She had taken a new temporary worker to the food court to show him around, and they were on their way back to their desks. When the bomb exploded, they heard a loud pop and the elevator stopped and began to descend. Then it stopped for good, trapping her and five other people. Smoke began to slowly coil in from below. Two men grappled with the door. A woman dropped to her knees and started praying, making Zedeño nervous. Then one of the men calmly directed everyone to get low and cover their faces. They all did as they were told.

Zedeño concentrated on keeping her breathing shallow and slow. But the more she tried to calm down, the harder her heart seemed to pound. Then they heard a man screaming in the elevator next to them. "I'm burning up!" he yelled as he banged on the metal box around him. But soon he was quiet. "I remember thinking, 'We're going to be next,'" Zedeño says. She visualized rescue workers finding them dead inside the elevator later. Just then, she thought she would lunge for the doors and start banging herself. But before she could, the temp had started doing it for her. He was screaming and banging. So Zedeño took charge of quieting him down. "Robert, calm down. You're going to inhale too much smoke," she told him. He started to cough and returned to the floor.

It was around then that Zedeño was filled with a wave of peace, inexplicably. "Regardless of the outcome, I knew everything was going to be OK," she remembers. "My breath became effortless. My mind no longer wandered. Suddenly, I wasn't there anymore. I was just watching. I could see the people lying in the elevator. The sounds were far away, and I was just hovering. I had no emotions."

When they'd been in the elevator for about an hour, a firefighter managed to rip open the door and pull them out. It turned out the car had returned to the lobby level, and that's where they'd been all along. Zedeño could not see the face of the firefighter who pulled her out; the smoke was too thick. She did as he instructed, grabbing onto a rope and following it out through the lobby and out the doors. She was stunned by the darkness in the lobby and the emptiness outside. She thought that once she had made it out of her own private catastrophe, everything would be normal, bustling and bright. She never imagined that a place could look so different.

In the basement below, a Ryder truck full of eleven hundred pounds of explosives had left a crater five stories deep. Six people had died. It was the largest full-building evacuation in U.S. history, and nothing had gone the way it was supposed to go. Smoke purled up the stairways. The power failed, rendering the emergency communications system useless and the stairways dark. People moved extraordinarily slowly. Ten hours after the explosion, firefighters were still finding people who had not yet evacuated in their offices.

After the bombing, glow-in-the-dark tape and backup power generators were installed in the Trade Center. Both helped save lives eight years later. But still no one fully answered the fundamental question: why did people move so slowly? And what did it mean about all of our assumptions about skyscrapers—and the Trade Center in particular? The 1993 bombing became a story about terrorism, as would the attacks on the same buildings eight years later, and rightly so. But they were also stories of procrastination and denial, the first phase of the human disaster experience.

A few days later, Zedeño was right back at work in a neighboring building. One month later, her office reopened on the seventy-third floor of Tower 1. She started riding the same elevator to work. But it was months before she could get the taste of soot out of her mouth. She thought about leaving the towers, but not with any conviction. "I remember saying, 'This could happen again.' And someone said, 'Lightning never strikes twice.'"

"Don't Worry. It's in Your Head!"

Zedeño has a small stature, round glasses, and Dizzy Gillespie cheeks when she smiles, which happens often. She came to America with her family from Cuba when she was eleven. Her parents had spent her entire childhood plotting to get away from Fidel Castro. When they finally got permission to leave in the early 1970s, they moved to West New York, New Jersey, where their daughter could see the brand-new Trade Center Towers sunning themselves almost everywhere she went.

When she was nineteen, Zedeño visited the Trade Center for the first time. She came to apply for a secretarial job with the Port Authority of New York/New Jersey. She had no idea what the Port Authority did—or even that it owned the Trade Center—but a girlfriend convinced her to fill out the application. When she returned for her second interview, her mother came with her. The boss hired her on the spot, and, on her lunch break, Zedeño ran to the plaza to tell her mother. "What will you do?" she asked her mother, who had no idea how to get home to New Jersey. "I will sit right here and wait for you," her mother announced. They took the train home together that evening.

Eventually, Zedeño got promoted to the finance section. Her office had regular fire drills, which consisted of gathering in the hallway to gossip. During a blackout in 1990, she and her office mates walked down the tower's stairs. That's how they learned that homeless people had been using the lower stairwells as bathrooms. "We were laughing and talking," she remembers. When Zedeño talks, her voice goes up at the end of her sentences, like a child telling you something outrageous. "The whole thing was a joke!"

Zedeño is a witness wherever she goes. She remembers life in surround-sound detail. When I ask her what it was like to leave Cuba as a little girl, she tells me about the day she left in April of 1971. Her mother was doing her hair when they heard the sound of a motorcycle. "Only one man in town had a motorcycle, and it didn't sound like that," she says. Suddenly, the sound stopped in front of their house. A soldier walked in the front door without knocking and told them to leave. Zedeño knew this was good news: they had finally won permission to go to America. Fifteen minutes later, they left their house forever. They were terrified the whole journey out, but they made it. When they arrived in Miami, Zedeño ran down the aisles of a supermarket yelling out descriptions of everything she saw.

By September 2001, Zedeño had worked in the towers for over twenty-one years. She was forty-one years old, and she managed five employees on the seventy-third floor of Tower 1. Her group oversaw the Port Authority's engineering consultants. On 9/11, Zedeño got to work a little after 8:00 A.M. She settled into her cubicle and listened to her voice-mail messages. In an hour, she would head up to the cafeteria to get some breakfast, as usual.

The Trade Center did not feel like a cluster of seven buildings; it felt like a city. Every day, fifty thousand people came to work there, and another two hundred thousand passed through. The plaza underneath held the largest shopping mall in Lower Manhattan. "You didn't need to leave for anything," Zedeño says. The complex had 103 elevators—and its own zip code (10048). Bomb threats and small fires were not uncommon. The engine company across the street sometimes got called to the Trade Center eight times a day. Zedeño got used to seeing firefighters in the elevators. Days later, she would hear that there had been smoke somewhere in the building. It might have been two football fields away from her.

At 8:46 A.M., an American Airlines Boeing 767 traveling 490 mph struck the building eleven floors above her. When the plane hit Zedeño's building, the effect was not subtle. It obliterated four floors immediately. From her desk, Zedeño heard a booming explosion and felt the building lurch to the south, as if it might topple. It had never done that before, not even in 1993. This time, she grabbed her desk and held on, lifting her feet off the floor. "I actually expected the ceiling to fall and the building to cave in," she remembers. At the time, she screamed, "What's happening?"

Talking about it now, in a deli across from the void where the towers once stood, Zedeño wonders why she didn't immediately run for the stairs. She'd been through this before, after all. But what she really wanted, quite desperately, was for someone to answer back: "Everything is OK! Don't worry. It's in your head!" At the moment of impact, Zedeño had entered a rarefied zone. The rules of normal life were suspended. Her entire body and mind changed. She would wind her way through a series of phases along the survival arc. First would be a thicket of disbelief, followed by frantic deliberation, and, finally, action. We will witness all three here, but more than anything else, Zedeño's story is one of denial.

Zedeño has revisited the moments of her escape from the Trade Center until they are worn and familiar. She now gives tours of Ground Zero to tourists from around the world. But still there are riddles she cannot decipher, behavioral glitches that don't make obvious sense. More than anything else, she is mystified by how slow she was to accept what was happening all day long.

After the plane hit the building, Zedeño told me, she wanted nothing so much as to stay. Like her, I was perplexed by this reaction. Shouldn't a primal, survival instinct have kicked in, propelling her to the door? I wondered if Zedeño was unusual. So I went to the National Fire Academy to find out more. The instructors at the school, located on the rolling grounds of a former Catholic college in rural Maryland, are veteran firefighters who have witnessed just about every conceivable form of human behavior in fire. I met Jack Rowley, who spent thirty-three years as a firefighter in Columbus, Ohio. When I told him about Zedeño, he told me that he saw this kind of curious indifference all the time. In fact, he came to consider one particular kind of fire a regular Saturday night ritual. His station house would get dispatched to a bar; he would walk into the establishment and see smoke. But he would also see customers sitting at the bar nursing their beers. "We would say, 'Looks like there's a fire here,'" he says. He'd ask the customers if they felt like evacuating. "They would say, 'No, we'll be just fine.'"

One of the few people who has extensively analyzed behavior at the Trade Center in both 1993 and 2001 is Guylène Proulx at Canada's National Research Council. And what she saw fit with Zedeño's memory exactly. "Actual human behavior in fires is somewhat different from the 'panic' scenario. What is regularly observed is a lethargic response," she wrote in a 2002 article in the journal *Fire Protection Engineering*. "People are often cool during fires, ignoring or delaying their response."

In a May 19, 2006, column in the *Wall Street Journal,* Matthew Kaminski wrote about a recent flight he'd taken from Paris to New York. Three hours out of Paris, halfway into the movie *Jarhead,* Kaminski heard a loud thud and felt the plane shudder and swerve. "The captain made no announcement. No one asked the flight attendants a thing," he wrote. And yet, wrote Kaminski, a veteran traveler, "My stomach told me to worry."

About an hour later, the pilot announced the plane would be making an emergency landing in St. John's, Newfoundland. It seems one of the plane's four engines had blown out. As the plane approached the landing strip, the passengers could see fire trucks and ambulances on the tarmac below. The French flight attendant's English was deteriorating fast. In a high-pitched voice, she ordered the passengers to "Brace, brace!" And what did about half the passengers do in this moment of exquisite tension? Did they panic or weep or pray to God? No. They laughed.

The plane, as it turned out, landed safely. And Kaminski was left to marvel at his fellow passengers' well-developed sense of irony.

Laughter—or silence—is a classic manifestation of denial, as is delay. Zedeño was not alone. On average, Trade Center survivors waited six minutes before heading downstairs, according to a 2005 National Institute of Standards and Technology (NIST) study drawn from interviews with nearly nine hundred survivors. (The average would likely be higher if those who died had been able to respond to the survey.) Some waited as long as forty-five minutes. People occupied themselves in all kinds of interesting ways. Some helped coworkers who were disabled or obese. In Tower 2, many people followed fatal instructions to stay put. Staying inside was, after all, the standard protocol for skyscraper fires. But ultimately, the threat should have demanded immediate attention. Eventually, almost everyone saw smoke, smelled jet fuel, or heard someone giving the order to leave. Even then, many called relatives and friends. About one thousand individuals took the time to shut down their computers, according to NIST. "The building started to sway and everything started shaking," one person on a floor in the sixties of Tower 1 told NIST. "I knew there was something wrong." Notice what comes next: "I ran to my desk and made a couple of phone calls. I dialed about five times trying to reach my [spouse]. I also called my sisters to find out more information."

Why do we procrastinate leaving? The denial phase is a humbling one. It takes a while to come to terms with our miserable luck. Rowley puts it this way: "Fires only happen to other people." We have a tendency to believe that everything is OK because, well, it almost always has been before. Psychologists call this tendency "normalcy bias." The human brain works by identifying patterns. It uses information from the past to understand what is happening in the present and to anticipate the future. This strategy works elegantly in most situations. But we inevitably see patterns where they don't exist. In other words, we are slow to recognize exceptions. There is also the peer-pressure factor. All of us have been in situations that looked ominous, and they almost always turn out to be innocuous. If we behave otherwise, we risk social embarrassment by overreacting. So we err on the side of underreacting.

But it would be a mistake to assume that we just waste time during this delay. Given time to think, people in disasters need information like they need shelter and water. Their brains lack the patterns they need to make a good decision, so they wisely search for better data. No matter what we are told by a man in a uniform, no matter how shrill the alarm, we check in with one another. This "milling" ritual is part of the second phase of deliberation. How and with whom you mill can dramatically influence your chances of survival. For now, it's fair to say that milling is a useful process that can take a painfully long time to complete.

"Get Out of the Building!"

Luckily, one of Zedeño's colleagues passed through the denial phase immediately. He screamed at her: "Get out of the building!" His brain worked faster, for reasons we'll go into later. Zedeño still wonders what she would have done if he hadn't told her to leave. As it was, she still found ways to delay a little longer. First, she reached for her purse. Then she started walking in circles in her cubicle. "I was looking for something to take with me. It was like I was in a trance." She picked up a mystery novel she'd been reading. Then she looked for more things to take. This gathering process is common in life-or-death situations. Facing a void of unknown, we want to be prepared with as many supplies as possible. And, as with normalcy bias, we find comfort in our usual habits. (In a survey of 1,444 survivors after the attacks, 40 percent would say they gathered items before leaving.)

Finally, Zedeño headed into the stairwell. She was taking action, the last stage in the process. But her journey had only just begun. She would cycle through the phases of "disaster think" over and over. Disbelief and deliberation would continue to stall her descent. "I never found myself in a hurry," she says. "It's weird because the sound, the way the building shook, should have kept me going fast. But it was almost as if I put the sound away in my mind."

On average, the estimated 15,410 people who got out of the Trade Center took about a minute to make it down each floor, the NIST findings show. A minute may not sound like a long time, but it was shocking to people who design and build tall buildings. It was twice as long as the standard engineering codes had predicted—and the buildings were less than half full. In a 110-story building, a minute per floor is just too slow.

Most of the people who died on 9/11 had no choices. They were above the impact zone of the planes and could not find a way out. Of the thousands who had access to open stairwells and time to use them, all but about 135 did manage to escape, the NIST report found. But the most important finding from the Trade Center evacuation is what did not happen. The attacks took place on the same day as the mayoral election in New York City. Many people had stopped at the polls to vote and were late to work. Others had taken their children into school for the first day of classes. Meanwhile, the New York Stock Exchange does not open until 9:30 A.M., so the trading firms were not fully staffed yet. And the Trade Center's visiting platform did not open to tourists until 9:30 A.M.

The fires caused by the 9/11 attacks were the deadliest in American history, killing 2,666 people. Had the buildings been full that morning, the slow evacuation would have translated into more than five times the casualties. It's hard to imagine that kind of body count. This was already an unprecedented tragedy for the United States, after all. But had the attacks happened at a different time, at least fourteen thousand people would have been killed, according to NIST's conservative estimates based on the rate of movement on 9/11. And the exasperating crawl of the evacuation would have been a topic of endless public debate.

Since the first skyscraper was built in 1885 in Chicago, these monuments to human engineering have been designed without much consideration for how human beings actually behave. The people who work in skyscrapers have never been required to undergo regular full-evacuation drills, which could dramatically improve their escape times. When they do have drills, most people see them as a waste of time. They overestimate how well their minds will perform in a real crisis. When the alarm goes off, they know they are being interrupted and inconvenienced, but they don't necessarily know how much they might one day appreciate the remedial help.

When she gives tours of Ground Zero, the number one question Zedeño gets asked is, How did people behave in the stairwell? Were people panicking? No one expects the answer they get. "Everybody was very calm, very calm," Zedeño tells them. Only one woman got hysterical—screaming and hyperventilating in the staircase. Zedeño gives her the benefit of the doubt. "I don't know what this woman saw," she says. The woman was walking with a man who had blood on his forehead.

The man kept repeating, "We were the lucky ones, we were the lucky ones." Zedeño and the rest of the crowd moved to the side in the narrow stairway so the two of them could go ahead.

Crowds generally become very quiet and docile in a true disaster. Of course, on 9/11, no one in the stairways expected the towers to collapse. We'll never know how they would have behaved had they known. But even in other, more overtly dire situations, crowds don't tolerate irrational panic behavior. Most of the time, people remain consistently orderly—and kind, much kinder than they would have been on a normal day. One of Zedeño's coworkers weighed over three hundred pounds and was in a wheelchair. He worked on the sixty-ninth floor in 1993—and in 2001. Both times, his coworkers carried him all the way down the stairs.

During the first thirty floors of her descent, Zedeño learned that the explosion she'd heard was a plane hitting the tower. She promptly made up a story for herself to explain what had happened. Her brain reached into its database of patterns for a reasonable explanation, in other words. "I said to myself, 'Poor pilot. He must have had a heart attack or a stroke.'" She would revise the story again and again that day, underestimating the gravity of the attacks each time.

At the forty-fourth floor, someone told Zedeño and the people near her to switch stairways. She's not sure who said this, but she remembers someone saying there were fires below in that staircase. So they all filed out into the sky lobby and queued up at another stairway entrance. Zedeño stood facing the windows of the sky lobby. About seventeen minutes had passed since the first plane hit.

Suddenly, another explosion shook the tower. Zedeño looked up and saw balls of fire and black smoke. "I don't remember the sound, for some reason," she says. Like many people in disasters, her memory and her senses switched on and off at certain key points. But she does remember somebody screaming: "Get away from the windows!" Zedeño turned and ran toward the center of the building.

Until now, Zedeño had been mostly calm and quiet. But as she ran from the explosion, she felt a new sensation. She was filled with a rush of anger. I ask her whom she was angry at, expecting her to say whoever was causing the explosions. But what she says, very slowly and deliberately, is this: "How . . . could . . . I . . . have been so stupid to put myself inside this building again after what happened in 1993? I should have known better." Zedeño was furious at herself. As she ran, she experienced a moment of clarity—which can be decidedly unhelpful. "I kept saying to myself, 'I'm on the forty-fourth floor of a building. Where am I going? I'm still way up high. I can't go anywhere!'"

Then everything changed again just as quickly. The group stopped running, the anger faded away, and things returned, instantly, to the previous calm. "Every single one of us turned around and marched right back to the stairway as if nothing ever had happened," Zedeño says. She smiles when she says this. She knows it sounds strange. Disaster victims often oscillate between horrifying realizations and mechanical submission. As Zedeño describes it, they can be remarkably obedient:

> We were like robots. There were no comments as to, "What do you think happened outside?" Nobody ran to the windows to see what was happening. Nobody pushed anybody. Nobody tried to get into the stairway before anyone else. Everybody just went right back as a group and continued to funnel into the stairway in an orderly fashion.

I ask Zedeño what she thought the sound of this second explosion was. At that moment, she says, she did not think about it at all. "As far as I'm concerned, I'm telling you, it was as if it didn't happen. It's not even that I forgot it. It's just that it was as if it never happened. Never." Psychologists call this "dissociation." Most often, you hear the word used to describe the way children distance themselves from physical or sexual abuse. But it happens in life-or-death situations too. It can be a coping mechanism—a productive and extreme form of denial, in a sense. As Zedeño puts it, "I could not afford to dwell on it. My job was to just take it one step at a time."

Soon afterward, though, Zedeño heard someone in the stairwell say that another plane had hit the towers. That information conflicted with her heart-attack theory. So she promptly made up a new story for herself. This, too, was a clever coping device. "I said, 'Those idiots! They were racing! And they ended up hitting us. I can't believe people are so stupid.'"

Several floors later, as the slow descent wore on, she heard some more disturbing information. A man behind her noted that one plane had hit about fifteen minutes after the other. She turned to him as if he had told her something new and surprising, and she announced to herself as much as to him, "It was intentional!" He looked back at her. "Yes," he said. Her carefully constructed narrative could not absorb this information. So Zedeño did the most pragmatic thing she could do: she ignored it. "I put it out of my mind as if it hadn't happened," she says. Denial can be remarkably agile.

Around the twentieth floor, Zedeño started passing a lot of firefighters coming up the stairs. Again, the instinct of the crowd was to be generous. "I remember thinking the firemen looked tired. I wished we had bottles of water to give them," she says. The evacuees kept moving to the side to give the firefighters more space, but the firefighters urged them to keep going down, don't stop, don't stop.

Zedeño remembers certain sounds from that descent with perfect clarity. There were two men, probably firefighters, coming up below her. At each floor, they would stop and yell, "Does anyone need help? Is there anyone here?" She heard their voices floating upward several minutes before she saw the men. Then they passed her and she heard their voices above her, getting farther and farther away. She doesn't know what happened to them. "Their voices stayed with me. I can still hear them now. Their voices haunted me for a long time."

Nothing imprints the brain more effectively than fear. Certain details from life-or-death events stay with us for the rest of our lives, like scars in our consciousness. They can cause debilitating problems. They can require years of therapy to repair. But, like most disaster behaviors, they can be helpful, too. They are there to protect us from getting into the same situation again.

A Woman in Red

Finally, about an hour after she had left her cubicle, Zedeño emerged into the light of the Trade Center lobby. She felt a flush of happiness. She was on the ground at last. She looked around and saw firefighters and other people moving in slow motion, a common distortion in extreme situations. Then she looked outside and gasped.

As when she'd emerged from the elevator after the 1993 bombing, she'd expected to see normal life, bustling on indifferently. Here is how Zedeño describes this powerful presumption that the trouble was limited to her immediate vicinity, which psychologists call the "illusion of centrality":

> When you're in trauma, the mind says, this is a very local problem. This is your little world, and everything outside is fine. It can't afford to say that everything outside is horrible. The sound that I heard on the seventy-third floor should have told me, this is bad. The feeling of the building shaking should have told me, this is bad. The explosion when I was on the forty-fourth floor: bad. The smell of debris in the lower stairways: bad. Yet in every single moment, I made it my little world here. And nothing else exists.

But on 9/11, when she looked out the windows of the Trade Center lobby, Zedeño could no longer suspend disbelief. Pay close attention to what happened next, as she walked toward the front doors, staring at the bodies lying motionless on the plaza. It is the story of how the human mind processes overwhelming peril:

> I'm slowing down because I'm starting to realize I'm not just looking at debris. My mind says, "It's the wrong color." That was the first thing. Then I start saying, "It's the wrong shape." Over and over in my mind: "It's the wrong shape." It was like I was trying to keep the information out. My eyes were not allowing me to understand. I

couldn't afford it. So I was like, "No, it can't be." Then when I finally realized what it meant to see the wrong color, the wrong shape, that's when I realized, I'm seeing bodies. That's when I froze.

"Freezing" is as common as fleeing in the repertoire of human disaster responses. But it's also a fascinating, complicated response. It has meant certain death for many thousands of people over the centuries. Zedeño, however, had a personal savior.

Just then, a woman—a stranger—appeared at Zedeño's side and linked arms with her. The woman said: "We're getting out of here." Zedeño looked down at the woman's arm. She still remembers the woman's dark skin tone, similar to her own, and the red sleeve of her shirt. And then, Zedeño stopped being able to see altogether. "Because of the smoke?" I ask her. "No, no, no. There was no smoke there. I didn't see anything at all."

Zedeño went temporarily blind at that moment. When she describes this remarkable occurrence now, she does it matter-of-factly. She was not frightened when this happened, she says. Just numb. She relied on hearing—and this woman in red, who began to pull her toward the doors. As they walked, the woman talked and talked. Zedeño can't remember a word she said. "It's funny how I tuned out everything she said. But she kept talking, she never shut up," she says, laughing. "It was so weird! She never shut up." But when the two of them got outside, Zedeño did hear her say, "Look, we made it." In response, Zedeño remembers saying: "Yeah, we're outside." But in fact she still couldn't see anything. She never saw the woman's face.

At that moment, Zedeño heard a new sound. It was a rumbling, and it was close by. It was 9:59 A.M. At the time, she thought, "It's another airplane." Three notions passed through her mind in rapid sequence: "Airplane, war, a building is coming down." With that, she screamed— either out loud or in her head, she can't remember which—"Inside!" Her vision returned, just when she needed it again. This time, there was no denial. She turned and saw the revolving door of Five World Trade, with Borders bookstore on her right. And she ran through the door. She never saw the woman in red again.

"The only thing I remember is the sound getting louder behind me, and I felt a strong wind. And when I felt the wind rushing right through me, I remember thinking, 'I'm not going to outrun this. It's too late. I can't run fast enough.'" As the other tower—Tower 2—collapsed like a locomotive running into the ground, the force knocked her off her feet.

Right after the tremendous crack of the collapse, there was total quiet. Zedeño remembers thinking she must be dead, perhaps because of that silent blankness. As soon as she realized she was still alive, she realized she couldn't breathe. The dense gray matter of Tower 2 was lodged in her nose, mouth, and ears. She dug her hand into her mouth to clear out the debris, but more debris took its place. "I kept trying to catch my breath, but I couldn't. Oh my God, it was horrible," she says.

During this moment, choking on great piles of ash, the anger she felt on the forty-fourth floor came surging back. This time, it was more than anger; it was rage, and it was directed not at herself but at God:

> *I was thinking, "I was outside already! I almost made it! Why couldn't I get out?" After all that trouble! I just didn't understand. And this anger, this overwhelming anger is saying, "Why can't you give me a break! I was there in 1993. I'm here now, I was almost out, and I'm still here! Ah! God almighty!"*

The dust started to settle. Zedeño was able to empty out her mouth, and as she leaned against a wall, she tried to clean her glasses and blow her nose. She couldn't see through all the dust, but she heard a voice asking her to move out of the way. It was a firefighter and he was trying to break through a wall to get them out. She moved and stumbled over some debris, falling on top of someone else. It turned out to be a police officer. He was screaming that his eyes were burning. And at the same time, he was telling her, "Don't worry, don't worry! We're gonna get out of here." Zedeño could see his hands shaking. But she never saw his face.

By then, her anger had vanished again. She got very quiet. It helped to have the police officer there, even though he was hurt. Then she heard a voice: "I found a way out. Everybody, hold hands." And that's what they did. They went into Borders and out through the door at the corner of Vesey and Church Streets. The books were still on the shelves, Zedeño noticed. "The idea of what had happened slipped away completely. Gone! I had no feeling anymore. It was almost like I was daydreaming."

Zedeño had traveled a long way. From the seventy-third floor to the ground, she had invented at least three different explanations for what was happening, all of which she had been forced to abandon. She had passed in and out of bouts of rage as her brain worked to make sense of it all. Denial both slowed her down, by distracting her with false hope, and kept her moving, by calming her down.

The Ten-Thousand-Pound Planters

Before the 1993 bombings, the fire safety plan for the Trade Center was naïve: each tenant company selected a volunteer to act as a fire marshal. Then the volunteer was allegedly trained to know what to do in a fire. That meant there was about one volunteer marshal for every fifty employees. As it turns out, the vast majority of the fire marshals had never left their own floor or the building in any previous alarm or drill, according to a NIST survey of all the marshals after the 1993 bombing. As a result, most of the fire marshals were unfamiliar with the stairs, despite the fact that they were the only ones "trained" to get out. In fact, they were trained only to meet in the corridor and wait for instructions. But no instructions ever came. The bomb, which was relatively weak compared with a 767 airplane, disabled the power and communications systems in the towers.

Afterward, many of the 1993 fire marshals complained about their lack of training. They hadn't known that two-thirds of the stairwells required people to wind through transfer hallways. No one had told them that it would take firefighters several hours to reach the upper floors. So they waited and waited, some for four hours before descending. Logically, the study's authors concluded: "Training should not be limited to members of the fire safety team. Many fire marshals weren't even in their areas when the incident occurred. . . . *All building occupants need some level of training or education* if they are going to react safely to a fire in a high-rise." It wasn't enough to rely upon volunteer fire marshals or even firefighters. People needed to be able to get out on their own.

After 1993, it was obvious that changes needed to be made. The Port Authority spent more than $100 million on improvements. But notice where the money went: the perimeter of the complex was ringed with ten-thousand-pound planters to prevent vehicles from getting too close. Some two hundred cameras went up. Truck drivers were photographed on their way into the truck dock. Dogs sniffed for explosives. The Port Authority also installed a repeater system to help boost the fire department's radios when firefighters had to go up into the buildings.

But the new vision for the World Trade Center did not feature a role for regular people. Alan Reiss, who was the director of the Port Authority's World Trade Department, which ran the World Trade Center, put it this way in his testimony to the September 11th Commission: "Evacuation protocols did not change after 1993, but training and equipment certainly did." Safety engineers' recommendations to widen the stairways were overruled. It would cost too much money in lost real estate. Fire drills were held twice a year, but the Trade Center's definition of a fire drill was to ask everyone to gather in the middle of their floors and pick up an emergency phone to obtain directions. Employees did not generally go into the stairwells, let alone down them.

Information and responsibility remained the province of the exclusive few—the building's fire safety director, the Port Authority police, and other first responders. The role of regular people was to await orders.

On 9/11, the ten-thousand-pound planters didn't help, unfortunately. Neither did the repeater: it was never correctly turned on, and, in the chaos of that morning, firefighters concluded it was broken. Meanwhile, the relatively cheap addition of glow-in-the-dark strips along the stairs after 1993 made the evacuation much easier, survivors reported. But many thousands of people did not even know where the stairs were. Fewer than half the survivors had ever entered the stairwells before, the NIST report found. Only 45 percent of 445 Trade Center workers interviewed after 9/11 had known the buildings even had three stairwells, according to the early results of a study conducted at Columbia University. "I found the lack of preparedness shocking. People were not thinking vertically. They were thinking horizontally," says lead investigator Robyn Gershon, a professor at Columbia. "Many people said they hesitated to get into the stairways because they didn't know where they would end up."

Most people had no idea how to navigate the transfer hallways on lower floors. Only half had known the doors to the roof would be locked, according to Gershon's findings. The 9/11 Commission Report concluded that people may have died as a result: "Once the South Tower was hit, civilians on upper floors wasted time ascending the stairs instead of searching for a clear path down, when stairwell A was at least initially passable."

After 1993, the fire-marshal system remained in effect. Zedeño was a marshal on 9/11. In fact, she was the only member of the fire-safety team on her floor that morning. Everyone else had yet to arrive to work. Keep in mind that each floor of the Trade Center was about an acre in size. Zedeño was a "searcher," meaning she was supposed to search the women's bathroom before she went into the stairs. In reality, she didn't search for anyone anywhere. She didn't even remember she was a fire marshal until months after the towers had collapsed.

It turns out that on 9/11, fire marshals did not know much more than regular people. Of those interviewed in the Columbia study, 94 percent had never exited the buildings as part of a drill. Only 50 percent said they were knowledgeable enough to evacuate on their own.

After she left Tower 1 on 9/11, Zedeño walked north with the police officer with the burning eyes. Eventually, they were picked up by ambulances. Zedeño was taken to Woodhull Hospital in Brooklyn, where she was given oxygen and a change of clothes. She then wandered from one train station to the next, trying to get back home. Around 7:00 P.M., she finally found her way back to New Jersey—and to her parents, who had watched from their balcony as her tower collapsed over eight hours earlier.

Over a period of three years, Zedeño met with me many times to relive her ordeal in microdetail. It can't have been pleasant for her. But she did it because she wanted her experience to be worth something. "In helping others understand," she once wrote in an e-mail, "I am reaffirmed as to the reason I survived."

Today, Zedeño still works for the Port Authority. Her office is now in Newark, New Jersey, on the eleventh floor of an eighteen-story building. She also helps run the World Trade Center Survivors' Network, which has over two thousand members. Two years after 9/11, Zedeño adopted a three-year-old boy from Newark. She named him Elias. Her sister shares custody of him, just in case anything ever happens to Zedeño again.

Through my long talks with Zedeño, I came to appreciate the duality of denial. I was amazed by how consuming it could be, even in the presence of smoke and flames. But, as I would come to learn about most of our disaster responses, denial could also be lifesaving. If Zedeño had been forced to reckon with reality all at once on 9/11, she might never have been able to make the long, tedious trip to safety. Denial created blinders for her brain, letting her see only what she needed to see.

But the more I learned about denial, the harder time I had identifying its boundaries. Where did it start and end? Did denial shape Zedeño's response the morning of 9/11? Or did it start its work long before, after she was trapped in an elevator in 1993 and decided it could never happen again? Denial is the most insidious fear response of all. It lurks in places we never think to look. The more I learned, the more denial seemed to matter all the time, even long before the disaster, on days that pass by without incident.

2

Risk

Gambling in New Orleans

O N SEPTEMBER 9, 1965, Hurricane Betsy slammed into Louisiana with winds of up to 125 mph. In Eastern New Orleans, Meaher Patrick Turner and his family did what they always did: his four children, wife, and elderly father rode out the storm together in their shotgun house. But this time, the ferocious category 3 hurricane breached the levees around Lake Pontchartrain, and the streets began to gurgle with water. As the water rose, first one foot, then another, the children noticed a faint meowing sound from under the floorboards. A cat had found its way into the crawlspace under the house. As the hours began to pass, its cries got louder. It would be days before the water receded. It was clear that the cat would either drown or starve, and they would have to listen to it die.

This would not do. Turner told the kids to get down on their stomachs and put their ears to the floor. Find the cat's exact location, he told them. After crawling around on their bellies, the kids concluded that the cat was under the washing machine. So Turner moved the washing machine into the kitchen and got his saw. Then he carved a circle out of the wooden floor, just like a character in a cartoon, and the cat bounded up out of the hole to safety.

Turner was a World War II veteran who had a job of some responsibility at the Federal Housing Administration. The rest of his life was about his family. He liked having them around, and he dedicated himself to the rituals that kept them together. Every Sunday, he cooked a big family dinner of roast beef with mashed potatoes and green beans. On holidays, even the minor holidays, he decked the house with ornaments. On St. Patrick's Day, he stationed leprechauns all around the house. On Valentine's Day, he hung little cardboard hearts from the bushes. It was known in the neighborhood as the little holiday house, and people would drive by to see it. Christmas was the grand finale. On Christmas Eve, Turner hosted a party for all his relatives. Nearly a hundred people would pack the house. Cousins flew in from San Francisco and Birmingham. Every year, no matter how warm it was, Turner put on a big, heavy red suit and played Santa Claus. He did this for forty-eight years. "He was very handsome," remembers his youngest daughter, Sheila Williams. "He had a full set of white hair."

But Turner was also stubborn. And the older he got, the more obstinate he became. "My dad was always right," Williams says. "He was strictly Catholic. There was no other religion that existed except Catholicism. And ooh, my gosh, don't say nothing bad about President [George W.] Bush. He kept his Christmas card Scotch-taped to the window in the kitchen."

Sometimes Turner's certainty masked his fear. He hated hospitals, for instance. "He was an Archie Bunker, a terrible patient," Williams says. He had a deep distrust of doctors, convinced they were using him for his Medicare reimbursements. He didn't often talk about his experiences in World War II, but the memories stalked him after dark. Several times a week, he used to wake up at night crying from nightmares. And he was also afraid of dying, Williams says. "I know he was scared."

When Hurricane Katrina began its approach toward New Orleans in August of 2005, Turner's children, now grown, knew it was serious. By Friday, three days before landfall, they had moved past denial and toward deliberation. They started calling motels in Mississippi, looking for rooms. Then Williams called her father, who was then living alone. "And that's when he started giving us trouble," she says.

"Let's wait," he said. "It's too early."

By Saturday, New Orleans mayor Ray Nagin was advising residents to evacuate. "Ladies and gentlemen, this is not a test. This is the real deal," he said at a news conference. Even in Nagin's lazy drawl there was a sliver of urgency. "Board up your homes, make sure you have enough medicine, make sure the car has enough gas. Treat this one differently because it is pointed towards New Orleans."

Williams called her father again. He said he had made up his mind: he was staying. "These storms always make that turn to Pascagoula," he told Williams. She argued with him. He laughed. "You are all very dramatic," he said.

On Sunday morning, less than twenty-four hours before the hurricane's landfall, Nagin called for an unprecedented mandatory evacuation. "We are facing a storm that most of us have long feared. This is very serious," he said on TV. "I want to emphasize, the first choice of every citizen should be to leave the city."

Turner went to Mass, just like he did every day. There weren't many people there. After the service, when the priest asked him what he was going to do, he said he would stay put. "My family's aggravating me, but I'm staying." Turner was stuck in denial, while everyone else around him moved on to deliberation and decision. It wasn't that he thought he was immortal. He thought often about death, especially as his siblings began to pass away. No, Turner was in denial about Katrina because something else scared him more.

Williams and her brother decided to ride out the storm in a neighbor's house, which was well built and far from any trees. That way, her father wouldn't have to deal with evacuating the city. She asked him to come spend the night with them. He would not. He invited her to come to his house, a one-story structure two blocks from Lake Pontchartrain, but she said no. "Something just came in the pit of my stomach," she says. She made one last request of him: "I said, 'Daddy, I don't know if you remember Hurricane Betsy. But they found claw marks in people's attics. People couldn't get out. If you're going to stay, please put some tools up there in your attic."

By this point, Turner was starting to get truly annoyed with his children and their entreaties. He'd already stopped watching the weather on TV. "I don't think he even knew the name of the storm," Williams says. It was around then that he took his phone off the hook.

Blind Spots

About 80 percent of New Orleans's population got out before the storm—a huge success compared with previous evacuations there and around the country. The vast majority of people navigated through the denial and deliberation phases and took action. But what happened to the remaining 20 percent? The consensus in most media reports was that people were simply too poor to leave. And it's true that the more resources you have, the more choices you have about how to evacuate and where to go. About 21 percent of New Orleans households were carless when Katrina hit, according to the Census Bureau.

But poverty does not explain what happened in New Orleans. An analysis of 486 Katrina victims by Knight Ridder Newspapers found that they were not disproportionately poor—or black. Michael Lindell, director of the Hazard Reduction and Recovery Center at Texas A&M University, has studied scores of evacuations, and he says people's behavior defies simple explanations. "If you're looking at 100% of the variance in evacuation behavior, income accounts for no more than 5–10 percentage points," he says. "What really accounts for the differences are people's beliefs."

Why wouldn't Patrick Turner leave? Turner had an old Chevrolet and a family full of people with cars headed out of town. In New Orleans, most people knew much of the city lay below sea level. In July 2002, the *New Orleans Times-Picayune* ran a five-part series on the inevitable. "It's a matter of when, not if," wrote reporters John McQuaid and Mark Schleifstein about a hurricane decimating the city. "It's happened before and it'll happen again." They described a precarious levee system and flooding that could kill thousands.

In hindsight, it's always easy to craft a narrative for any disaster: to see all the signs stacking up like dominoes, if only we'd been paying attention. But that's not what happened with Hurricane Katrina. It was that most unusual of fiascoes: almost nothing was a surprise. "This was not a comet hitting us," says Stephen Leatherman, director of the International Hurricane Research Center in Miami. "This is Hurricane Alley." Leatherman has studied hurricanes for thirty years. In 2002, he wrote a paper warning that Louisiana had lost many of its natural defenses against storms and New Orleans was particularly vulnerable. When we spoke just days after landfall, while tens of thousands of people remained stuck at the Superdome in New Orleans, he sounded sick with vindication. "You do all these computer models, but [now] you have a human face on it," he said quietly. "It's something. It really hurts."

We gauge risk literally hundreds of times per day, usually well and often subconsciously. For more predictable calamities, the first phase of disaster think actually begins with this calculus. We start assessing risk before the disaster even happens. We are doing it right now. We decide where to live and what kind of insurance to buy, just like we process all kinds of everyday risks: we wear bike helmets, or not. We buckle our seat belts, smoke a cigarette, and let our kids stay out until midnight. Or not.

To deconstruct how we place these bets, I called Nassim Nicholas Taleb, a man obsessed with risk. Taleb spent twenty years as a trader in New York and London, earning money off other people's blind spots. While other traders indulged in big short-term risks in hopes of big, short-term gains, Taleb set up his investments so that he could never win big—nor lose big. He was hedged every which way. "I never have blown up, and I never will," he likes to say.

One autumn day, Taleb and I met for tea in Washington, D.C. Taleb, who has a balding head and a gray beard, is an author and a professor now, in addition to holding a large stake in a hedge fund. He likes to do many things at once, and he speaks so quickly that it is sometimes hard to keep up. That afternoon, he had come from the Pentagon, where he had briefed officials on his theories about uncertainty. The Pentagon was a strange place for him to be, since Taleb is a self-described pacifist. But he's the kind of pacifist the Pentagon can tolerate—which is to say, the stoic kind. "I am a peace activist simply out of rationality," he explains.

Taleb grew up in Lebanon, a country haunted by war's unintended consequences. He has concluded that human beings are unable to handle war in the modern age. "We're not really able to assess how long wars will take and what the net outcome will be." The risk is too complex for our abilities. Once upon a time, we were better at war. "In a primitive environment, if someone is threatening me, I go kill him," he says in his clipped, matter-of-fact way. "And I get good results most of the time." He calls this environment "Mediocristan," a place where it is hard to kill many people at once; a place where cause and effect are more closely connected. *Homo sapiens* spent hundreds of thousands of years living in Mediocristan. We rarely needed to understand probability because, most of the time, life was simpler, and the range of possible events was narrower.

But today, we live in a place Taleb calls "Extremistan," subject to the "tyranny of the singular, the accidental, the unseen and the unpredicted." Technology has allowed us to create weaponry that can strafe the planet in minutes. Lone individuals can alter the course of history. People kill each other every day without much physical exertion. And, at the same time, we have become ever more interdependent. What happens on one continent now has consequences for another. World War I, Taleb points out, was expected to be a rather small affair. So was Vietnam. In fact, the twentieth century was, and now the twenty-first century is, characterized by wars of unforeseen results. America's war in Iraq was certainly not intended to create more terrorists bent on attacking the United States. But that is what happened, as a national intelligence estimate completed by U.S. government intelligence agencies concluded in April 2006.

Risk is often counterintuitive in Extremistan. Our old tricks don't work. For example, just like Turner, many of Louisiana's oldest residents had survived Hurricane Betsy in 1965. They had also survived Hurricane Camille, a category 5 storm that struck in 1969. Turner rode out both storms without a problem. So he saw no reason to leave for Katrina. He hunkered down in denial.

As it turned out, the veteran Louisianans were half right: Katrina was indeed less powerful than Camille. Had the world stood still since then, they would have been just fine. In Mediocristan, they would have survived.

But since Camille, rapid development had destroyed much of the wetlands that had created a natural barrier against storm surge. The force field, in other words, was down. Humankind had literally changed the shape of the earth, and we had done it faster, thanks to technology, than we could have throughout most of history. This fact was well reported in popular media. But the firsthand experience of Camille was more powerful than any warning.

As it turned out, the victims of Katrina were not disproportionately poor; they were disproportionately old. Three-quarters of the dead were over sixty, according to the Knight Ridder analysis. Half were over seventy-five. They had been middle-aged when Hurricane Camille struck. "I think Camille killed more people during Katrina than it did in 1969," says Max Mayfield, director of the National Hurricane Center. "Experience is not always a good teacher."

After Katrina, a poll of 680 New Orleans residents asked why they had not evacuated before the storm. The respondents could give multiple explanations. A slim majority did indeed cite a lack of transportation. But that was not the biggest reason. The most popular explanation, given by 64 percent, was that they did not think the storm would be as bad as it was. In fact, in retrospect, half of those who hadn't evacuated said that they could have found a way to leave if they had really wanted to, according to the study, conducted for the Henry J. Kaiser Family Foundation and the *Washington Post*. Motivation, in other words, mattered more than transportation.

A Baseball Bat and a Crucifix

At 7:00 A.M. on Monday, August 29, Katrina made landfall in Louisiana with winds of up to 140 mph. At 9:00 A.M., Turner's children dialed his number again. Sometime before then, as the storm screamed by his window, he'd put his phone back on the hook.

Turner answered the phone. "It's real windy," he told his son. The electricity was out. And he was worried about the big tree in his backyard. Then he said something he rarely ever said: "I think I made a mistake."

His son told him to hang in there. They'd drive out to get him as soon as they could. "My daddy was in very, very good health. No pacemakers, no surgery, nothing," says Williams. "We figured as soon as they'd cleared the roadways, we could get him." They hung up.

But then the floodwaters came, breaching the levees in half a dozen places and charging through the streets. Then the five-mile bridge that crosses Lake Pontchartrain broke into pieces, cutting Turner off from his children. And finally, the phones went out for good.

Turner's neighborhood, like much of New Orleans, was in a bowl. Water poured in from the lake, rising to five feet in his one-story house. All of his possessions—the photographs, the Santa suit, all the reminders of his wife, who had died three years before—everything was sinking. Turner pulled the stairs down and went up into his attic. He brought up a gallon of water, a bucket, and two candles.

For nine days, the phones stayed down and the roads remained uncrossable. All of Turner's children except Williams had lost their homes. They were desperate to get to their father, but they could not. Finally, the phones came back on and Williams made a frantic call to a radio station. She pleaded for someone, anyone, to go check on her father. Three hours later, she got a call from rescue officials. They had found her father in the attic, with a baseball bat and the crucifix he kept by his bed. He was dead at age eighty-five, apparently killed by a heart attack. Time of death was unknown.

In those early, chaotic days, rescue personnel were under orders to prioritize bodies that were in the water. Turner was not in the water, so it would be two weeks before they took his body away. About a month after the storm, Williams went to the house. She found the Santa suit hanging in her father's bedroom closet, in its normal place. It had gotten wet, along with everything else, but her brother decided to hang it outside of the house as a reminder to those who passed that this had been the little holiday house. "We wanted people to see it," Williams says. "I don't know. When people passed by, maybe people who knew him as Santa Claus or whatever, would remember."

In the confusion that followed the storm, the authorities lost Turner's body. For five months, his family tried to find him. Morgue workers called Williams repeatedly to describe the bodies of dead men, none of whom were her father. "I kept telling them, 'He doesn't have a tattoo!'" Five months after he died, Turner's body was found again and handed over to his family.

When we spoke a year and a half after the storm, Williams was having trouble forgiving her father. "It makes me so mad," she said. "It didn't have to happen. I took such good care of him for him to do something like that." Since his death her family has not been nearly as close, she says. She wonders if they will ever reconnect. She agreed to be interviewed for this book because, she said, she wants other people to know how one decision can make all the difference.

Turner was nobody's fool; he had accumulated a lot of wisdom in his long life. When Katrina came, he made a trade-off that is more complicated than it looks. As I came to know Turner through his daughter, I wanted to know more about his decision. Why had his risk calculus failed him this time—after working so well for so long? Could we predict these kinds of blind spots in our own risk equations? And if so, couldn't we overcome them?

The Science of Risk

How are you most likely to die? Think for a moment: Given your own profile, what do you really think is most likely to kill you?

The facts depend upon your age, genetics, lifestyle, location, and a thousand other factors, of course. But overall, here are the leading causes of death in the United States:

1. Heart disease
2. Cancer
3. Stroke

Now ask yourself whether these most-likely scenarios are also the ones you worry about more than any other. Are these the risks you actively work hardest to avoid? Do you start each day with twenty minutes of meditation? Do you work out for at least thirty minutes a day? When you swim in the ocean, are you more terrified of getting sunburned than you are of getting bit by a shark?

The human brain worries about many, many things before it worries about probability. If we really were just concerned with preventing the most likely causes of death, we would worry more about falling down than we would about homicide. The nightly news would feature back-to-back segments on tragic heart-attack deaths. And we might spend more money on therapists than police (you are twice as likely to kill yourself than you are to be killed by someone else during your lifetime). It's as if we don't fear death itself so much as dying. We fear the how, not so much the what.

Curiously, we have only recently begun to understand how we process risk. For centuries, philosophers and especially economists assumed that people were rational creatures—if not individually than certainly overall. To measure risk, it was thought, humans simply multiplied the probability of something happening by the consequences of it happening.

It took two psychologists to point out that this was simply not true. In the 1970s and 1980s, Daniel Kahneman and Amos Tversky published a series of revolutionary papers on human decision making. They explained that people rely on emotional shortcuts, called "heuristics," to make choices. The more uncertainty, the more shortcuts. And the shortcuts, while very useful, lead to a slew of predictable errors. For example, in one study, they found that a majority of subjects judged a deadly flood triggered by a California earthquake to be more likely than an equally deadly flood occurring somewhere else in North America on its own. The notion of a California earthquake resonated more than the prospect of a flood—and so it was assigned a higher probability by the people in the study.

In fact, the chances of a flood occurring for some other reason is far greater. But that kind of workaday flood—the kind that kills people every year—does not trigger the same cascading series of emotional shortcuts. It is less scary for a reason, which isn't to say that it's rational.

At first, Kahneman and Tversky were labeled pessimists. At a time when most Americans were enchanted by technology, they had concluded that people were in fact irrational. They were attacked for exaggerating the flaws of the human brain. More than one critic pointed to the fact that man had walked on the moon. How could a species that has evolved to walk on the moon be plagued by irrationality? But their work forever altered the study of risk. In 2002, six years after Tversky's death, Kahneman was awarded the Nobel Prize in Economics for their work.

Today, most people who study decision making agree that human beings are not rational. "We don't go around like risk assessors—doing calculations, multiplying probabilities. That's been disproved," says Paul Slovic, a psychology professor at the University of Oregon and one of the world's most respected experts on risk. Instead, people rely on two different systems: the intuitive and the analytical. The intuitive system is automatic, fast, emotional, and swayed heavily by experiences and images. The analytical system is the ego to the brain's id: logical, contemplative, and pragmatic.

One system can override the other, depending on the situation. For example, consider this question:

A coffee and a donut cost $1.10 in total. The coffee costs $1 more than the donut. How much does the donut cost?

If your first answer was ten cents, that's your intuitive system talking. If you then caught yourself and came to the correct answer (five cents), that's your analytical system policing your intuition.

Notice how deft the intuitive system is! It moved at lightning speed, and if the question were a mountain lion about to lunge at your throat, it might have saved your life—or at least distracted the lion for a minute.

But it was also wrong. And this is where we come to the truth-telling moment: we all make mistakes when we judge risk. Our risk formula, especially when it comes to disasters, almost never looks this rational:

$$Risk = Probability \times Consequence$$

No, if we could reduce our risk calculation to a simple formula, it might look more like this:

$$Risk = Probability \times Consequence \times \textbf{Dread}/Optimism$$

Dread. Rarely does a label used by scientists so aptly fit the emotion it describes. Think of dread as humanity in a word. It represents all of our evolutionary fears, hopes, lessons, prejudices, and distortions wrapped up in one dark X factor.

After talking about dread with risk experts, I started to imagine it as a sum of many other, powerful factors. Dread had its own equation. Each factor in the equation could raise or reduce the sensation of dread, depending on the situation. It seemed important to break dread into its parts in order to understand its imperfections. So here, with apologies to those experts for reducing their findings to a formula, is what I think the equation for dread might look like:

$$Dread = Uncontrollability + Unfamiliarity + Imaginability \\ + Suffering + Scale\ of\ Destruction + Unfairness$$

Chances are the thing that most terrifies you is high in several of these factors. Dread explains why we fear plane crashes so much more than we fear heart disease or car crashes. First, planes (unlike cars) are not under our personal control, so that bumps up the dread factor. Second, planes are very unfamiliar to human beings; we are not comfortable at twenty thousand feet, perhaps because we have spent only a tiny fraction of our evolutionary history at such a height. So the dread score goes up again. At the same time, accidents are easy to imagine, given the salience of plane-crash images in movies and in the news media. On a plane, there's also a chance the suffering might be prolonged, at least compared to a car crash, in which you have little or no warning. Who hasn't felt a sudden drop in altitude and imagined what it might portend? Minutes might pass between the anticipation of death and the end itself. The crash would also likely kill many people, not just one, further compounding the horror under the dread equation. (The importance of scale helps explain why we are more distressed by a bus accident that kills fifty people than we are by the one hundred people killed individually in cars on the same day.) A plane crash can also be brutally unfair if, for example, it is perpetrated by terrorists who turn a commercial jetliner into a weapon.

Terrorists understand dread. Unpredictable attacks on civilians are an extremely efficient way to create dread. And dread is a good way to get a population agitated. In fact, the number of Americans killed by international terrorism in the past fifty years is fewer than the number killed by food allergies. But terrorism is by nature a mind game.

After 9/11, many thousands of Americans decided to drive instead of fly. Driving felt safer, and, given the spasm of new security rituals in airports, certainly easier. In the months after 9/11, planes carried about 17 percent fewer passengers compared with the same period before the attacks. Meanwhile, the number of miles driven increased about 5 percent, according to government estimates.

But something terrible happened in the name of common sense. In the two years after 9/11, an estimated 2,302 *additional* people were likely killed because they drove instead of flew, according to a 2006 study of road accidents in America by three Cornell University professors. The study compared the total number of road fatalities in the years before 9/11 with the period after. It controlled for other things that might explain a spike in accidents—like bad weather. And after all of that, the researchers found 2,302 deaths above and beyond the "normal" tally of car-accident casualties; that's 2,302 people who, if not for 9/11, almost certainly would have lived. These were the lesser-known, secondary victims of 9/11, casualties of the adjustments we make in times of great uncertainty. "The greatest cost of terrorism may be the public's response to the attacks rather than the attacks themselves," the authors note.

In reality, even after 9/11, driving remained much, much more dangerous than flying. The chance of dying on a major domestic commercial flight from 1992 through 2001 was roughly 8 in 100 million, according to a 2003 analysis in *American Scientist*. Driving the same distance as the average flight segment is, by comparison, about sixty-five times riskier.

Hierarchy of Fears

Justin Klabin, a partner in a manufacturing firm in New Jersey, is not a coward. He has ridden motorcycles, played competitive rugby, and fought fires. In 2005, he even tried out for the America's Cup bobsled team; that is, he willingly hurtled down an iced, steeply banked course at speeds up to 90 mph in a fiberglass sled controlled almost exclusively by gravity. But after 9/11, Klabin decided to stop flying on airplanes. He had watched the Twin Towers collapse from across the Hudson River in New Jersey, and he had responded to Ground Zero with his fire department. That was all he needed to see. "I'd like to get on a plane," he says. "It would be a lot easier." But he is convinced that plane travel is just not worth the risk. "Flying is so many things combined—claustrophobia, fear of heights, fear of being out of control," says Klabin. Given all of those factors, the statistics mean little to him. "Even if the odds are 1 in 15 million, that's one person. People like me think there's no reason it can't happen to me."

In October 2001, when Klabin and his girlfriend went on a planned trip to Florida, they drove instead of flying. They traveled more than a thousand miles in his pickup truck. On the way back, at the end of a long day of driving, they stopped in South Carolina. As Klabin pulled the truck into a parking space, he heard a loud pop. The tie-rod, which connects the wheel to the steering column, had snapped. Both front tires were turned in toward each other, like snowplowing skis. The truck could not be driven a foot farther. Staring at the inverted tires, Klabin started laughing at himself. Here he was trying to be safe by driving instead of flying. But had the rod snapped just a few minutes earlier, when they were on the highway, the truck would have been uncontrollable at 80 mph. "There's no question we would have been dead," he says.

After his near miss, Klabin decided to do something radical. He took flying lessons. He thought he might feel better about flying if he understood the mechanics. So he went up in a Cessna plane (which is far more dangerous than a commercial jet). Surprisingly, he felt absolutely fine. He wasn't scared!

Why wasn't Klabin terrified? People who drive because they fear flying are not really looking for physical safety, explains Tom Bunn, a former commercial airline pilot who now counsels people with a fear of flying. "What they're looking for is emotional safety."

In the Cessna, Klabin felt in control. The dread factor plummeted. But he had no control on commercial planes. So he remained just as frightened as ever. When we spoke more than five years after 9/11, Klabin still had not set foot on a passenger plane.

"Hazards have personalities," says Paul Slovic, the risk expert, "kind of like people." In the mid-1980s, Slovic was studying the potential impact of building a nuclear waste repository at Yucca Mountain, Nevada. The more he talked to people about their concerns, the more he realized that anything with the word *nuclear* in it disturbed people—regardless of what the actual dangers were. The same goes for chemicals. When people are asked what comes to mind when they hear the word *chemicals,* the most frequent response by far is "dangerous"—or a synonym, like "toxic," "hazardous," "poison," "deadly," or "cancer." Up to 75 percent of the public agrees with the following statement: "I try hard to avoid contact with chemicals and chemical products in my everyday life."

Some of the most common disasters are the least feared. Fire, for example, usually kills more Americans each year than most other disasters combined. There is, at this point, very little we don't know about fires. We know where and when they happen. We even know how to prevent them. Most fatal fires happen in people's homes in December and January and are caused by arson or smoking. Deaths peak from midnight to 5:00 A.M. In 2005, according to the National Fire Protection Association, 3,675 Americans died in fires. If all homes had sprinklers and smoke detectors with working batteries, that number would probably drop by at least a third.

Lightning is another underappreciated threat. It may be the most dangerous natural hazard in rich industrialized countries like the United States. About one hundred lightning strikes hit the earth every second, and in many years, these bolts of fire kill more people than any other kind of weather. But lightning is not something most of us worry about very much.

Ironically, the most destructive single disasters are usually the least surprising. Hurricanes, for example, happen at the same time every year in the same general locations. And yet we are shocked at the devastation, every year. Between official declarations of emergencies, we build and re-build, upping the ante for the next storm season. By 2010, an estimated 70 percent of Americans will live within a hundred miles of a coast—where hurricanes, floods, and tropical storms are annual rites. Floridians, in particular, live dangerously. But they aren't alone. Texas and California are the country's other riskiest states. (The least hazardous are Vermont, Delaware, and Rhode Island. Fabulously boring places.)

Now think back to Patrick Turner, the man who refused to evacuate before Hurricane Katrina even though he had the means to do so. Turner was quite capable of feeling dread when it came to hospitals or doctors. But hurricanes did not move him. Why? For one thing, most of us fear natural threats less than those created by humans. Even though most of the devastation caused by hurricanes *is* humanmade (due to the overpopulation of the coasts, faulty levees, and depleted wetlands), the direct threat (wind and rain) is natural. If we consider the equation for dread, this makes sense: nuclear and chemical waste are far less familiar to us than weather, and they carry the potential for mass-scale casualties and suffering. If hazards have personalities, nuclear waste is the di-sheveled man standing on the street corner swearing. No one wants to get near him, regardless of how harmless he is. Hurricanes, on the other hand, are the slow, plodding types that the neighbors will later say looked perfectly harmless.

There is something else we need to understand about Turner. The year before Katrina, he had given in to his children's pleadings. He had evacuated for Hurricane Ivan. But the experience was traumatic. The traffic jams were horrendous, partly due to poor planning on the part of city and state officials. A trip from New Orleans to Baton Rouge that normally took eighty to ninety minutes took as long as ten to twelve hours. Turner rode with his other daughter all the way to Austin, Texas, in a car jammed with people and possessions, and he vowed never to do it again. Firsthand experience was more powerful than any official warning could be; the palpable risks of evacuating seemed stronger than the abstract risks of staying.

Turner lived a life of small rituals. He went to Mass every day at 8:00 A.M. Every Tuesday, he played golf with his brothers. On Saturday, Williams came over to clean his house. And every Sunday, she took him to the cemetery to pay respects to her mother. They never missed a Sunday. Turner didn't like the idea of disrupting his routines. The day before Katrina hit, he told his daughter he didn't want to evacuate because he wanted to be able to go to Mass on Monday morning.

Remember Zedeño's fog of disbelief after a Boeing 767 smashed into her building on 9/11? That disbelief, a natural and often helpful product of the human brain, sets in well before the crisis. In certain people facing certain threats, the fog can be impenetrable. "It just didn't adjust in his head" is how Williams puts it.

Elderly people don't like to evacuate. In 1979, after the accident at the Three Mile Island nuclear power plant in Pennsylvania, retirees and people over age seventy were least likely to evacuate—regardless of how close they were to the reactor. That's partly because, even if they have a good means of leaving, older people do not like change, generally speaking. Turner had lived in his house for over three decades. Like his old shotgun house, it was well built, and it had survived many hurricanes. So why wouldn't it survive this one?

It turned out that Turner's house did survive. It flooded with five feet of water, but the walls and the roof held strong. It was the man that the hurricane claimed.

Overconfidence

When it comes to old-fashioned risks like weather, we often overestimate ourselves. Of the fifty-two people who died during Hurricane Floyd in 1999, for example, 70 percent drowned. And most of them drowned in their cars, which had become trapped in floodwaters. This is a recurring problem in hurricanes. People are overconfident about driving through water, even though they are bombarded with official warnings not to. (This tendency varies, of course, depending on the individual. One study out of the University of Pittsburgh showed that men are much more likely to try to drive through high water than women—and thus more likely to die in the process. But more about the individual profile of a risk taker in Chapter 4.)

Less than one year after Katrina, a research team from the Harvard School of Public Health interviewed 2,029 people who live in high-risk hurricane zones in eight states. They asked them what they would do if government officials said they had to evacuate before a major hurricane. Incredibly, with the images of the Superdome still on rotation on the evening news, one quarter said flat out that they would not leave. An additional 9 percent said they weren't sure what they would do. So that means a third of people interviewed admitted they may not evacuate before a major storm.

Even more surprising was their reasoning: the number one rationale, given by 68 percent of those surveyed, was that they thought their homes were well built enough to survive a storm. Mobile home owners were no more likely to say they would evacuate. Like campers tucked into polyester tents in the deep woods, we seem to derive a false sense of protection from even the flimsiest shelter. And, as suggested by the early Katrina data, income did not predict behavior. In fact, the groups most likely to say they would ride out the storm were homeowners (39%), whites (41%), and long-term residents (45%).

Even in times of calm, we trend toward arrogance. About 90 percent of drivers think they are safer than the average driver. Most people also think they are less likely than others to get divorced, have heart disease, or get fired. And three out of four baby boomers think they look younger than their peers. People have a tendency to believe that they are, well, superior. Psychologists call this the "Lake Wobegon effect"—after the fictitious Minnesota town invented by Garrison Keillor, who described it as a place "where the women are strong, the men are good-looking, and all the children are above average."

The Lake Wobegon effect may be warped, but it helps us deal. We can process horrible events more readily if we assume we will be exempt from future suffering. Shortly after 9/11, a survey of a thousand Americans found that they thought they had a 21 percent chance of being injured in a terrorist attack within the next year. That's way too high. But it's nowhere near as high as the 48 percent chance that they assigned to the rest of us.

Hurricanes are especially tricky because we have to respond to them before things get ugly. We have to evacuate when the skies are clear and blue. Going back to the dread equation, it's hard to *imagine* the violence to come. Without any tangible cues, denial comes easily. But as coastal cities get bigger and bigger, people have to evacuate earlier and earlier. The infrastructure is not set up for a fast exit, so ten- and twenty-hour traffic jams are becoming common—making people even more reluctant to leave on a sunny day, forty-eight to seventy-two hours before the actual storm.

Experts are vulnerable to the same biases, by the way. Subtle cues set a background mood that makes us more or less cautious. The stock market, perhaps the ultimate laboratory for studying the human risk equation, offers a particularly fascinating example. Five years ago, two business-school professors, David Hirshleifer and Tyler Shumway, were curious about what effect the weather has on stock trades. So they gathered weather data for twenty-six international cities from 1982 to 1997. Then they compared stock returns for each city on each day. What they found is remarkable: sunshine strongly correlated with daily stock returns—in ways that couldn't easily be explained by any other factors. If it was sunny in the morning, stocks were more likely to go up.

Risk analysts call these nuanced emotional judgments "affect"—or, as Slovic puts it, "faint whispers of emotion." Slovic has tremendous respect for affect. It is at once "wondrous and frightening." Wondrous because, once upon a time, making decisions based on such subconscious atmospherics would have made great sense. In small communities focused on short-term survival, the weather was an excellent indicator of safety. But in complex financial markets—or dense coastal cities—affect works like a broken compass.

Of course, too much dread can be as problematic as too little. Coming less than a month after Katrina, and striking many of the same places, Hurricane Rita hit a profound resonance in the cultural psyche. For a brief period, the worst-case scenario was easy to imagine. Though only 1.25 million people were told to evacuate, 2.5 million did so. A carefully planned evacuation quickly devolved into mass frustration. One-hundred-mile-long traffic jams clogged the freeways around Houston. A spokesman for the State Transportation Department, Mike Cox, told reporters that no one had predicted how many Texans would be so frightened by Katrina. "Not one of our fifteen thousand employees is a psychologist," he said, nicely summarizing the big problem.

The Man Without Dread

It's tempting to throw our hands up and conclude that people are simply irrational, a lost cause. But dread is not so easily dismissed. In some cases, it sends us reeling, making life less safe and less productive. But other times, like so many of our disaster reflexes, it is the wisdom of ages imbedded right there in our heads.

Neurologist Antonio Damasio encountered a baffling patient in the 1970s at the University of Iowa College of Medicine. The patient, whom he calls Elliot to protect his identity, was an accomplished businessman, father, and husband until he developed a brain tumor. The tumor, which was the size of a small orange when it was discovered, was successfully removed through surgery. And Elliot appeared cured: he could talk, move around, and remember things just as he had before. He took an IQ test and scored in the superior range.

Elliot was rationalism personified. He *knew*, as Damasio puts it, but he didn't *feel*. Ah, finally a human with 20/20 risk perception, right? Wrong. Elliot seemed normal in so many ways. But the more Damasio talked with him, the more the neurologist realized that something was missing. Elliot relayed the story of his life like a historian describing a long-ago tragedy. Listening to him talk, Damasio found himself getting more upset than Elliot. And Elliot's life was a mess. He could not seem to function in the world. He had trouble making decisions and tended to fixate on details that didn't really matter. He couldn't plan the day, much less the week. He got fired from his job and then divorced. He lost his life savings in a dubious business venture that his friends had warned him was doomed.

Damasio studied Elliot's brain and saw that the tumor had damaged both frontal lobes—and especially the right frontal lobe. Everything else was intact. Then Damasio found twelve other patients with prefrontal damage similar to Elliot's. Every single patient exhibited the same combination of indecision and emotional flatness.

The more Damasio learned, the more he came to appreciate so-called irrational sentiments. Emotions and feelings were not impediments to reason; they were integral. "Reason may not be as pure as most of us think it is or wish it were," he wrote. "At their best, feelings point us in the proper direction, take us to the appropriate place in a decision-making space, where we may put the instruments of logic to good use."

Once we factor in emotion, then, the human risk equation is actually more sophisticated, not less. Damasio's discoveries convinced me that the way for people to get better at judging risk is not to avoid emotion—or wish it away—but to capitalize upon it. Dread, properly tapped, can save our lives.

Secure Your Own Mask First

Dennis Mileti has been studying how to warn people against threats like hurricanes and earthquakes for more than thirty years. He knows how to do it, he says. That's not the problem. The problem is getting people—in particular governments—to take his advice.

Today Mileti lives in the California desert. He is retired from his long-time teaching post at the University of Colorado at Boulder, but he's still complaining to anyone who will listen. "In this great, highly educated, affluent country, we do not have adequate warning systems," Mileti says. "We should have more than luck. We can have more than luck. We've been studying warnings for half a century, and we have it nailed."

Like a lot of disaster researchers, Mileti is perpetually disappointed. Luckily, he also has a sense of humor. After he says something particularly provocative, he laughs with a loud bark, showing off unnaturally white, straight teeth. When he is asked to give speeches, which is often, he sometimes shows up in a Hawaiian shirt. Then he unleashes sweeping condemnations and calls to action. For all these reasons, in the small and sometimes tedious world of disaster research, Mileti has something of a cult following.

In July of 2006, at the annual disaster summit held at the University of Colorado at Boulder, Mileti appeared at a panel titled "Risk-Wise Behavior." The auditorium was packed with 440 disaster experts. Mileti, who spoke last, was the only one without a PowerPoint presentation. He just got up and started ranting. "How many people do you need to see pounding through their roofs before we tell them how high the floodwaters can be, how hard the ground can shake? How many citizens must die to get us to do it?" he nearly shouted. "If you can't create the political will, do it anyway." The crowd went crazy.

As a smoker, Mileti likes to point out that the nation does take *some* risks seriously: "Do you know how many no-smoking signs you see in an airport? We've just not chosen to do the same thing for natural disasters," he said. "Why can't we put up signs that say, 'This is a tsunami inundation zone' [along the coast] of California? If we're not doing it for other hazards, I say take the no-smoking signs out of the airport."

Later, over hamburgers next to the Boulder Creek, Mileti rattled off other counterexamples: "You know how everyone knows not to take an elevator in a fire? How did that happen? In Hawaii, it's now part of the culture to get to high ground if you feel an earthquake. It should be the same in Santa Monica. You need to acculturate a tsunami warning system." Like most people at the workshop, Mileti was heartbroken by Hurricane Katrina—a catastrophe that did not have to happen. Unlike some of the younger attendees, Mileti fully expects to be heartbroken again. "We know exactly—exactly—where the major disasters will occur," he says, smiling. "But individuals underperceive risk. The public totally discounts low-probability, high-consequence events. The individual says, it's not going to be this plane, this bus, this time."

We still measure risk with the ancient slide rule that worked for most of our evolutionary history, even though we have calculators at our side. Likewise, we still eat chocolate cake even though we no longer need to hoard calories. But we can learn to eat less cake, and it is possible to become better judges of risk.

So how do we override our worst instincts? First and most important, the people in charge of warning us should treat us with respect. It's surprising how rarely warnings explain *why* you should do something, not just *what* you should do. Once you start noticing this problem, you'll see it everywhere. In fact, I think that the mistakes the public makes in calculating risk are primarily due to this pervasive lack of trust on behalf of the people charged with protecting us. They are our escorts through Extremistan, but they don't level with us often enough.

For example, you have heard flight attendants explain how to put on an oxygen mask, should it drop down from the ceiling of the plane. "Secure your own mask before helping others," the warning goes. But the flight attendant does not tell you *why*. Imagine if you were told that, in the event of a rapid decompression, you would only have ten to fifteen seconds before you lost consciousness. Aha. Then you might understand *why* you should put your mask on before you help your child. You might understand that if you don't put your mask on first, you'll both be unconscious before you can say, "how does this thing work?" Suddenly the warning would not just sound like a nagging legalese; it would sound like common sense. It would motivate.

In the late 1990s, the U.S. government conducted a large and priceless survey of 457 passengers involved in serious airplane evacuations. Over half of them said that they had not watched the entire preflight safety briefing because they had seen it before. Of those who did watch most of the briefing, 50 percent said it had not been helpful to them when the emergency came to pass. In retrospect, they wished they had been told more about exit routes, how to use the slides, and how to get off the wing after fleeing through the overwing exit. They wanted a more vivid, practical warning than they got.

Carry-on bags are a major problem in plane crashes. About half of all passengers try to take their carry-on with them in an evacuation, even though they have been ordered by flight attendants to leave everything behind. (This is the same gathering behavior exhibited by Elia Zedeño in the World Trade Center, when she felt compelled to take things, including a mystery novel, before she left her office.) Later, plane-crash survivors report that these collected carry-on bags posed a major obstacle to getting out quickly and safely. People tripped on them as they groped through the darkness, and the bags became weapons as they hurtled down the evacuation slides. The solution to this problem may not be that complicated, however. In a recent study in the United Kingdom, one volunteer suggested that flight attendants, instead of asking passengers to "leave all hand baggage behind," tell passengers *why* they should do so. They should simply say this, the volunteer suggested: "Taking luggage will cost lives."

Why don't the airlines give people better warnings, even when plane-crash survivors tell them how to do it? For one thing, they are in business. They don't want to scare customers by talking too vividly about crashes. Better to keep the language abstract and forgettable. But there's another, more insidious reason. Airline employees, like professionals in most fields, don't particularly trust regular people. "Like police, they think of civilians as a grade below them," says Daniel Johnson, a research psychologist who has worked for the airlines in various capacities for more than three decades. At aviation conferences, he still has trouble getting experts to appreciate the human factor. "They would rather talk about hardware and training manuals—and not worry about what I consider equally important, which is the behavior of the actual people." If the worst does happen, this distrust makes things harder still for regular people. "Often the pilots and the flight attendants do not want to inform the passengers about an emergency for fear of upsetting them," Johnson says. "So they let them sit there in ignorance, and when the accident does happen, no one knows what the hell is going on."

On the D.C. subway system recently, I heard this taped announcement: "In the event of a fire, remain calm and listen for instructions." That's it. Hundreds of conversations and thoughts were interrupted for that announcement. What was the message? That the officials who run the subway system do not trust me. They think I will dissolve into hysterics and ignore instructions in the event of a fire.

Consider what the people who created this announcement did *not* do: they had an excellent opportunity to tell me how many subway fires happen in the D.C. system each year. That would have gotten my attention. They also had a chance to explain *why* it's almost always better to stay in the subway car in case of a fire (because the rails on the track can electrocute you, and the tunnels are, in some places, too narrow to fit through if a train is coming). But instead, they just told me not to panic. Ah, thank you so much. And here I'd been planning on panicking!

Trust is the basic building block of any effective warning system. Right now, it's too scarce in both directions: officials don't trust the public, and the public doesn't trust officials either. That's partly an unintended consequence of the way we live. "Our social and democratic institutions, admirable as they are in many respects, breed distrust," Slovic wrote in his 2000 book, *The Perception of Risk*. A capitalist society with a free press has many things to recommend it. But it is not a place where citizens have overwhelming confidence in authority figures. Distrust makes it harder for the government to compensate for its citizens' blind spots—one of government's most vital functions.

Overcoming the trust deficit requires some ingenuity. But it can be done. The easiest way to mesmerize the brain is through images. Anecdotes, as any journalist or advertiser knows, always trump statistics. That's why lottery advertisements feature individual winners basking in the glow of newfound wealth. "Ramon Valencia celebrates Father's Day by winning a cool $1 million!" reads a California Lottery announcement. Probabilities pale in comparison to Ramon Valencia, father of four, from La Puente.

Usually, people think in binary terms: either something will happen or it won't. Either it will affect me, or it won't. So when people hear they have a 6 in 100,000 chance of dying from a fall, they shelve that risk under the label "won't happen to me," even though falling is in fact the third most common cause of accidental deaths in the United States (after car crashes and poisoning). It would be much more powerful to tell people about Grant Sheal, age three, who fell and cut himself on a vase while playing at home in February 2007. The toddler died from his injuries. Or about Patryk Rzezawski, nineteen, who fell down and hit his head that same month while walking near his home. He was pronounced dead at the scene. These deaths are almost always described in news accounts as "freak accidents," despite the fact that they are relatively common.

When people imagine good things happening to them, they become more prone to take risks—regardless of the odds. In human brain imaging studies, part of the brain called the "ventral striatum" is highly active in gamblers and drug addicts. Within this region, something called the "nucleus accumbens" lights up when people just anticipate winning money. When this region is activated, people have a tendency to take more risks. So all a casino has to do is get you to anticipate winning—even if you never actually experience it. This might explain why casinos ply gamblers with minirewards like cheap food, free drinks, bonus points, and surprise gifts. Anticipating those rewards can activate the nucleus accumbens, which in turn can lead to more risk taking.

Another part of the brain lights up when people imagine losing. The "anterior insula" is active when people calculate the risk of bad things happening—like disasters. This region also shows activation when people are anticipating upsetting images. So it makes sense that insurance advertisements might encourage risk-averse behavior (i.e., buying policies) by activating the anterior insula through scary images.

This isn't to say people need to be terrified into planning for disasters. Subtlety can work too. In Old Town Alexandria, Virginia, lines etched into a large renovated factory mark how high the Potomac River has risen in previous floods. At the Starbucks next door, one of the photos on the walls shows floodwaters surrounding the café and a man in a yellow rain slicker canoeing past. There are creative ways to institutionalize memory in everyday life.

In fact, it's important not to overwhelm people with a warning that's *too* frightening. Eric Holdeman ran King County's Office of Emergency Management in Washington state for eleven years. He has found that there's a fine line between getting people's attention and losing them to a sense of futility. In 2005, an organization in his state issued a big report about what would happen if a massive earthquake occurred on the Seattle fault. The fault could deliver a 7.4 earthquake. But the report's authors deliberately proposed a less-frightening hypothetical (a magnitude 6.7 quake, which would kill an estimated 1,660 people), betting they would get more attention. Says Holdeman: "Sometimes it's hard to get people to do worst-case planning because the worst case is so bad. People just throw up their hands."

But given reasonable, tangible advice, people can be very receptive. In the nation of Vanuatu, east of Australia, the residents of a remote part of Pentecost Island have no access to modern amenities. But once a week, they get to watch TV. A truck with a satellite dish, a VCR, and a TV comes to town and everyone gathers round for some entertainment. After a 1998 earthquake in Papua New Guinea, the TV truck showed a UNESCO video on how to survive a tsunami. In 1999, the islanders felt the earth shake, just like in the video, and they ran for high ground. Thirty minutes later, a giant wave inundated the town. But only three people out of five hundred died.

But all over the world, even in developing nations, officials have an unfortunate preference for high-tech gadgetry over simplicity. In coastal Bangladesh, after a 1970 cyclone killed more than three hundred thousand people, the government devised a complex warning system. Volunteers were trained to hoist flags representing one of ten different warning levels. But a 2003 survey of rural villagers found that many took no notice of the semaphore system. "I know there are disaster signals ranging from Signal No. 1 to 10," Mohammud Nurul Islam told a team from the Benfield Hazard Research Centre, based at University College of London. "But I have no idea what they mean." He does have his own personal survival system, however. "I can predict any disaster coming when the sky turns gloomy, bees move around in clusters, the cattle become restless, and the wind blows from the south."

Even a child can do better than a fancy warning system, if she has been trusted with some basic information. English schoolgirl Tilly Smith was vacationing with her parents and sister in Thailand in 2004 when the tide suddenly rushed out. Tourists pointed at the fish flopping on the sand. Out on the horizon, the water began to bubble strangely, and boats bobbed up and down. Smith, ten, had just learned about tsunami in her geography class, two weeks earlier. She had watched a video of a Hawaii tsunami and learned all the signs. "Mummy, we must get off the beach now. I think there is going to be a tsunami," she said. Her parents started warning people to leave. Then the family raced up to the JW Marriott hotel where they were staying and alerted the staff, who evacuated the rest of the beach. In the end, the beach was one of the few in Phuket where no one was killed or seriously hurt.

The best warnings are like the best ads: consistent, easily understood, specific, frequently repeated, personal, accurate, and targeted. Now compare that description to the U.S. Department of Homeland Security's color-coded alert system. It is indeed easy to understand, and it gets repeated frequently. But other than that, the alerts are inconsistent, unspecific, impersonal, and untargeted. "That isn't a warning system," says warnings expert Mileti. "That's the first 10 percent of the system. It's a risk classification system. It would be equivalent to saying, 'It's orange today for floods.'" Warnings need to tell people what to do. Since people aren't sure what action they should take in response to an Orange Alert for terrorism, the color codes are unsatisfying—like someone clinking a glass to give a toast and then standing there in silence.

So what can regular people do to improve their own risk perception? When I asked risk experts this question, they told me their own tricks.

When it comes to financial risk, Taleb, the mathematical trader, refuses to read the newspaper or watch TV news. He doesn't want to tempt his brain with buy-sell sound bites. Likewise, Slovic avoids short-term investments; he invests broadly and then walks away. Similarly, when it comes to disaster risk, there's little to be gained by watching TV news segments: stories of shark attacks will distract your brain from focusing on far likelier risks. (Sharks kill an average of six people worldwide every year. Humans kill between 26 and 73 million sharks. This is not a battle humans are losing.)

"I tell people that if it's in the news, don't worry about it. The very definition of 'news' is 'something that hardly ever happens,'" writes security expert Bruce Schneier. "It's when something isn't in the news, when it's so common that it's no longer news—car crashes, domestic violence—that you should start worrying."

Repeatedly absorbing disaster images on TV can be particularly damaging. After 9/11, studies showed that the more hours of coverage adults and children watched, the more stress they experienced. In general, TV makes us worry about the wrong things. Your brain is better at filtering out media hype when it is reading. Words have less emotional salience than images. So it's much healthier to read the newspaper than watch TV.

The time to let your emotions run free is when you can't get good data. Long ago, that would have been all the time. You would have needed to rely on your emotions every minute of every day. "If you're back in a time before books and statistical research, and you need to know which mushrooms are poisonous, going by rumor and hearsay is a good strategy," says Gerd Gigerenzer, director of the Center for Adaptive Behavior and Cognition at the Max Planck Institute in Berlin. But when data are available—and they are now more available than any time before—there is no better complement to raw emotion.

David Ropeik, coauthor of *Risk: A Practical Guide for Deciding What's Really Safe and What's Really Dangerous in the World Around You,* does not totally repress his own instincts. He allows his emotions to help him make decisions. "We're always going to use our feelings. We're never going to have all the facts. So we have to use emotions to kind of fill in the blanks," Ropeik says. "But, and this is the challenge, that can be dangerous. If you go with how a risk feels, and that flies in the face of the facts, you could die." So Ropeik tries to check himself whenever his feelings clash with known facts. For example, he is emotionally opposed to wearing a bike helmet. He feels strongly that he looks "goofy and stupid" in a helmet. But he forces himself to wear one anyway. He knows his emotions clash with the data, so he suppresses his feelings, just the way he suppresses the desire to eat a piece of chocolate cake (most of the time).

The next time you hear about something that scares you, look for data. Be suspicious of absolute numbers—or no numbers at all. For example, new parents are now inundated with warnings about sudden infant death syndrome (SIDS), the name given to the unexplained death of a baby under age one. Given the enormous stakes, and the ready availability of preventive measures (like putting the baby to sleep on his or her back), these warnings make sense. But it would be much better if the scary pamphlets handed to new parents at the hospital put the risk into perspective. For instance, perhaps the warnings could include language like this: "SIDS is still not well-understood. But it is at an all-time low, partly because parents like you have been following basic precautions described in this pamphlet. Fewer than one baby per 1,000 dies this way (four times as many infants die from birth defects and low birthweight). So you don't need to get up seven times in the middle of the night to check if the baby is breathing. Just follow these simple rules—and concentrate on sleeping, which will make you a much better parent, with near 100 percent certainty."

Of course, even when people really do understand the risks, that doesn't mean they will make low-risk choices. Mileti, one of the nation's foremost experts on hazards, lives along one of the biggest earthquake faults in North America. I ask him if this is wise. "No, it makes no sense," he says. But, unlike 86 percent of Californians, Mileti has earthquake insurance. He also has several days' worth of supplies. And instead of paying off his house, he has stashed his savings in the bank, so he'll have cash if he needs it. He isn't mired in denial. He's made an informed gamble: until the megaearthquake he fully expects to occur one day, he gets to live in Palm Springs, California.

Part Two
Deliberation

3

Fear

The Body and Mind of
a Hostage

THE DOMINICAN REPUBLIC'S embassy in Bogotá, Colombia, occupied a large but rather shabby building outside of the usual diplomatic enclave. It would take U.S. ambassador Diego Asencio, his
driver, and four bodyguards at least half an hour to drive there. But the
Dominican ambassador was celebrating his country's independence
day, and by tradition, every diplomat attended everyone else's party. Be-
sides, it was Asencio's job to pan for treasure at cocktail parties. There
was always the chance he would carry home some small rumor, floated
theory, or unkind whisper that might prove valuable.

At age forty-eight, Asencio was "used to the low lighting of comfortable offices," as he would later put it. He had grown up in working-class
Newark, New Jersey, the son of Spanish immigrants. Through charm,
hard work, and fluent Spanish, he managed to tunnel his way into the
squirearchy of diplomacy. He graduated from the Georgetown University School of Foreign Service in Washington, D.C. Then he worked in
embassies in Mexico, Panama, Brazil, and Venezuela before going to
Colombia. Around the State Department, Asencio was known as a gre-
garious, pipe-smoking character unafraid to offer his opinion on delicate

matters. He liked dirty jokes, "the dirtier the better," according to one newspaper account from the time. By February 27, 1980, the day of the party, he had been the U.S. Ambassador to Colombia for two and a half years.

Asencio swept into the party around noon with a short agenda: greet the host, say hello to a few friends, and then gracefully exit in time for lunch. About sixty people had already arrived. The banter, as usual at such functions, was collegial but calculated. Asencio began making his rounds. Ambassadors from Israel, the Soviet Union, Egypt, and Switzerland, as well as the pope's representative, exchanged kisses and handshakes and picked at the canapés. Around the time the Venezuelan ambassador pulled Asencio aside to debate a proposal affecting the local beef industry, Asencio sensed it was time to go. He started to glide toward the door and compose his good-byes.

Just then, two well-dressed couples walked in through the front door, past Asencio's armored Chrysler Imperial limousine and his bodyguards. The couples wore unusually serious expressions for such an affair, but attracted no special attention. There were bound to be a few professional party crashers in attendance—a tradition at diplomatic functions in Colombia.

But the four young arrivals were members of M-19, a group of violent, nationalist rebels, and they had come to take the diplomats hostage. Lining up in the front of the room, they opened up their jackets, pulled pistols from their belts, and started firing at the ceiling. There was total quiet at first, as plaster fell to the floor. Then a few women started screaming. Men shouted. Despite his rather portly build, Asencio did not hesitate. He dove to the ground and crawled between a sofa and a wall. Others did nothing at all, silently watching the world collapse around them.

From the ground, as the gunfire continued, Asencio looked up to see his host, the Dominican ambassador, run shrieking from the room—followed immediately by the countershriek of his wife, who yelled, "Mallol, act like a man!" and sent her husband spinning back inside. Meanwhile, another twelve young people who had been casually kicking a soccer ball around across the street ran into the embassy, pulling shotguns, carbines, and pistols from their gym bags and firing at Asencio's bodyguards outside the door.

The security men returned fire, but they were now badly outnumbered. As the sixteen terrorists barricaded themselves inside the embassy, the cacophony of screaming, swearing, and gunfire was overwhelming. Bullets shattered the tall window above Asencio, raining glass down onto his head. He could hear the thud of bullets slamming into the wall behind him. The terrorists held more than fifty captives—one of the largest groups of diplomatic hostages in history.

Over the previous two months, there had been a dozen embassy seizures in Latin America alone. At that very moment, Iranian militants were occupying the U.S. embassy in Tehran. Asencio had read accounts of diplomats held hostage, and he himself had recently been involved in negotiations to free a Peace Corps officer held by Colombian guerrillas. Given all that he knew, he did not anticipate things going well for him. "My feeling was that there was absolutely no way I was going to survive," he remembers. "I was for all intents and purposes, dead."

The Physiology of Fear

What does it feel like to face death? What happens in our brains as the ground buckles under our feet? Fear guides our reactions in every station of the survival arc. But we'll consider its effects here, in the beginning of the deliberation phase, because fear is typically at its peak once we've grasped the danger we face. Any deliberation that follows will happen through the prism of fear. People's behavior in a disaster is inexplicable until we understand the effect of fear on the body and mind.

The human fear response looks a lot like the fear response of other animals. So scientists understand fear better than, say, guilt or shame. "Fear is so fundamental," says brain expert Joseph LeDoux. "There are key environmental triggers that will turn it on and well-worked-out responses that help you cope with it. These things have stuck around through zillions of years of evolution."

The first rule of fear is that it is primitive. Consider the fact that our hair stands on end in a terrifying situation. What purpose could that possibly serve? Well, none—for us. But scientists believe it may be related to the flashing of feathers in birds or fin extensions in fish—all of which aid in the survival of those creatures. Over the long arc of history, fear has served us very well, and it still does, with some exceptions.

Here is how fear moved through Asencio's body: first, an unexpected sound registering 90 decibels or louder sets off an instinctive alarm in human beings. A rifle shot registers around 120 to 155 decibels. As soon as Asencio's ears detected the booming gunshots, before he even realized what they were or that he was afraid, a signal traveled to his brain by way of the auditory nerve. When the signal reached his brainstem, neurons passed along the information to his amygdala, an ancient, almond-shaped mass of nuclei located deep within his brain's temporal lobes that is central to the human fear circuit. In response, the amygdala set off a cascading series of changes throughout his body. In a flash, Asencio transformed into survival mode—without any conscious decision making on his part.

If Asencio responded like most people, the chemistry of his blood literally changed so that it would be able to coagulate more easily. At the same time, his blood vessels constricted so that he would bleed less if he got hurt. His blood pressure and his heart rate shot up. And a slew of hormones—in particular cortisol and adrenaline—surged through his system, giving his gross-motor muscles a sort of bionic boost. (The hormones are so powerful that, after a life-or-death situation, many people report having an odd, chemical taste in their mouths.)

But the next rule of fear is that for every gift it gives us, it takes one away. Like a country under attack, the human body has limited resources. The brain must decide what to prioritize and what to neglect. Our muscles become taut and ready. Our body creates its own natural painkillers. But our abilities to reason and perceive our surroundings deteriorate. Cortisol interferes with the part of the brain that handles complex thinking. We suddenly have trouble solving problems, even simple ones—like how to put on a life jacket or unbuckle a seat belt. All of our senses are profoundly altered. A few of us, like Elia Zedeño in the World Trade Center, even go temporarily blind, as we saw in Chapter 1.

Not all of the diplomats dove for cover like Asencio. While the gun battle raged on, the Costa Rican consul general wandered the room, still clutching his drink, until one of his assailants pulled him down to the ground. Another ambassador, who had only arrived in Bogotá three weeks before, stood immobilized on the staircase where she'd been when the terrorists entered. Glass showered down on her from above, but still she didn't move. Finally, one of the attackers screamed at her repeatedly: "Get down! You'll get shot!" With that, the ambassador slumped into a crouch.

The amygdala learns about danger in two ways. We have already seen the first way, which neuroscientist LeDoux calls the "low road": Asencio's ears sent a signal directly to his amygdala to trigger the sympathetic nervous system reaction. The low road is "a quick and dirty processing system," as LeDoux writes in his excellent book, *The Emotional Brain*. But the sound of the gunshots also sent a signal that traveled through the cortex, the outer layer of gray matter involved in Asencio's higher brain functions. The cortex recognized the sound as gunshots and sent a more nuanced message to the amygdala. This is the "high road." It is a more accurate depiction of what happened, but it is also slower.

The more time we have to respond to a threat, the more we can recruit the brain's more sophisticated abilities. We can put the threat in context, consider our options, and act intelligently. But these higher functions are always slower and weaker than the primal response of the amygdala. As with risk, so with fear: emotions trump reason. "Emotions monopolize brain resources," says LeDoux. "There's a reason for that: If you're faced with a bloodthirsty beast, you don't want your attention to wane."

In Asencio's case, as the gunfight pounded on, he tried to breathe evenly. His brain had just enough time to think. The drama of the situation was powerful enough that he vaulted right over the traditional first phase of denial and moved on to deliberation. He had no one to mill with, back there behind the couch. So he did what most people do in this kind of crisis: he had a conversation with himself. And it didn't go as he would have predicted. First, crouched on the floor, he consciously compared what he was feeling with what he would have expected to feel at such a time. "I was trying to take my own temperature," he told me. To his surprise, his life did not flash before his eyes. Instead, he suddenly remembered how in Norman Mailer's novel *The Naked and the Dead* men under fire had had trouble controlling their bowels. And, in the midst of the bedlam, he noted that this problem, thankfully, had not happened to him. His brain searched its memory for script to address this situation and successfully pulled up a relevant data point. But it turned out to be inaccurate. He actually thought to himself, "Mailer was wrong."

Technically, Mailer was right. Under extreme duress, the body abandons certain nonessential functions like digestion, salivation, and sometimes bladder and sphincter control. One firefighter in a U.S. city (I promised the chief I wouldn't reveal the location), spent ten years soiling his pants every time his station was called to an alarm. The other firefighters still remember the stench. Finally, this unfortunate man had a heart attack and switched careers. In a study of U.S. soldiers in World War II, 10 to 20 percent admitted they had defecated in their pants. The true percentage is probably much higher, since incontinence is not something most soldiers like to acknowledge. But it doesn't happen to everyone, as Asencio discovered.

Asencio did experience another classic fear response, however: the slowing down of time. "Time and space became entirely disjointed," he wrote later. "The action around me, which had seemed speeded up at first, now turned into slow motion. The scene was like a confused, nightmarish hallucination, a grotesque charade. Everything I saw seemed distorted; everyone, everything, was out of character."

As he huddled behind the sofa, the gunfight escalated. A bullet grazed the head of one of the female hostage-takers. But she kept shooting, blood streaming down her face. Another guerrilla fighter, a seventeen-year-old high school student standing near the front door in a green sweatsuit, took a bullet to the head and crumpled to the ground. Asencio stared at the boy's head, covered in blood, and felt oddly detached. "It was unreal," he says. "Here was this young man, dead, right in front of me, and it just seemed surrealistic somehow."

This curious sense of aloofness, called "dissociation," can feel subtle. In a study of 115 police officers involved in serious shootings, 90 percent reported having some kind of dissociative symptom—from numbing to a loss of awareness to memory problems. At its most extreme, dissociation can take the form of an out-of-body experience. That's when people describe feeling as if they were watching themselves from above. The exact same phenomenon is reported by patients with epilepsy, depression, migraine, or schizophrenia, which tells us that the sensation probably has something to do with a breakdown in the brain's ability to integrate a flood of data. (In at least one case, scientists have even been able to induce an out-of-body experience by electronically stimulating part of a patient's brain.) Extreme dissociation seems to be the brain's last line of defense, and it is particularly common among victims of childhood sexual abuse. "It's a way to survive," says Hanoch Yerushalmi, an Israeli psychologist who has worked with many victims of trauma. "People are saying, 'You have my body, but you don't have my soul.'" Like all defense mechanisms, dissociation exacts a cost. A series of studies has found that the more intense the dissociation during the crisis, the harder the recovery will be for the person who survives.

Asencio thinks the fiercest part of the gunfight went on for at least thirty minutes. But to this day, he's not really sure how long it lasted. "It seemed interminable to me," he says. As the shots became more sporadic, he could hear the groans of the casualties scattered around him. Continuing his internal dialogue (which psychologists call "self-talk"), he decided he would behave with honor, if he possibly could. "I knew there was no way I could return to my wife and children, to my friends and colleagues in the Foreign Service after collapsing in a heap and saying, 'I can't cut it.'" With that decision made, Asencio felt slightly better.

People in life-or-death situations often think of their children or how others will perceive them after the crisis is over. Gasping for air in turbulent seas or groping their way out of a burning plane, they hear the voices of their family members in their heads. Sometimes the voices are even mocking. In *Guests of the Ayatollah,* a book about the 1979 Iran hostage crisis, writer Mark Bowden describes one Marine major's conversation with himself as his helicopter curled into flames around him during a doomed rescue effort. The passage illustrates just how compelling these conjectures can be: "The pilot shut down the engines and sat for a moment, certain he was about to die. Then for some reason an image came into his mind of his fiancée's father—a man who had always seemed none too impressed with his future pilot son-in-law—commenting during some future family meal about how the poor sap's body had been found cooked like a holiday turkey in the front seat of his aircraft, and something about that horrifying image motivated him. His body would not be found like an overcooked Butterball; he had to at least try to escape." He ejected from the window and ran, burning, from the wreckage.

In Colombia, the gunfire finally stopped altogether. The leader of the guerrillas gathered Asencio and the rest of the captives together. He was a serious young man with glasses who called himself "Commandante Uno." He ticked off the group's goals: they were seeking the release of 311 M-19 prisoners, $50 million in cash, and publicity for charges of brutality against the Colombian government. Listening to this list of fantasies, Asencio remained certain that his death was near. Somehow, that knowledge left him feeling strangely fearless. It was only days later, when it seemed possible that he might actually survive, that he became frightened again.

A Plane Crash Imagined

In order to imagine what it might feel like to lose your senses under stress, I visited the Federal Aviation Administration's training academy in Oklahoma City, Oklahoma. In a field behind one of their labs, they have hoisted a section of a jet onto risers. One afternoon, I boarded the mock-up plane along with thirty flight-attendant supervisors. Inside, it looked just like a normal plane, and the flight attendants made jokes, pretending to be passengers. "Could I get a cocktail over here, please? I paid a lot of money for this seat!" But once smoke started pouring into the cabin, everyone got quiet.

As most people do, I underestimated how quickly the smoke would fill the space, from ceiling to floor, like a black curtain unfurling in front of us. The smoke was nontoxic, but it still had the desired effect. Most people have no concept of how little they will be able to see in a fire, and how much harder the brain will have to work as a result. We would get a very mild preview.

In less than twenty seconds, all we could see were the pin lights along the floor. As we stood to evacuate, there was a loud thump. In a crowd of experienced flight attendants, someone had hit his or her head on an overhead bin. Under a minor amount of stress, our brains were already performing clumsily. As we filed toward the exit slide, crouched low, holding on to the person in front of us, several of the flight attendants had to be comforted by their colleagues. Then we emerged into the light, and the mood brightened. The flight attendants cheered as their colleagues slid, one by one, to the ground.

Next, we headed to the indoor pool for a water rescue. We wore regular clothing, just like passengers, and jumped into the pool—yanking a cord to inflate our life jackets as we entered the water. (In real crashes, people usually ignore instructions and inflate their life vests while they're still on the plane—an understandable mistake, given the stress of the situation. But the inflated vest is an unwieldy, bloated affair that takes up valuable space in a plane and makes it hard to walk and see.) The first exercise involved getting picked up by a "helicopter" in a basket lowered from the ceiling. Once again, there was a lot of clapping and cheering.

But then we moved on to the life-raft exercise. Just getting into the giant, yellow raft was an ordeal. We had to heave each other up and into the raft. In the tumult, one flight attendant got a black eye and had to sit out the rest of the simulation. Once inside the boat, the strong smell of vomit (from the chemically treated plastic of the raft) heightened the realism. Then we had to unfurl the raft's unwieldy tarp over our heads to create a shelter against the frigid "waves" crashing down on top of us (courtesy of a merciless FAA trainer with a hose). In the dim light, a female flight attendant with a loud, low voice shouted out instructions from a rescue kit while the rest of us bailed water and held on to the tarp.

It was hard to hear or think with the constant thud of the water hitting our precarious plastic shelter. Every thirty seconds or so, when a spray of ice-cold water leaked through, my fellow survivors would erupt in shrieks. At that moment, I remembered once being told by a military researcher that very cold or very hot environments tend to degrade human performance very, very quickly. The effect tends to be geometric. Sitting there for just five minutes in the wet, stinking huddle, I felt suddenly exhausted. I knew I'd be out of there in time for dinner. I knew my life wasn't even remotely in danger, and I did not feel afraid. But still, I felt surprisingly drained. My brain must have been working harder than I consciously realized. At that moment, the idea of quietly surrendering in a real disaster didn't seem quite so unimaginable.

Down the Rabbit Hole

In life-or-death situations, people gain certain powers and lose others. Asencio found he suddenly had crystal-clear vision. (In fact, his sight remained stronger for several months after the siege, leading his optometrist to temporarily lower his prescription.) Other people, a majority in most studies, get tunnel vision. Their field of sight shrinks by about 70 percent, so that in some cases they seem to be peering out of a keyhole, and they lose track of anything going on in their periphery. Most people also get a sort of tunnel hearing. Certain sounds become strangely muted; others are louder than life.

Stress hormones are like hallucinogenic drugs. Almost no one gets through an ordeal like this *without* experiencing some kind of altered reality. In one study of shootings of civilians by police officers, 94 percent of officers experienced at least one distortion, according to criminologist David Klinger's interviews with the officers involved. But very few knew what to expect beforehand. So their distortions distracted and even embarrassed some of them.

One of the most fascinating distortions, reported in more than half of the police-shooting cases, is the strange slowing down of time. Time distortion is so common that scientists have a name for it: tachypsychia, derived from the Greek for "speed of the mind." Drivers remember the bumper stickers of the car they rear-ended. Mugging victims remember how many chambers the robber's gun had. Consider this officer's memory from a gun battle, as told to police psychologist Alexis Artwohl: "I looked over, drawn to the sudden mayhem, and was puzzled to see beer cans slowly floating through the air past my face. What was even more puzzling was that they had the word *Federal* printed on the bottom. They turned out to be the shell casings ejected by the officer who was firing next to me."

Why does time seem to slow down in moments of terror? What is happening in our brain? And might it be saving our lives, whatever it is? When David Eagleman was in third grade, he and his older brother went exploring in a house under construction in their neighborhood. His father had explicitly told them not to play there, but the jungle gym of lumber was too tempting. As he scrambled across the roof, Eagleman lost his footing. He found himself falling twelve feet to the ground.

But the descent felt nothing like he would have expected. "The thing is, the fall took forever," he remembers. And instead of being afraid as he floated through space, Eagleman found that his brain was just busy trying to figure out what to do. He felt totally calm. "I had this whole series of thoughts that I can remember even now, two-thirds of a lifetime later." Like Asencio, he rifled through his mental database in search of a script. But he could not find one that was of much help. First he considered grabbing for the edge of the roof, but then he realized that it was too late for that. Then, as he watched the red brick below get closer and closer, he suddenly thought of *Alice in Wonderland*. "I was thinking that this must be what it felt like when she fell down the rabbit hole," he says. It was only after he landed, face-first and bloodied, that he felt fear. He jumped up and ran to a neighbor's house.

Eagleman grew up to be a neuroscientist. Today he works at Baylor College of Medicine in Houston, where he spends a lot of time trying to re-create that slow-motion fall. "I'm trying to figure out how the brain represents time," he says. We don't think about it, but under normal circumstances, your brain is already "controlling" time. Your sense of touch, vision, and hearing all operate using different architectures. Imagine your brain as a clock store: Data comes in at slightly different times, so no two clocks tick at exactly the same pace. But your brain synchs everything up so you are not confused. How does the brain do this? And what is it doing differently when things seem to move in slow motion?

Nobody really knows. So in 2006, Eagleman, then at the University of Texas, decided to try to figure it out through a rather unusual experiment. He designed a plan to scare people so badly that they might experience slow-motion time. The goal was to measure whether people actually saw things in slow motion—or whether it just seemed that way in their memories afterward. "We study vision by studying illusion, which is when the visual system gets things wrong," he says. "I'm trying to do the same thing with temporal distortion."

After eight months, Eagleman got approval for the study from his university's committee on human experimentation. ("It was an absolute miracle," he says.) And one fine spring day, he took twenty-three volunteers to the top of a 150-foot tower in Dallas. It was blustery outside—all the better for Eagleman's purposes. One by one, he strapped each subject into a harness, dangled each over the side of the tower, and then dropped each one—backward—into the air. It was important that they fall backward, Eagleman felt, for maximum fear factor. Plummeting toward the ground, the volunteers reached speeds of 70 mph before safely hitting the net below. Eagleman tried out the contraption himself. It was just like falling off the roof! "It is freaking scary. I felt like a changed man afterwards. Whew! Oh, boy," he says. "It goes against every Darwinian instinct you have to not have anything to grab on to."

Now that he could trigger the fear response, Eagleman needed to measure the time distortion. So each volunteer was outfitted with a special watch. The screen flashed a number faster than the human eye could normally see it. As the students fell, they looked at the watch and tried to read the number. If the students could see it, Eagleman reasoned, then perhaps we humans actually do have superpowers under extreme stress: our brains can see better than normally, creating the sensation that time is actually slowing down.

The results were humbling. "You're not like Neo in the *Matrix*," Eagleman says. All of the volunteers did indeed *feel* like they were moving in slow motion. "Everybody reports it was the longest three seconds of their lives," Eagleman says. But none of them could see the number. Eagleman thinks this means that time distortion primarily exists in our memory. "Time in general is not slowing down. It's just that in a fearful situation, you recruit other parts of the brain, like the amygdala, to lay down memories. And because they are laid down more richly, it seems as though it must have taken longer." In other words, trauma creates such a searing impression on our brains that it feels, in retrospect, like it happened in slow motion.

Eagleman is planning more free-fall experiments. Among other un-explained mysteries, he's curious about why some people report time slowing down, while others feel like it speeds up. (Asencio, remember, felt both sensations at different times.) Eagleman is also perplexed by the way our hearing changes under extreme stress. In studies of police shootings, many officers say sounds became muted or disappear alto-gether. Sometimes, this can be problematic—when police involved in shootings have no recollection of firing their guns, for example. But it can also be ingenious: just when we need to focus, the brain shuts off any sound that might distract us.

The ultimate question is whether any of these reflexes can be inten-tionally turned on—or off. If they could, imagine what we could do. We could hone our brains to become precision, instead of blunt, instru-ments, to know which abilities to enhance and suppress at just the right moment. To do, in other words, what we already do most of the time, but to do it all the time—even in acutely modern crises that we haven't evolved to survive.

The Making of a Gunfighter

Jim Cirillo was a gunfighter. Among police officers and combat instruc-tors, he was a legend, a retired New York City Police Department officer who, according to that legend, was in more gunfights than any cop, cow-boy, or mafia kingpin in the history of gunpowder. We spoke in October 2006 for this book. He was generous with his time and wisdom, and he asked me to send him a signed copy of the book. Nine months later, Cir-illo was killed in a car crash near his home in Upstate New York at the age of seventy-six. It was a sudden and tragic end to a long life. I am grateful to have had the chance to interview him, and I regret that I won't be able to do it again.

When we spoke, it was clear that Cirillo did not consider himself a legend. He declined to say how many shoot-outs he'd been in, though double-digit numbers have been printed elsewhere. "I hate to mention the number," he said. "People start thinking there must be something wrong with you." Actually, he said, he thought of himself as kind of cowardly. "I never even gave blood at the department," he confessed. "I didn't want them sticking needles in me."

When he joined the NYPD in 1954, Cirillo hoped to never have to shoot anyone. And he succeeded for over a decade, working as a firearms instructor. He fired his gun thousands of times, but never at a real person. Then in the late 1960s, a rash of violent corner-store robberies rocked the city. Police found one store owner shot execution style in his establishment. He had a concentration-camp number tattooed on his arm. "This poor bastard comes over here to get killed, right?" Cirillo says, still disgusted after all these years.

Under pressure to do something, police commissioner Howard Leary started up a new special unit: the Stakeout Squad. The department asked Cirillo and the other instructors to volunteer. Given the risks, almost all of them, including Cirillo, declined. But after some goading from his partner, who insisted that the assignment would be prestigious, warm, and dry, Cirillo signed on.

Two hours into his first stakeout, he realized he'd made a mistake. He and his partner were standing vigil over a large dairy store in Queens that had been held up by the same robbers several times. The officers settled in on top of the manager's booth, and camouflaged their position with ads and coupons. Sure enough, four men walked in, looking nervous. Cirillo could just tell they were going to hold up the place. He knew he would have to do something. But the realization came with a shock of fear. "I felt like I was becoming unglued, like my arms were going to fall off, like I was going to slip down like a river of water," he told me. "I knew I was a good shot, but I didn't know what would happen if someone was shooting back at me." Cirillo also felt, at the same time, ashamed of his own reaction. So when three of the robbers took out guns and held them to the heads of the cashier and manager, he forced himself to pop up above the wall of coupons.

As he stood, the crotch piece on his bulletproof vest fell off, clattering to the floor. The robbers turned around and pointed their guns at him. What happened next was nothing short of a miracle, Cirillo said. His training took over. His pistol sights came into focus, nice and steady, just like at the shooting range. He found he could count the serrations on his front sight. Everything began to move in slow motion. But as he took aim, he saw one of the robbers wave something light in color. His conscious mind responded this way: "I'm saying to myself, 'Oh, is he giving up? Is that a handkerchief?'" Suddenly, he heard a shot and saw a flash of fire spark out from his own gun barrel. "My subconscious was saving my ass." He felt the revolver buck in his hand several times. And his conscious mind said, "Who the hell is shooting my gun?"

When the smoke cleared, he found that three of the men had run off. (Two were arrested soon afterward, seeking medical attention for bullet wounds.) The fourth lay behind the cashier, dying from Cirillo's gunshot. What he had thought might have been a white flag of surrender was actually a nickel-plated revolver, now cradled in the robber's hands. The man had managed to fire one bullet, which was found embedded in a can of Planters Peanuts just in front of Cirillo's position.

Later, Cirillo learned that his partner, standing right beside him during the melee, had fired a shotgun six inches from his head. Cirillo didn't see him, and he barely heard the shot. Between the two of them, they got off seven shots. But Cirillo's ears did not ring afterward! It seemed that his brain had not only suppressed the sound of the shots; it had somehow sealed off his ear so that it suffered no physical effects.

How did Cirillo perform so well, despite the fear coursing through his body? As an instructor, he had taken training very seriously. He had created subconscious muscle memories for holding his gun in one hand, two hands, every conceivable position, so that he did not need to think when the time came to fire.

As he did more stakeouts, Cirillo started to appreciate his subconscious more and more. He realized that it worked best if he got out of its way; in other words, he needed to turn off his conscious mind to avoid distracting thoughts that would sap precious mental resources. So he started training himself with only positive imagery, to clear his mind of any self-doubting conscious thoughts. After five gunfights, Cirillo said, "I had it all figured out. It got familiar, and it didn't shake me." On stake-outs, instead of feeling liquefied by fear, he felt vaguely exhilarated. "Sometimes I almost wished these guys would walk in."

Cirillo began training other officers with positive visualization exercises. Instead of telling them, "If you jerk the trigger, you will miss the target," he would say: "As you focus on the sights while compressing the trigger smoothly, you will easily achieve a good shot." After he retired, Cirillo traveled the country, teaching police officers to make their skills subconscious. "Your subconscious mind is the most fascinating tool in the world," he said. "You can do things you could never do consciously."

The Survival Zone

The body's first defense is hardwired. The amygdala triggers an ancient survival dance, and it is hard to change. But we have an outstanding second defense: we can learn from experience. Among experts who train police, soldiers, and astronauts, nothing matters as much. "The actual threat is not nearly as important as the level of preparation," police psychologist Artwohl and her coauthor, Loren W. Christensen, write in their book, *Deadly Force Encounters*. "The more prepared you are, the more in control you feel, and the less fear you will experience."

Of course, it's easier to train professionals for a range of probable threats than it is to train regular people for any threat. But the larger point holds: fear is negotiable. So even civilians can benefit from some preparation. Whether or not their preparation is perfectly tailored to the actual incident, the preparation will have increased their confidence, thereby decreasing their fear and improving their performance. "A police officer facing a shooting is really going through the same process as someone who is being mugged or facing a car crash or a plane crash," Artwohl told me. "How that person responds will have something to do with their genetics, but also the sum total of their life experiences—which is basically training."

People who knew where the stairwells were in the World Trade Center were less likely to get injured or have long-term health problems. That's partly because they had the training they needed to take action under extreme stress. And, later, they could take comfort in their own competence. The same is true with police officers or firefighters. If they have the skills they need, they not only have a higher chance of survival; they fare better psychologically after the crisis. They've saved themselves once; they can do it again.

It makes intuitive sense that the more you expose yourself to safe stress, the less sensitive you would be to its effects. Just as athletes have a "zone," in which they achieve maximum performance, so do regular people. Each individual's zone is shaped a little differently, as we will see in the next chapter. But everyone's zone looks like a bell curve: at first, stress makes us perform better; but too much starts to yield diminishing returns. Beyond a critical inflection point, we begin to unravel altogether.

Sports psychologists were among the first to figure this out. Then, in the 1980s, a police academy instructor in St. Louis, Missouri, named Bruce Siddle began to take what they had learned and apply it to combat situations. He found that people perform best when their heart rates are between 115 and 145 beats per minute (resting heart rate is usually about 75 bpm). At this range, people tend to react quickly, see clearly, and manage complex motor skills (like driving).

But after about 145 bpm, people begin to deteriorate. Their voices begin to shake, probably because their blood has concentrated toward their core, shutting down the complex motor control of the larynx and leaving the face pale and the hands clumsy. Vision, hearing, and depth perception can also start to decline. If the stress intensifies, people will usually experience some amnesia after the trauma.

A young Israeli Blackhawk helicopter pilot told me that he learned this lesson on his first mission. This pilot (the Israeli military does not allow journalists to use the first or last names of its members) was awakened at 5:00 A.M. to respond to an emergency. The adrenaline yanked him out of his bed. He'd just completed six months of intense training in the elite unit. He headed for the helicopter. This call was not particularly dangerous, but now that the mission was real, he found that he was virtually useless. On the helicopter, he couldn't seem to clear his head. "I sat down and looked around. I started doing what I was supposed to do, but very, very slowly. I was two steps behind," he says. His body moved in slow motion, just like the people evacuating the Trade Center. At one point, instead of turning off one of the radios, he accidentally shut off the ignition to one of the engines. He'd overdosed on stress hormones. Luckily, he had a copilot with more experience. The mission was completed without incident.

But even veteran pilots can still experience a brain drain. Laurence Gonzales, in his book *Deep Survival,* quotes his father, a bomber pilot in World War II, explaining what happens to the mind as it prepares to fly a mission: "When you walk across the ramp to your airplane, you lose half your IQ."

Everybody is different, of course. The performance ranges will vary depending on the individual. But the heart rate of untrained people in life-or-death situations can instantly shoot up to 200 bpm—a stratospheric level that is hard to negotiate. The trick is to stretch out your zone through training and experience. Even a little preparation—like noticing where the exit is before things go awry—can go a long way. "If you give people an option, something to anchor onto when they don't know what to do, that small help is huge. That is the difference," says Ephimia Morphew-Lu, a human factors specialist at NASA until 2004.

Tunnel Vision

Sometimes the fix is astonishingly simple. In the 1970s, airplane pilots started to realize that tunnel vision was a serious problem in the cockpit. The more stressed they got, the less they saw. And the problem went beyond just vision; as stress increased, they tended to become mentally obsessed with one data point to the exclusion of all others.

On the evening of December 29, 1972, an Eastern Air Lines jet coming from New York City began its final approach to Miami International Airport. The flight had been uneventful, and the weather in Miami was clear, with unrestricted visibility. The landing should have been perfect. The plane carried 163 passengers, most of them returning from or leaving for holiday vacations.

But when the pilots tried to lower the landing gear, they didn't get a green light indicating that the gear was fully down. At 11:34 P.M, the captain, who had more than three decades of experience, called the Miami control tower to explain that he would have to circle while they worked on getting the green light. The plane climbed to two thousand feet and began a wide U-turn over the airport.

For the next eight minutes, the flight crew tried to figure out what was wrong. Why wouldn't the light go on? The captain ordered two different people to try to visually confirm that the gear was down, but they couldn't see anything in the dark. The first officer pulled out the nose-gear light to inspect it, but had problems putting it back in. All the while, the captain offered advice and issued orders. The entire cockpit crew was focused on getting that green light on.

At 11:40, a half-second alarm tone went off in the cockpit, indicating that the plane had deviated from its altitude. The transcript from the cockpit voice recorder shows that no one said anything about the alarm. It was as if they hadn't heard it at all. The crew continued to speculate about possible reasons for the light problem. But then, two minutes later, the first officer noticed another problem.

"We did something to the altitude," he said.

"What?" the captain said.

The first officer backtracked: "We're still at 2,000, right?"

Then the captain said, "Hey, what's happening here?"

Another warning sound began to beep, more insistently this time. Two seconds later, the plane crashed into the Everglades, nineteen miles from the airport.

Investigators would find that the plane had been in fine working order—except for the lightbulbs in the landing-gear indicator, which had burned out. While the flight crew worried about the light, the plane had dipped toward the earth. When it sliced into the soggy marshland, it disintegrated on impact. The wreckage was scattered over an area 1,600 feet long and 330 feet wide. A total of 101 people died.

The crash, and several other unnervingly similar accidents in the 1970s, convinced aviation researchers that pilots needed to be trained to avoid such myopia—or what is known in the industry as "task saturation." "This happens to everybody under stress," says Rogers V. Shaw II, who trains pilots for the FAA. "If there's not enough training, you get channelized on one thing, and you forget the whole big picture."

Today, Shaw trains pilots to proactively scan their instrument panels, over and over again, to counteract the tendency to fixate on one problem. He also teaches pilots to make sure one member of the flight crew remains focused on flying the plane at all times. And he hammers home the importance of open communication and dissent. "In the early '70s, the captain was God," says Shaw. "Now a lot of people send their captains to charm school, if you want to call it, so that they can create a climate where everybody feels that, if they see something they don't like, they can discuss it."

It would be a mistake to say tunnel vision is no longer a problem in cockpits. But it is a more manageable problem. On July 19, 1989, a United flight en route from Denver to Chicago suffered a catastrophic engine failure while cruising at thirty-seven thousand feet. The plane became almost impossible to control. But the flight crew, working together, managed to spontaneously invent ways to rein in the bucking plane. Forty-five minutes later, they crash-landed the plane in Sioux City, Iowa. Of the 296 people aboard, 184 survived. The plane's captain, Alfred C. Haynes, credits luck and the crew's training for the high survival rate. Immediately after hearing the initial explosion, Haynes checked to make sure someone was tasked with flying the plane, according to an account he wrote after the crash. When he saw that his first officer was focused on doing just that, he turned to investigating the cause of the explosion. "There were 103 years of flying experience in that cockpit when we faced our end . . . but not one minute of those 103 years had been spent operating an aircraft the way we were trying to fly it," Haynes wrote. "If we had not worked together, with everybody coming up with ideas . . . I do not think we would have made it to Sioux City."

Police officers, like pilots, are sometimes trained to repeatedly scan their horizon to avoid fixation. (Police have also learned to exploit tunnel vision in others by intentionally stepping to the side to get into a suspect's blind spot.) Just knowing enough to identify certain stress reactions can improve people's performance. But most regular people don't know to expect tunnel vision—even though they experience it every day. You have suffered from a mild version of tunnel vision yourself, maybe even on your way to work today. When you talk on your cell phone while driving, your range of sight narrows significantly, according to a 2002 University of Rhode Island study. The distraction is so strong that your case of tunnel vision continues well after the phone conversation has ended. The brain is built to focus on one thing at a time, whether in a traffic jam or during an emergency landing. We have built technology for multitasking, but the brain has not changed.

Bulking Up the Brain

The best way to negotiate stress is through repeated, realistic training. The military used to train soldiers to shoot bull's-eye targets, and it didn't work very well. Now soldiers train using highly realistic targets and video games, as retired Lieutenant Colonel Dave Grossman explains in his book, *On Combat*. Advanced police training now relies on actual gunfights—using gunpowder-propelled, paint-filled plastic bullets that actually sting when they hit you. Self-defense courses use "model muggings," in which a pretend assailant, wearing heavy padding, relentlessly attacks the student. Fire drills work the same way, especially for children, who tend to get the best training for disasters in our society. "Kids remember 'stop, drop, and roll' because we make them rehearse it—not because we make them say it," says Richard Gist, a psychologist who works for the Kansas City, Missouri, Fire Department. The trick is to embed the behavior in the subconscious, so that it is automatic, almost like the rest of the fear response.

The idea that we can negotiate our fear response is a fairly radical one. For most of history, human beings have assumed a bright line between instinct and learning. But the past decade of brain research has proven that we are actually a magnificent work in progress. The brain literally changes in structure and function throughout our lives, depending on what we do. Blind people who read Braille increase the size of the brain region that processes touch. A small but charming 2004 study published in *Nature* found that people who learned how to juggle actually increased the gray matter in their brains in certain locations. When they stopped juggling, the new gray matter vanished. A similar structural change appears to occur in people who learn a second language. Just like a novice cab driver in New York City, the brain starts out slow and inefficient and finds shortcuts as time goes on. This way, we can compensate for our own weaknesses. Even if our fear response is ancient, we can continually upgrade it for modernity.

Some reflexes cannot be entirely overridden, of course. The human startle response, for example, is something we possess from the womb. The first 150 milliseconds of the startle response begin with a very small but reliable reaction. We blink. Like almost all of the fear responses, blinking serves a useful purpose—by potentially protecting our eyes from harm. (In laboratory experiments, people blink even more rapidly when they see unpleasant images.) Meanwhile, our head and upper body automatically lean forward, and the arms bend at the elbow—positioning the body to fight, cower, or flee. Instantly, the hands begin to tighten into fists—generating about twenty-five pounds of pressure in adults.

For years, police academy instructors tried to train officers *not* to flinch. In 1992, a Canadian police officer and trainer named Darren Laur decided to see if the training was working. He ran eighty-five police officers through an experiment in which they were unexpectedly confronted by a knife-wielding attacker. Laur videotaped all of the confrontations. What he saw was disconcerting: a majority of the officers completely ignored their training. They collapsed into a crouch, brought both their hands up to protect their head, and backed away from the attacker. They flinched, in other words.

After watching the tapes, Laur realized it made more sense to train around the flinch, instead of against it. Shooting instructors have learned the same lesson. Above roughly 145 bpm, most people's movements become symmetrical: whatever one hand does, so does the other. If they are startled, that automatic fist-tightening response will happen in both hands, and they will almost certainly fire their guns at anything in front of them. Today, many police officers are trained to never keep their fingers on their gun triggers. That way, the flinch has fewer consequences.

Combat Lamaze

On 9/11, Manuel Chea, a systems administrator on the forty-ninth floor of Tower 1, did everything right. As soon as the building stopped swaying, he jumped up from his cubicle and ran to the closest stairwell. It was an automatic reaction. As he left, he noticed that some of his colleagues were collecting things to take with them. "I was probably the fastest one to leave," he says. An hour later, he was outside.

When I asked him why he had moved so swiftly, Chea offered several theories. He knew where the stairway was because he used it all the time to go to the cafeteria. He was familiar with the escape route, a huge advantage. Also, he had experience with fire. The previous year, his house in Queens, New York, had burned to the ground. He had escaped, blinded by smoke. As a child in Peru, he had been in a serious earthquake. Then, later, he'd been in several smaller quakes in Los Angeles. He was basically a disaster expert.

Most of us, I think it's fair to say, have no obvious way to train for life-or-death situations that may never happen. Other than fire drills, which are usually not very realistic anyway, there aren't many opportunities to get to know your disaster personality in a safe environment. There should be disaster amusement parks filled with simulation rides. Ride in a funnel cloud! Feel the g-forces of an earthquake! Survive a tsunami! And sign this waiver!

But for now, there are simpler ways to train the fear response. One of the most surprising tactics, taught in all seriousness to some of the scariest, gun-wielding men in the world, is breathing. Over and over again, when I ask combat trainers how people can master their fear, this is what they talk about. Of course, they call it "combat breathing" or "tactical breathing" when they teach it to Green Berets and FBI agents. But it's the same basic concept taught in yoga and Lamaze classes. One version taught to police works like this: breathe in for four counts; hold for four counts; breathe out for four counts; hold for four; start again. That's it.

Keith Nelson Borders was shot ten times in six shoot-outs as a police officer in Oklahoma and then Nevada from 1994 to 2005. Every time he got shot, he breathed deeply and methodically, and he swears by the strategy. "It keeps you very calm. You don't start to hyperventilate or panic. Everything just kind of goes in slow motion for you," says Nelson, who is now retired at age forty due to injuries. "You say, OK, here's what's going on, I can handle this. I got shot in the head, and I'm still alive, things are working, so it's not that bad."

How could something so simple be so powerful? The breath is one of the few actions that reside in both our somatic nervous system (which we can consciously control) *and* our autonomic system (which includes our heartbeat and other actions we cannot easily access). So the breath is a bridge between the two, as combat instructor Dave Grossman explains. By consciously slowing down the breath, we can de-escalate the primal fear response that otherwise takes over.

Charles Humes, a police officer in Toledo, Ohio, has devised a clever way to combine breathing with realistic training. As a young officer, he found he lost control of his body and mind in high-speed car chases. "I was a threat to myself and others," he remembers. "My voice would go up several octaves. My radio communications would become unintelligible, tunnel vision would take over, and my reasoning and common sense would go right out the window." To try to tame this response, he started using breathing tactics he had learned in martial arts. Every day, he played a tape recording of a police siren for five or ten minutes. As the siren shrieked, he breathed deeply—in for four, hold for four, out for four. He wanted to make his breathing an automatic response to the siren. "It all goes back to the Pavlovian theory," he says. "It's not rocket science." After about a month of this, he sounded like a different person over the radio. "I even have some of the radio tapes from some of my old pursuits, and you could tell, just listening to the tone of the voice and clarity, that I was much more under control. I wasn't getting nearly as hyped up."

There is a wonderful scientific study that shows how rhythmic breathing and mindfulness can actually alter the topography of the brain. A few years ago, an instructor at Harvard Medical School named Sara Lazar scanned the brains of twenty people who meditate for forty minutes a day. These weren't Buddhist monks. Just regular people who had a long history of meditating. When she compared their brain images to those of nonmeditating people of similar ages and backgrounds, she found a highly significant difference. The meditators had 5 percent thicker brain tissue in the parts of the prefrontal cortex that are engaged during meditation—that is, the parts that handle emotion regulation, attention, and working memory, all of which help control stress.

Meditators, like deep-breathing cops, may have found a way to essentially evolve past the basic human fear response. In other words, they may have discovered a bridge in the brain—between their conscious and subconscious—that most people don't know exists. What's most interesting is that just knowing they have such powers might be valuable in itself.

Laughter, like breathing, reduces our emotional arousal level as well. It also has the benefit of making us feel more in control of the situation. Again and again, studies have shown that people perform better under stress if they *think* they can handle it. In studies of rats, scientists have taken this discovery one step further: the medial prefrontal cortex appears to detect whether a threat is under the rat's control. If the brain concludes that the stressor is indeed under its control, the brain blocks some of the more devastating effects of extreme stress. Self-confidence, in other words, can save your life. Says Massad Ayoob, a veteran police officer and instructor: "The single strongest [weapon] is a mental plan of what you'll do in a certain crisis. And an absolute commitment to do it, by God, if the crisis comes to pass."

The Hostage-Taker

On February 27, 1980, Rosemberg Pabón, age thirty-one, put on a pinstriped suit and tucked a pistol into his waistband. Pabón, also known as Commandante Uno, had never been in a gunfight before. He'd never even been to Bogotá until now. The night before, when he met his M-19 accomplices for the first time, he was given one last chance to back out of this operation. But the camaraderie in the room had fortified him. "All the compañeros said really beautiful things—like they were proud to have been chosen, that they were doing it for a better country. So I heard that and I was filled with courage," he remembers. "The only thing I thought was to ask God to help me not to be afraid."

But Pabón was afraid, terribly so. That morning, the group waited at a hideout house nearby for the final go-ahead order. They would not leave until they heard that the American ambassador, Diego Asencio, had arrived at the party. "Without him, it wasn't worth it to run the risk of the operation. He was the key." The call came around 11:30 A.M. Asencio was there. Pabón, another man, and two women, dressed to look like diplomats, got into a car and headed for the embassy. The car let them off at the corner. Pabón took the arm of one of the female terrorists, and they headed for the front door.

Already, there was a problem. Soldiers had occupied the National University across the street to quell a disturbance. That meant that armed men would respond immediately to the siege, which was not part of the plan. Pabón and his comrades had counted on having at least fifteen minutes to subdue the crowd without serious opposition. "The situation was difficult from the very first moment," he says. And so the terrorists had few illusions about their chances. "There was nothing other than death awaiting us there. We knew it. We knew it would be very hard to get out alive."

It's easy to forget that the victims are not the only tremulous people at a crime scene. Fear transforms everyone, from the police officer to the bank robber. Many of the terrorists who took over the embassy that day were later killed in other conflicts. But Pabón is still alive to tell his version of the takeover. In the kind of comeback story that could only happen in a society that is exceedingly generous with its former insurgents, Pabón now works as a midlevel functionary for the Colombian government. He occupies a large, wood-paneled office in a dingy building in downtown Bogotá. In November of 2006, from behind a polished wooden desk, under a crucifix and a portrait of the Colombian president, he recounted his memories of the siege. He wore a dark, pin-striped suit, just as he had the day of the takeover. This time, he was well accessorized—with a red-and-white-striped shirt and a yellow tie. He spoke matter-of-factly, revealing only an occasional glint of pride in the role he had played in an international hostage incident.

Walking from the corner to the embassy, Pabón remembered, he had slipped into the same kind of time warp he was about to impose upon his victims. "I felt like those fifteen meters from the corner to the door were interminable," he says, using the very same adjective Asencio used to describe his impressions of that morning. "They stretched on and on and on." He followed the other couple, but they seemed to be going very slowly. He felt like he was walking in place. "The movie of my life came to me. With every step I took I remembered my childhood, my adolescence, everything—like it was a farewell. It was like having the eyes of a fly with a thousand lenses, and in each lens, there was a different image. That's what I felt."

When he got to the front door, a man asked him for his invitation. Pabón took out his gun. With that, the fog lifted. "I felt as if I was back in reality." But as he walked through the front door, he was stunned to see a man to his left with a gun. He felt a new surge of fear, this time tinged with betrayal. He had been promised that once they entered the embassy, none of the diplomats would be armed. So who was this man in a suit gripping a pistol? Pabón dropped to the floor instinctively. So did the other man. Pabón opened fire; so did the other man. "I lifted my head, and he lifted his head. I fired again, and so did he," Pabón says. The man was unstoppable.

Then one of his comrades stopped him; Pabón was firing at a mirror, scared of his own shadow. Fear short-circuited his higher-level brain functioning, just as it did for the hostages and the soldiers who tried to rescue them. Telling the story now, Pabón laughs gently at himself. "I had good reflexes, but I was very nervous. I didn't recognize myself. I just saw a gun and started shooting."

As the gunfire and the screaming rose to an unsustainable climax, a sudden vision of the next day's newspaper flashed across Pabón's mind. He saw a head shot of himself and another picture of the people in the embassy on the floor, all of them dead. The images popped into his head, and then vanished, just as quickly. Pabón's brain was contemplating the possible outcomes of his actions, just as Asencio imagined what it would be like to face his family and colleagues if he exhibited inadequate courage under fire.

When the shots finally began to fade out, Pabón and his comrades divided the hostages into groups, depending on their political worth. They had before them a crowd of valuable assets. The terrorists chose five diplomats to form a committee to represent the hostages. The committee included Asencio, the U.S. ambassador. "They had all this experience in diplomacy, and this was all about diplomacy at the highest level," Pabón explains.

Asencio, meanwhile, was already a man who did not want for confidence. In this situation, he recognized that he had a skill the terrorists needed. In his role on the committee, he became more comfortable. He began to joke with the other hostages and his captors. As the days wore on, he even got into animated debates with the guerrillas about U.S. foreign policy. One day, when he and the other diplomats learned about a long diatribe that the terrorists were planning on issuing at their next negotiating session with government officials, they told the terrorists that their strategy was flawed. They wrote up a more nuanced draft of their own, and the terrorists used it, Asencio says.

Pabón does not remember the hostages actually writing any documents. But he does remember that they were helpful. "They taught us how to read between the lines of the messages that the government sent us. When things got really confusing and somber, they helped us to see the light at the end of the tunnel, and they showed us how to stay positive."

The siege of the Dominican embassy would last sixty-one days. When it finally ended, it happened very differently from how Asencio or Pabón would have predicted that first, bloody day. The Colombian government agreed to allow international observers to monitor prison conditions and trials. And the terrorists eventually gave up their demand for prisoner releases. They did receive $1 million in ransom (supposedly from private donors, but Pabón believes the ransom may have been paid by the government). And they were permitted to fly to Cuba with twelve of their hostages (including Asencio), whom they then released.

For students of disasters, the story of the Dominican embassy siege was astonishing. It proved that hostages can in fact be very useful actors. They do not automatically melt down into helpless victims. Nor do they necessarily fall prey to the so-called Stockholm syndrome, whereby hostages become perversely loyal to their captors. The Stockholm syndrome, named after a 1973 bank robbery in Stockholm in which the hostages ended up defending their captors, rarely happens in real life, Asencio believes. But belief in the Stockholm syndrome made his countrymen discount his input when he was being held hostage, he says. The memory of that sense of helplessness remains bitter for him. "My requests were being either ignored or very distinctly opposed," he says. After his release, Asencio was honored at the State Department, and he continued to rise through the ranks of professional diplomacy. But he still argues with his colleagues about the existence of the Stockholm syndrome. "I have had many conversations with counterterrorism experts at the State Department about this. And I haven't had any luck," he says. The experts, as is so often the case, underestimate the victims.

Asencio now lives in Mexico City, where he works as a contractor to the U.S. Agency for International Development. The Dominican embassy has been torn down, and an apartment building constructed in its place.

In Cuba, Pabón and his fellow rebels did not retire to the hills. They repeatedly returned to Colombia to carry out more operations. In 1981, Pabón was captured by the Ecuadorian military as he attempted to cross back into Colombia. "We committed thousands of mistakes," he says now. Ecuador sent Pabón back to Colombia, where he spent twenty-two months in prison. Luckily for him, Colombians adore their rebels. Over the past century, the country has negotiated eighty-eight peace deals with different insurgent groups. In 1982, the new president, Belisario Betancour, declared an unconditional amnesty for political crimes. That December, Pabón walked out of prison a free man.

Seven years later, M-19 disarmed and formed a political party. Pabón was elected to the constituent assembly, which drafted a new constitution for the country. M-19 got the second-largest number of seats in the body. In 1998, Pabón was elected mayor of Yumbo, a city of seventy-one thousand in southwestern Colombia. Two years later, he was voted the country's best mayor by two major newspapers. He returned to national office in September 2006, when he was sworn in as director of Dansocial, an agency that promotes economic cooperatives and volunteer work.

Asencio and Pabón have not spoken since the siege. But through their stories, we see the striking similarities in the body's reaction to fear, even from two very different points of view. The fear response is profound, and it colors every moment of a crisis, to varying degrees, for every victim, perpetrator, and rescuer at the scene. The next logical question then is about the varying degrees. Why did Asencio respond so appropriately to the gunfight, ducking down below the couch and remaining still, while other diplomats did decidedly unhelpful things? After all, they were all terrified, worldly professionals at a cocktail party. So what made the difference? To find out, I figured it made sense to go to one of the places in the world where stress is part of the texture of life, embedded in the stones and atomized into the air, a place where people have absorbed a lot of fear, on all sides.

4

Resilience

Staying Cool in
Jerusalem

BRIGADIER GENERAL Nisso Shacham commands the police force in the southern half of Israel, a triangle of land bordering the Gaza Strip, the West Bank, Egypt, and Jordan. It may well be the most stressful job anywhere. In 2000, Shacham was in charge of keeping the peace in the holy places of Jerusalem. He was the only police officer who warned against Ariel Sharon visiting the Temple Mount. His concerns were dismissed, and Sharon's visit, in September 2000, sparked the second intifada. "If you want to get a doctorate in stress, I'm the case," Shacham says.

We meet at his home, located, appropriately enough, on a precipice in the hills outside Jerusalem. Shacham spends the first thirty minutes in the kitchen. First, he assembles a plate of sliced peaches, grapes, and cherries. Next come neat squares of chocolate cake. Then he insists on making Turkish coffee. Finally, he settles down at the table with a cigar and starts telling stories. Shacham speaks fluent English but feels less self-conscious when speaking Hebrew, so my colleague Aaron Klein, from *Time*'s Jerusalem bureau, acts as a translator. When Shacham's teenage son comes home from school with his report card, Shacham interrupts the interview and slowly and silently reads through the document. Then he plants a big kiss on his son's cheek. Other than the glowering, equine dogs lying next to the front door, there were no indications that this was the home of a man who had repeatedly been the only thing standing between shrieking Jewish and Muslim fundamentalists in the Old City.

Shacham became a police officer out of curiosity, he says. "I was like a good guy, a nerd. I never had any experience with criminals." But he did have a ponytail and earrings, so his superiors chose him for the undercover unit. His first and hardest job was to earn the trust of gang leaders. He was afraid all the time in those days. "The gangs tested me every day because I was new."

One day, Shacham made contact with one of the most dangerous criminals in Jerusalem, a major dealer who had been linked to multiple murders. "He was a psychopath by definition," says Shacham. After their meeting, the dealer asked him for a ride downtown. Shacham's cover story was that he worked as a messenger in an office and sold drugs on the side. In the car, the dealer suddenly asked Shacham to show him his office. It was a test. Shacham headed toward the large building where he was supposed to work. He had never been inside. No one there knew him. As he drove, he tried to control his fear. His mind raced through all the possible outcomes, all of them bad. He had no training for this scenario.

When they pulled up to the building, the parking garage was blocked by an electronic gate requiring a code. Next to the gate was a guard. Shacham didn't know the code. "What am I going to tell him, this guard?" He slowed the car to a stop and paused. Then he flashed his headlights. The guard opened the gate. "It was a miracle."

Now what? How would he get inside? Where would he go if he did? Shacham had another idea. He stopped the car next to the guard and asked, "Is John inside?" The guard looked bored. "I don't know. Go inside and check," he replied. It worked. The dealer in the passenger seat had seen enough. "Let's go," he said. Shacham turned the car around. He had passed the test.

There are people whom psychologists call "extreme dreaders"—people who have a tendency to live in a state of heightened anxiety. Then there are people like Shacham. What makes him able to negotiate extreme fear so well? How does he navigate through the fog of deliberation without a map? When I ask him this question, he says it's not that he doesn't feel fear; he does, every time. But a calmness resides just adjacent to the fear. "You have to be very cold-blooded," he says. But what makes someone "cold-blooded"? Is it genetics? Experience? A chemical imbalance? What makes the difference?

The Profile of a Survivor

The answer is out there, I was told by trauma psychologists and other disaster experts in Israel and the United States. But it is slippery. We all have ideas about what we might do in an emergency. But we are probably wrong. There are ways to predict behavior under extreme duress, and they aren't what you might expect. People who are leaders or basket cases on a normal day at the office aren't necessarily the same in a crisis.

But before behavior even comes into play, our basic profile can dramatically alter our odds. Our handicaps tend to be the same ones that plague us in normal day-to-day life. If you are very overweight, for example, you will almost certainly have a lower chance of survival in most disasters. In car crashes, we know that heavy people are more likely to die than thin people. That's partly because very overweight people have more health problems in general. So they have a harder time recovering from any injuries. Their bodies also have more difficulty handling intense heat. For the human heart, the strain of a crisis can be far more deadly than the actual threat. That's why more firefighters die from heart attacks and strokes than from fires.

There is the cruel reality of physics, too. Overweight people move more slowly and need more space, so they have more trouble escaping. On 9/11, people with low physical abilities were three times as likely to be injured while evacuating the Trade Center. This problem has gotten worse as Americans have gotten bigger. Body fat even changes crowd dynamics. When people walk down a staircase, they sway slightly from side to side, taking up more space than their actual body width. The heavier people are, the slower they move and the more they sway—and the fewer people can fit down a staircase.

Sex matters too. It is far better to be a man in certain disasters, and a woman in others. Men are more likely to be killed by lightning, hurricanes, and fires. Nearly twice as many men die in fires, according to the U.S. Fire Administration. That's partly because men tend to do more dangerous jobs. But it's also because men take more risks overall. They are more likely to walk toward smoke and drive through floods. "Women tend to be more cautious," says Susan Cutter, director of the Hazards Research Laboratory at the University of South Carolina. "They are not going to put themselves or their families at risk. They are going to be out of an area before the rains come."

Remember that equation for dread? It's different for men and women. Almost every survey ever done on risk perception finds that women worry more about almost everything—from pollution to handguns. On a superficial level, this makes sense. Women are physically weaker, on average, and traditionally more responsible for caring for others. Maybe they should worry more. But when risk expert Paul Slovic tried to explain the gender gap this way, he ran into problems. The stereotype didn't quite fit. For example, African American *men* worried just as much as women generally did. So unless African American men are born nurturers, nature didn't entirely explain the difference. Slovic tried other variables. Are women and minorities less educated and so more emotional in their risk assessments? Well, no. When Slovic controlled for education, the sex and race differences persisted. In fact, when he asked scientists who study risk perception for a living to rank hazards, women scientists still tended to worry more than their male counterparts. Maybe women and minorities just have less faith in government authorities. Do they worry more because they don't trust other people to do it for them? But there again, when the researchers controlled for such attitudes, it didn't fully explain the worry gap.

Eventually, Slovic realized he was obsessing over the wrong people.

Men were the ones throwing off the curve, not women or minorities. And not all men, but a small subgroup.

As it turns out, about 30 percent of white males see very little risk in most threats. They create much of the gender and race gap all on their own. So then Slovic began to study these white men. They had a few subtle things in common. "They liked the world of status, hierarchy, and power," says Slovic. They believed in technology. They were more likely than any other group to disagree with the statement that people should be treated more equally. Usually, they were white men, but not always. The more important factor was how they viewed the world and their place in it. If a white male felt discriminated against or marginalized by society, then he would likely switch sides, joining women and minorities in their worry.

So does that mean it's better to be a woman who worries than a man who doesn't? In some disasters, worrying definitely helps. It can motivate people to evacuate before it's too late. For example, it's relatively easy to convince women with children to leave their homes before a hurricane. In other cases, though, worrying is not nearly enough, and other, more egregious gender differences matter more. In many countries hit by the 2004 tsunami, for example, women did not know how to swim, and men did. The survival rates varied accordingly. In four Indonesian villages surveyed by Oxfam after the tsunami, male survivors outnumbered females by a ratio of almost three to one.

Sometimes gender handicaps are embarrassingly banal. On 9/11, women were almost twice as likely to get injured while evacuating, according to the Columbia study. Was it a question of strength? Confidence? Fear? No, says lead investigator Robyn Gershon. "It was the shoes." Many women took off their heels halfway through the evacuation and had to walk home barefoot. Survivors reported tripping over piles of high-heeled shoes in the staircases.

Often, other disadvantages overwhelm the effect of worry. Of all the people who die in fires each year, 25 percent are African American—twice their share of the population. The disparity is most glaring when it comes to children: African American and American Indian children are nearly twice as likely to die in a fire than white or Asian children.

Fire, as it turns out, is mostly about money. "I never fought a fire in a rich person's home," says Denis Onieal, who became a firefighter in Jersey City, New Jersey, in 1971 and is now superintendent of the National Fire Academy. Fires are more likely in places with shoddy construction where people use portable heaters to stay warm and where smoke detectors are absent or not working. In poor neighborhoods, then, fire is part of the hazardscape, says Onieal. "You got addicts on the corner, you got people who steal your lunch money, and you got fires."

The simple truth is that money matters more than anything else in most disasters. Which is another way of saying that where and how we live matters more than Mother Nature. Developed nations experience just as many natural disasters as undeveloped nations. The difference is in the death toll. Of all the people who died from natural disasters on the planet from 1985 to 1999, 65 percent came from nations with incomes below $760 per capita, according to the Intergovernmental Panel on Climate Change. The 1994 Northridge earthquake in California, for example, was similar in magnitude and depth to the 2005 earthquake in Pakistan. But the Northridge earthquake killed only sixty-three people. The Pakistan earthquake killed about a hundred thousand.

People need roofs, roads, and health care before quibbles like personality and risk perception count for much. And the effect is geometric. If a large nation raises its GNP from $2,000 to $14,000 per person, it can expect to save 530 lives a year in natural disasters, according to a study by Matthew Kahn at Tufts University. And for those who survive, money is a form of liquid resilience: it can bring treatment, stability, and recovery.

But in rich countries like America, where the GNP is about $42,000 per person, individual traits can make a difference. In fact, your personal makeup can be more important than the facts of the disaster. "What will eventually determine chronic stress in a discrete event is genetics and personality more than the details of the event," says Ilan Kutz, a trauma expert and psychiatrist in Israel. All other obvious things (like gender, weight, and income) being equal, some people outperform others. They are simply hardier. The grand mystery is why.

The Finer Distinctions

At an upscale restaurant in downtown Portland, Oregon, two women are eating together at a table by the window. In the middle of their conversation, a drunken homeless man stumbles up to the window, unzips his pants, and pulls his penis up to the table. After a short period of gasps and guffaws, the police are called. Officer Loren Christensen arrives at the scene and finds two extremes. One of the women, he says, is "laughing her head off." The other is slumped on a bench in the lobby with someone fanning her.

In his twenty-five years as a police officer, Christensen noticed this kind of variance often—particularly among female victims of flashers. "One would laugh it off. Another would be enraged. Still another would be emotionally traumatized." Christensen, who has retired from the police force and now works as an author and martial-arts instructor, has always had trouble discerning what makes one person react so differently from another—even in war, when he was a military policeman. "In Vietnam, I saw people psychologically impacted in the extreme who worked as cooks. Cooks! And I saw infantrymen who had seriously faced the dragon who appeared, at least on the surface, to be fine."

Resilience is a precious skill. People who have it tend to also have three underlying advantages: a belief that they can influence life events; a tendency to find meaningful purpose in life's turmoil; and a conviction that they can learn from both positive and negative experiences. These beliefs act as a sort of buffer, cushioning the blow of any given disaster. Dangers seem more manageable to these people, and they perform better as a result. "Trauma, like beauty, is in the eye of the beholder," says George Everly Jr., at the Johns Hopkins Center for Public Health Preparedness in Baltimore, Maryland.

This makes sense. A healthy, proactive worldview should logically lead to resilience. But it's the kind of unsatisfying answer that begs another question. If this worldview leads to resilience, well, what leads to the worldview?

The answer is not what we might expect. Resilient people aren't necessarily yoga-practicing Buddhists. One thing that they have in abundance is confidence. As we saw in the chapter on fear, confidence—that comes from realistic rehearsal or even laughter—soothes the more disruptive effects of extreme fear. A few recent studies have found that people who are unrealistically confident tend to fare spectacularly well in disasters. Psychologists call these people "self-enhancers," but you and I would probably call them arrogant. These are people who think more highly of themselves than other people think of them. They tend to come off as annoying and self-absorbed. In a way, they might be better adapted to crises than they are to real life.

Less than a year after the civil war ended, George Bonanno at Columbia University interviewed seventy-eight Bosnia-Herzegovina citizens in Sarajevo. Each person in the study rated himself or herself when it came to psychological problems, interpersonal skills, health problems, and moodiness. Then each person was rated by his or her peers. A small group of people rated themselves significantly higher than others did. And these were the people found by mental health professionals to be better adjusted.

After 9/11, Bonanno found a similar pattern among survivors who were in or near the World Trade Center during the attacks. Those with high senses of self-worth rebounded relatively easily. They even had lower levels of the stress hormone cortisol in their saliva. Their confidence was like a vaccine against life's vicissitudes.

Several studies have found that people with higher IQs tend to fare better after a trauma. Resilient people may be smarter, in other words. Why would that be? Perhaps intelligence helps people think creatively, which might in turn lead to a greater sense of purpose and control. Or maybe the confidence that comes with a high IQ is what leads to the resilience to begin with.

The more important point is that everyone, regardless of IQ, can manufacture self-esteem through training and experience. That is what soldiers and police officers will tell you; that confidence comes from doing. As we saw in Chapter 3, the brain functions much better when it is familiar with a problem. We feel more in control because we are more in control. But in certain situations, like the one in which Shacham found himself as a rookie cop, sitting next to a violent criminal who had called his bluff, neither experience nor training could rescue him. He drew upon something else, something more fundamental.

Special Forces Soldiers Are Not Normal

The U.S. military has spent millions of dollars trying to figure out how to profile people like Shacham—people who will stay lucid in life-or-death situations and then remain resilient afterward. Charles Morgan III is an associate clinical professor of psychiatry at Yale University and the director of the human performance laboratory at the National Center for Posttraumatic Stress Disorder. He has spent the past fifteen years studying differences in how people react to extreme stress. He started out studying Vietnam and Gulf War veterans. The ones with posttraumatic stress disorder behaved a lot differently from the ones without, as you might expect. The vets with posttraumatic stress disorder were jumpier. They also dissociated more, reporting that colors appeared brighter or things moved in slow motion, even in normal life. It was as if their brains, having once entered crisis mode, remained perpetually stuck there. They even had higher levels of certain stress hormones in their blood than other people.

In the 1990s, the consensus among most scientists was that these people had been damaged by their experiences. Their brains, their blood, and their personalities had been altered by trauma. But a handful of researchers were not satisfied with that theory. "We were making assumptions," says Morgan. "We really didn't know." Which came first, these scientists wondered: the trauma? Or the person susceptible to being traumatized?

To find out, Morgan needed to study people *before* they were exposed to the trauma. At the Military Survival School at Fort Bragg in North Carolina, he found a laboratory for stress. After a period of classroom training, soldiers at the school are released into the woods to try to avoid capture. They have no food, water, or weapons. Instructors hunt them down, fire on them with blanks, and, eventually, catch them. Then they take the soldiers, hooded and roped together, to a mock prisoner of war camp, where they are systematically deprived of food, control, and dignity. The conditions are meant to resemble the experiences of U.S. POWs in World War II Europe, Korea, and Vietnam. Over seventy-two hours, the soldiers are only allowed to sleep less than one hour.

Survival School is so realistic, it's actually frightening. When Morgan took the soldiers' blood, he found that their stress levels exceeded previously recorded averages taken in extreme situations. The soldiers had, for example, more cortisol in their system than people who are about to jump out of an airplane for the first time. On average, Survival School participants lose fifteen pounds during the course.

Right away, Morgan noticed big differences between the soldiers. The Army Special Forces soldiers, also known as Green Berets, consistently outperformed the other, general infantry soldiers. "They seemed to remain more mentally clear," says Morgan. "They didn't get as stupid as fast as the rest of us under stress." That's not surprising. Special Forces are an elite population; less than a third of those who try to join get selected.

What was more surprising was how different the Special Forces soldiers were *chemically*. When Morgan analyzed their blood samples, he found that the Special Forces soldiers produced significantly more of something called "neuropeptide Y," a compound that helps you stay focused on a task under stress, among other things. Even twenty-four hours after a mock interrogation, the Special Forces soldiers had returned to normal levels of neuropeptide Y, while the other soldiers remained depleted. (In civilian life, people with anxiety disorders or depression tend to have lower levels of neuropeptide Y.) The difference was so marked that Morgan could literally tell whether someone was a member of the Special Forces unit just by looking at their blood results. So then the question was, which came first? Were Special Forces soldiers just inherently different? Or did their training make them that way?

Let's pause to acknowledge that Special Forces soldiers are not normal. They seem to have certain immunities to extreme stress but, on average, Special Forces soldiers don't tend to be the he-man types, either;

they tend to be the ones with the beards who speak Arabic and can melt into a foreign population. "They like the challenge and the thrill but not in a thrill-seeking way. They're pretty quiet and meticulous and focused as a group," Morgan says. "If you've ever seen that movie *Black Hawk Down*, it really does portray Green Berets accurately. They really are different kinds of animals."

But it was surprising how predictably—and even biologically—different they appeared to be from other soldiers. In fact, Morgan discovered, he didn't even have to take their blood to tell the difference. It turned out a simple questionnaire could predict who would produce more neuropeptide Y.

He asked the soldiers questions from a standard psychological test measuring dissociative symptoms. For example, thinking back over the past few days, he asked, have you ever experienced any of the following symptoms?

1. Things seemed to move in slow motion.
2. Things seemed unreal, as if in a dream.
3. You had a feeling of separation from what was happening, as if you were watching a movie or a play.

That's just a sampling of the questions, of course. If you answered yes to all of the questions above, it doesn't necessarily mean you will perform poorly in a crisis. It depends, as is so often the case, on the crisis.

Over the past several years, Morgan has administered the questionnaire to more than two thousand soldiers before they began Survival School. He wanted to see which ones had a habit of dissociating—even under normal conditions. On average, about 30 percent scored high on the test. Even without extreme stress, about a third said they had felt some kind of detachment from reality. This is higher than Morgan might have expected, but he has repeatedly found the same ratio among military populations. And those soldiers who had scored high on the dissociation test were consistently less likely to make it through the school.

One day, soldiers may routinely pop pills to help them deal with extreme fear. Synthetic neuropeptide Y may be handed out to soldiers with their boots. The hormone oxytocin, released in mothers after they give birth and also available synthetically, has been shown to calm the brain's fear hub and promote trust. In one study, men who sniffed oxytocin before undergoing a brain scan exhibited less amygdala activity than they did without oxytocin.

But before we get too carried away with the pharmaceuticals, it's worth mentioning that dissociation is not always a bad thing. During the worst moments of the Survival School, all of the students—even the Special Forces soldiers—experienced dissociative symptoms. Some dissociated more than people taking hallucinogenic drugs. As Zedeño learned during her escape from the World Trade Center, dissociating can be a highly adaptive response to trauma. Jim Cirillo, a master gunslinger, dissociated as he shot a man for the first time. In Chapter 7, we'll see how an extreme form of dissociation might actually be an ancient survival mechanism.

There are different kinds of resilience. If all you need to do is walk down the stairs, moderate dissociation might be a perfectly fine response. If, however, you need to manipulate equipment or solve problems, you might have more trouble. "Military folks have to actively engage in their environments to go find an enemy or do something. So the tendency to pull away impairs their performance," Morgan explains. When we dissociate, the parts of our brains that handle spatial mapping, working memory, and concentration start to fail. If you are, say, a Special Forces soldier in a hostage rescue unit—tasked with entering buildings undetected, navigating in low light, and shooting the hostage-takers, not the hostages—losing these particular skills is problematic.

Before, during, *and* after the mock captivity, Special Forces soldiers reported fewer and less-intense dissociative symptoms than everyone else. The correlation was clear: the less a soldier dissociated—especially under normal conditions—the more neuropeptide Y he produced, and the better he performed.

Strangely, Special Forces soldiers also reported more trauma in their backgrounds overall. They reported a greater incidence of childhood abuse, for example. This was unexpected. Normally prior trauma predicts worse performance under stress. Among Special Forces soldiers, however, previous trauma hadn't left them any less able to handle future trauma. In fact, it seemed to have left them more capable. How could this be? It was a sort of paradox. In one group of people, trauma led to an unraveling. In another, it seemed to instill coping mechanisms.

Every year, about nine hundred soldiers apply to join the Army Special Forces. They are weeded out through a three-week assessment program that tests physical endurance, problem solving, and leadership abilities under stress. It is more physically demanding than Survival School, but a little less psychologically stressful. Only about a third of the candidates actually finish the course.

Was it the training itself—or the confidence that comes with knowing you are a Special Forces soldier—that gave these guys the extra boost in performance? To find out, Morgan decided to study men before they got selected. When the candidates arrived at the course, Morgan gave them his questionnaire. He wanted to know which ones had dissociated the week *before* they came to the course. As with the Survival School participants, about a third of the Special Forces candidates reported experiencing some kind of dissociation before their arrival. Morgan has tested 774 men so far, and the results are stunning: anyone who reported dissociating during normal times turned out to be significantly less likely to pass the course. If someone responded positively to eleven or more of the questions, Morgan could predict with 95 percent accuracy that the person would fail out of the course.

With this simple test, then, Morgan could potentially save soldiers the trouble of even trying to endure the Special Forces selection process. "If you just screened those people out at the beginning, it would save the Army millions of dollars," he says. But the generals aren't keen on that idea for philosophical reasons. "The Army doesn't like the idea that someone might be prevented from doing something he or she really wants to do," Morgan says. So today, everyone still gets to try out for the Special Forces, regardless of chemistry.

Still, another mystery remained: if these individuals were different before they joined the Special Forces, then how did they get that way? Were they born resilient? Or had they all undergone some kind of childhood experience to make them that way?

Whenever a psychologist (or anyone else, for that matter) tries to identify causality, things can go badly. Nature and nurture just don't divide cleanly, no matter how much we want them to. Both are intertwined, like strands of DNA. And still, we want to know. Even if we can't entirely isolate nature or nurture, can't we at least say which one matters more? Even a little bit?

When all else fails, there is one last way to find out. But it is a long shot. Subjects are few and far between. If it works, however, the twin study is a lovely thing to behold—as elegant and pure as pi.

The Thompson Twins

Even now, it's hard to tell Jerry and Terry Thompson apart. They stopped dressing the same in the seventh grade, but they still sometimes meet somewhere and realize they're wearing matching outfits. The identical twins live in Ardmore, Oklahoma, about fourteen miles away from each other. They both drive Toyota Tacoma pickup trucks. When I spoke to Jerry one summer Friday, he was waiting for Terry to help him pull his tractor out of the mud.

But the Thompson brothers have less in common outside of their DNA. "You can talk to us just briefly and know right off we're two different personalities," Jerry says. "I'm an on-time guy; he's a late guy. I'm real picky about the inside of my truck; he throws his trash down on his floorboard." Growing up in Southern California in a family of six children, they battled for supremacy. Their father bought them boxing gloves when they were two years old, and they're still going at it. "He pushes my buttons," Jerry says about Terry. "When we fight, he always lets me know how intelligent he is. He's eight minutes older than I am, and you can tell 'cause he's got his master's, and I have a little associate's degree." Jerry is retired now, while Terry runs a business making and selling jerky.

Another difference between the brothers is that Jerry went to Vietnam. They both joined the Marine Corps after high school. "It was more or less to fight for our country," Jerry says. "We had military on both sides of the family, so I couldn't have been a draft dodger, and I didn't really know enough about war to be one anyway." But only Jerry was sent to war. He arrived in Vietnam on June 3, 1970. Seven weeks later, he got caught in an ambush. He was shot in his right arm and riddled with shrapnel. "They threw one grenade at me and blew me into the air, and then another blew me backwards." He spent five weeks recovering and received a Purple Heart. Then he went back into combat. "You don't know how much of an animal you turn into," he says. "I cut some ears off and scalped some dudes."

Jerry was sent back the States nine months after he left. His ear collection got confiscated at the Da Nang airport. When he got back to California, he moved home. But his parents couldn't understand him. "I was in a different world when I came home." He quit a series of jobs and then dropped out of college, too. Then he got married and divorced. "I couldn't communicate with her or nobody else," Jerry says. "I'm still sorta that way. That's probably why I live out in the country and stay to myself. I got sorta numb."

In 1975, Jerry was diagnosed with Vietnam Stress Syndrome. But no one seemed to know how to help him. After a bad experience at a veterans' hospital in Waco, Texas, he didn't seek out help again until 1992. He joined a program for vets with posttraumatic stress disorder, as it's now called, at the Veterans Administration Hospital in Oklahoma City, Oklahoma. He drove two hours there and back for six weeks because he was finally getting the treatment he needed.

In the mid-1990s, scientists discovered that people with posttraumatic stress disorder didn't just behave differently; their brains actually *were* different. The hippocampus, located deep within the brain near the amygdala, was a little smaller in people with posttraumatic stress disorder. The hippocampus is intimately involved in learning and memory, and it helps us decide whether something is safe or not. In a disaster—and afterward—it can boost our resilience. (London cab drivers, who must memorize all the city's streets, have unusually large hippocampi.) Most scientists assumed that trauma had shrunk the hippocampus of the people with posttraumatic stress disorder. After all, that was what happened when animals were exposed to extreme stress: the hippocampus got smaller. But no one really knew for sure.

In 1998, the Thompsons got a phone call about an ingenious plan to study Vietnam veterans with twin brothers. Psychologist Mark Gilbertson and his colleagues at the Veterans Administration Medical Center in Manchester, New Hampshire, wanted to study the human brain before and after trauma. They wanted to see if people who developed posttraumatic stress disorder had started life with different brain structures than those who had not developed the disorder. In particular, they wanted to measure the hippocampus—the part of the brain that helps process danger signals and that is believed to be involved in dissociation.

Of course, it is hard (and extremely expensive) to track a large sample of people for decades. So Gilbertson and his team came up with a way to essentially turn back time on Vietnam vets. They would study sets of twins—in which one brother had gone to war and one hadn't. "It was a good analog for looking at this chicken and egg problem," he says. Through the Veterans Administration's twin registry, Gilbertson and his colleagues painstakingly tracked down eighty men like Jerry and Terry. It took three years to find and test them all, but it was a beautiful sample. Because they were identical twins, the size of the brothers' hippocampi should have been the same—unless some kind of trauma had altered their brains' terrain after birth. In other words, the brain of the nonveteran twin provided a snapshot of the brain of the veteran *before* he went to war. The sample included seventeen men who had developed posttraumatic stress disorder in Vietnam (and their seventeen brothers without combat experience); the rest of the vets and their brothers had never developed the disorder at all.

Two by two, the brothers flew in from around the country to Manchester or Boston to have their brains imaged through an MRI. "That was sort of fascinating," Gilbertson says. "Most of these guys, even in their fifties, looked so much alike. As soon as they'd come in, I'd have to tag a piece of clothing so that I could tell them apart." Many of the nonveterans saw the study as a sort of reunion and a way to serve their brothers who had been damaged by war. For some of the veterans, the process itself was a trial. Going through the claustrophobic MRI machine caused a spike in anxiety. The healthy brothers were in turn very protective of their twins. "Some of the brothers would stand guard at the foot of the MRI while their brother was undergoing the procedure," Gilbertson remembers.

Jerry and Terry flew to Boston together for the study. They stayed at the Holiday Inn at Logan Airport and had a fine time until Jerry had to actually get inside the MRI machine. The loud banging sound inside the machine sounded just like a .50-caliber gun. He had a flashback of being on a helicopter when one of the other American soldiers decided to eject three Vietcong prisoners they had captured. The helicopter was several thousand feet in the air, and Jerry vividly remembers watching the men pleading for their lives and then falling, falling.

The tech administering the MRI asked Jerry some basic questions to make sure he was doing OK. The test showed that he had some shrapnel behind his ear that he hadn't known about. The tech asked Jerry if he felt a burning sensation. When Jerry didn't answer, the tech figured he had fallen asleep in the machine. But really he was just lying there silently crying in the dark.

Jerry has now participated in five different studies on posttraumatic stress disorder. "I guess they like us a lot. We're sort of talkative type guys. Plus, we always bring jerky for everyone." He hates flying, as does his brother, and being in a big city is intensely stressful for him. But he goes through the ordeal because he wants doctors to learn more about the illness so they can help soldiers coming home from Iraq. "This is far worse than Vietnam. These guys are going to have severe problems. So I need to help."

Almost a third of Vietnam vets suffered from posttraumatic stress disorder after the war, according to the 1988 National Vietnam Veterans Readjustment Study. That's a lot of people. It would make sense to conclude that these men had simply experienced more horrendous trauma than the others. They were only scarred because of what had happened to them, not because of who they were.

But Gilbertson found something different. When he looked at the images, he saw that, *within* the twin sets, the hippocampi were about the same size. The trauma of war had not significantly altered the size of the hippocampus in the brothers who had gone to Vietnam. But there were significant differences *between* sets of twins. The twin sets that included vets with posttraumatic stress disorder had smaller hippocampi than the twin sets that included veterans without the disorder. In other words, a smaller hippocampus seemed to *predate* the trauma. Certain people were at higher risk of developing posttraumatic stress disorder before they even left for Vietnam. We can deduce, then, that certain people will likely have a harder time processing fear in a disaster—and recovering from that trauma later.

Jerry, for one, is not too surprised by the results. He knows that Vietnam damaged him. "I loved people. Damn, I was very popular in high school. It just changed after I got home." But he also says his problems predated the war. Depression runs in his family, he says. His senior year of high school, his girlfriend broke up with him, and he remembers telling her he was going to go to Vietnam to get killed. "Mentally, I was depressed even before Vietnam. Personally, I think that's why it messed me up so much."

The hippocampus is just one factor in the sprawling equation for posttraumatic stress disorder. Other things matter too, Gilbertson stresses. The amount of trauma, the degree of family support for the victim—all of these things can massively compound or contain the damage. Suffering accumulates, like debt.

Plus, having a smaller hippocampus isn't necessarily a negative in every situation. Gilbertson suspects that a smaller hippocampus might actually help some people in a life-or-death situation—by making them hypervigilant, for example, and less prone to waste time in denial. It's easy to imagine how a smaller hippocampus might have been an evolutionary advantage in some situations, and a handicap in others. So he doesn't think we should screen people with MRIs before they join the military or the police. The brain is too complicated to be reduced to the size of one of its parts.

My Naked Brain

We all wonder how we would react in a disaster. As I learned more about specific traits that may predict resilience, I couldn't help wondering about my own profile. I don't think I dissociate more often than average, but I don't always find meaningful purpose in life's turmoil either. Sometimes I just find turmoil. I can be overly anxious in certain situations. And I don't think anyone would call me relentlessly optimistic. But now I had a way to test my hypothesis.

To find out how my hippocampus measured up, Gilbertson generously agreed to scan my brain and run me through a full day of cognitive testing. I was a little nervous, admittedly. Did I really want to know the answer? Rationally, I knew size wasn't everything. But if I had a small hippocampus, wouldn't it make me lose confidence in my own ability to endure hardship? Would it become a self-fulfilling prophecy? But given the chance, passing up the MRI was like trying to walk past a mirror. I couldn't help but check myself out.

A few days before the MRI, Gilbertson e-mailed me to make sure I had no shrapnel in my body. I did not. He never once complained, but I could tell that he had had to placate a platoon of lawyers and bureaucrats in order to take a look at my brain. As a reporter, I fell well outside of the normal research-subject category. He had me sign a long consent form that he had designed just for me. "This is mostly just in case we find something," he said. "Oh, like a tumor?" I said. "Yes," he said. Insanely, I remained more worried about the size of my hippocampus. Why wasn't he worried they would find no hippocampus at all? What then?

On a rainy Sunday morning in May of 2007, we met in Boston at Brigham & Women's Hospital. I got terribly lost in the maze of Boston streets and showed up a half hour late, sweaty and apologetic. Gilbertson, wearing a sports jacket and tiny rectangular glasses pushed up on his forehead, smiled and told me not to worry. He suggested that I take a moment to relax. I thanked him and joked that I had been late on purpose; I'd wanted to make sure my brain had marinated in stress hormones before the exam. He laughed. I was hoping he would reassure me by stating the obvious—that my hippocampus remains the same size, regardless of how late I am. But he didn't. As we rode up in the elevator, I was sure I could feel my hippocampus shrinking. I asked him if he'd ever scanned his own brain. "No, I haven't," he said pensively, as if the idea had never occurred to him.

At the MRI suite, I was fitted with a bracelet and officially admitted into the hospital. Then, just before I climbed into the machine, Gilbertson shook my hand: "Good luck! I'll be watching your brain!" I scanned his face for sarcasm, but there was none. This is a man who has seen hundreds if not thousands of brains by now. But he seemed genuinely excited.

After a half hour of clanking and drilling, the test was over, and I was handed a CD of my brain. Then Gilbertson briefly showed me my hippocampus on the screen. "You have them!" he announced. (There are actually two in your brain, one on each side.) I chuckled, deeply relieved, and we left for his office in New Hampshire. It would take about a week for him to complete the precise measurements.

In the meantime, there was another way to test how well my hippocampus was functioning. The next day, I met Gilbertson at his office at the Veterans Administration Medical Center in Manchester, New Hampshire. I arrived early this time. He had planned a full day of cognitive testing—dozens of more old-fashioned ways to measure the size and functioning of my hippocampus. Gilbertson led me into a room with a wide monitor and a La-Z-Boy chair covered with soft blankets. Beverlee, a nurse in his office who administers some of the tests, encouraged me to put my feet up. The researchers in Gilbertson's office pride themselves on treating their subjects with great care. Normally, they are dealing with combat veterans, many with posttraumatic stress disorder.

The first test was a nicer version of what mice and rats have been doing in stress labs for many years. It's called the Morris Water Task. The rodents have to swim around a murky pool and find a submerged platform, hopefully before they die. In my case, I just had to navigate around a bright blue computer-generated pool with a joystick until I came across the underwater platform. Then the test repeated itself—over and over. Each time, I started off in a different part of the pool and had to find the submerged platform, which was always in the same place. I had to use clues to remember where the platform was. There were colorful windows and, for some reason, a bookshelf around the side of the pool. Beverlee sat quietly at my side, watching me make many, many mistakes.

The computer, unbeknownst to me, was tracking everything I was doing—not just whether I found the platform. Each time, it measured how long I took to get started, the length of my route, how long I took to find the platform, and how much time I spent in each quadrant of the pool. The test was forcing me to use my hippocampus to orient myself with my short-term memory and contextual cues. The theory is that the better I can do this, the more capable I will be at processing and integrating information during and after a life-or-death situation. Animals that do well on this task also tend to have larger hippocampi.

After the pool test came a much longer and more frustrating pattern test. I had to identify the "correct" one of two patterns in each set. It was surprisingly difficult to place the correct patterns in different contexts. Again, my hippocampal skills were being challenged. Only after about thirty-six different tries did I consistently choose the right pattern over and over. I was hoping Beverlee wasn't secretly appalled.

Next I sat down with a clinical psychologist for a battery of more old-fashioned tests of memory and IQ. The worn cards and 1960s-era pictures were almost quaint. The psychologist asked me to match strangers' faces, to put a series of cartoon frames in order, to re-create a shape with colored blocks, to repeat seven different digits—backward—over and over. She said I was doing great, but that was before the animal identification test. I had to name each animal depicted in silhouette on each card, and I was terrible at it. I still would argue about the duck—no duck in nature looks like that, I am telling you—but the truth is I was just miserable at this task.

After six hours, I was wrecked. My brain was clearly not used to this kind of exercise. I don't even like crossword puzzles. Gilbertson offered me some coffee and then sat me down to discuss the results. He pulled up the results of the pool test from that morning. Men normally do better on these kinds of tests, which measure spatial processing, among other things. "So you're already working with a handicap," Gilbertson said. I supposed that was reassuring. He showed me screen after screen of drawings retracing the routes I took to the submerged platform. Some were fairly direct; others look exceptionally loopy. "This is quite good," Gilbertson said. "It's actually remarkable. You clearly know where the platform is."

I figured he was just being nice until he showed me the results of an anonymous combat vet. The vet sometimes got it right, plowing straight toward the platform. But more often, he went round and round, tracing hexagons in the water and sometimes zigzagging back and forth far from the platform. His hippocampus was not reliably making sense of where he was and where he needed to go.

Of course, this was not a fair comparison. I was younger than Gilbertson's normal participants and female, not to mention the fact that I had never been to war. But for all these reasons, it was especially reassuring that the results were promising.

A week later, Gilbertson got the results of my brain scan. My total hippocampal volume was 7.38 milliliters, or about the size of a small marble, Gilbertson informed me several weeks later. That is significantly larger than the vets with posttraumatic stress disorder. Of course, we are talking about very tiny numbers here. On average, the vets with posttraumatic stress disorder had a hippocampal volume of 6.66 milliliters. So my measurement was only about 10 percent larger. What does this all mean? Well, the implication is that my brain, thanks to the relatively large size of my hippocampus, may be more resilient in certain ways during and after a life-or-death situation. Theoretically, at least. When compared with soldiers who went to war and never got posttraumatic stress disorder—men who were, in other words, quite resilient—my hippocampal volume was very similar (only about 1–2 percent bigger, which is not significant).

As for the other tests, my level of overall cognitive functioning ranked in the ninety-fifth percentile for the general population in my age group. That is also a good predictor of resilience. My concentration and memory scores were also very high, even though it hardly seems obvious to me in real life. Both skills also correlate with resilience.

I'd done better than I had expected. It was a good reminder that our presumptions about how we might behave in a disaster are not necessarily reliable. "If I had to put money on it, I'd probably say that your hippocampus is operating pretty darn well!" Gilbertson wrote in an e-mail. The inclusion of the word *darn* reminded me all over again that Gilbertson is fundamentally a very nice guy. Maybe he had been unable to tell me the truth about my teeny hippocampus. Maybe I was part of a whole new psychological experiment. Either way, I was grateful.

From Israel to New Hampshire, I'd observed an impressive spectrum of human performance. There are people who have been damaged by trauma, and people who seem to have been susceptible to the damage before the trauma began. I met unusually resilient characters like Nisso Shacham, the Israeli police commander, who get energized and focused under extreme duress. Then there were the troubled Vietnam veterans who found themselves reliving nightmares again and again, as their brains struggled to put what they were seeing and hearing in context.

The evidence for biological resilience was strong. But if the topography of our brain and the chemistry of our blood have such significant effects on our ability to deal with fear, then how many choices does that leave us to do better? Do we all walk into disasters with a probability attached to our names? Surely other things matter more—like our lifetimes of experience and the people fighting for survival right next to us.

Taking an MRI exam is a lonely experience. We quietly offer up our brains, lying passively under a magnetic eye, trying not to move. But disasters don't happen to us when we're alone. Disasters happen to groups of strangers, coworkers, friends, and family who persuade, bolster, and distract each other. I have yet to meet anyone who made it out of the World Trade Center on 9/11 without having memorable interactions with at least one other person. Which parts of their brains lit up when they had those conversations? How did their behavior change after they exchanged bits of information and helped each other up off the ground? Disasters, by definition, do not happen to individuals. The only way to fully understand our behavior, then, is to look around at the people beside us.

5

Groupthink

Role Playing at the
Beverly Hills Supper Club Fire

THE BEVERLY HILLS Supper Club sat up on a bluff five miles south of Cincinnati, regal and unexpected, like an exiled queen. Pale statues were profiled on the long driveway. The labyrinth of dining rooms, ballrooms, fountains, and gardens covered one and a half acres. The architect had visited Las Vegas for inspiration, and it showed. The lobby was a collage of mirrors and tiger-striped fabrics. There used to be illegal gambling here too. Back in the 1930s, six men with submachine guns forced a car full of club employees off the road and made off with $10,000.

By the 1970s, the Beverly Hills had become the Midwest's Tavern on the Green. There were bar mitzvahs and fashion shows in the private dining rooms, and Frank Sinatra, Ray Charles, Jerry Lewis, and Milton Berle had all played in the ballrooms. "An atmosphere of refinement," proclaimed an advertisement. "Show Place of the Middle West." It was the kind of place women bought a new dress to go to.

Darla McCollister was about ten years old when she first went to the Beverly Hills. Her father wore a tuxedo, and the club sparkled like a Christmas ornament in her eyes. It was the first time she ate a Caesar salad. The waiter made it right at the table with the flourishes of a symphony conductor, and she ate it slowly, like something to be taken very seriously. "It was very elegant," she remembers. "It was what Las Vegas used to be when the gold was real gold, not plastic." When she was in high school, she told her boyfriend she dreamed of getting married at the Beverly Hills one day. "He got that panicked look," she remembers. "'Maybe not to you,'" she told him.

On the night of May 28, 1977, McCollister pulled her white dress, which she'd designed and made herself, over her head. She was twenty-one and getting married—to a different boyfriend—at the Supper Club. It was a humid spring night, and nearly two hundred of her friends and relatives were gathering in the garden below. Her six bridesmaids buzzed around her, getting their own hair and dresses ready. That was when they noticed how unusually warm it was in the room. By then it was almost 7:30 P.M., time for the ceremony to begin, and they bustled downstairs, holding McCollister's train aloft.

Under the gazebo in the garden, McCollister got married. She remembers being excited and nervous. In the photographs, she looks like she was crying as she walked down the aisle. After the ceremony, the couple sat for pictures by the fountain as the guests milled about, eating appetizers. Then came the receiving line, and just before 9:00 P.M., the party began to move inside for dinner. The band began to play. That was when a waitress appeared at McCollister's side and told her there was a small fire in the building.

The electrical fire had started in the Zebra Room, adjacent to the bride's dressing room. The flames would tear through the Beverly Hills, led by a roiling advance of smoke. There were nearly three thousand people packed into the sprawling club on this Saturday night of Memorial Day weekend. Upstairs, ninety members of the Afghan Dog Owners Club were having a banquet in the Crystal Rooms. A group of doctors dined together in the Viennese Room. About four hundred people had gathered for an awards banquet in the Empire Room. But the vast majority of guests were in the Cabaret Room, the ballroom located off the garden. Most of the people who died that night would die in the Cabaret Room. All told, the fire would kill 167 people.

Everyone at the Beverly Hills that night had arrived with friends and family, and they would try to leave the same way. No one in the club that night would act alone. People would look to one another for direction and support. Their individual profiles mattered, but the group, and the parts they played in it, mattered just as much.

"I'm a Survivor. I Hope You're a Survivor Too"

Contrary to popular expectations, this is what happens in a real disaster. Civilization holds. People move in groups whenever they can. They are usually far more polite than they are normally. They look out for one another, and they maintain hierarchies. "People die the same way they live," notes disaster sociologist Lee Clarke, "with friends, loved ones, and colleagues, in communities."

So far, we've watched human beings grope their way through denial and then deliberation. We've seen how genetics and experience can make certain people more or less risk-averse—or resilient. But disasters happen to masses of people, not individuals. Disaster victims are members of a group, whether they want to be or not. And we all behave differently in a group than we would on our own.

When people are told to leave in anticipation of a hurricane or flood, most check with four or more sources—family, newscasters, and officials, among others—before deciding what to do, according to a study by sociologist Thomas Drabek. That process of checking in, or milling, sets the tone for the rest of the evacuation. Who you're with matters a great deal.

On April 18, 1906, psychologist William James was awakened in his Stanford University apartment by a violent shaking. As he wrote later, in an essay titled, "On Some Mental Effects of the Earthquake," his reaction to the shaking was nothing like he would have imagined. "My first consciousness was one of gleeful recognition. I felt no trace whatever of fear; it was pure delight and welcome." Once the "waggling" stopped, James did what everyone does in a disaster: he sought out other people. "Above all, there was an irresistible desire to talk about it, and exchange experiences."

In airplane crashes, passengers have died because they ignored a closer exit to follow the rest of the crowd. Others have risked their lives because they climbed over seats to regroup with the rest of their family before evacuating. On 9/11 at least 70 percent of survivors spoke with other people before trying to leave, the federal government's study found. They made thousands of phone calls, checked TV and Internet news sites, and e-mailed friends and families. Many people even took milling breaks on their way down the stairs, stopping off on random floors to call their spouses again and check CNN one more time.

That morning, Louis Lesce was on the eighty-sixth floor of the North Tower. He was a career counselor teaching a class to Port Authority employees. Before class started, he was sitting alone in a conference room reading through resumes. He felt the initial shake when the plane hit the tower. Having lived in Tokyo, he figured it was an earthquake. He kept reading. But then there was an explosion, and tiles started falling from the ceiling. The resumes scattered into the air. He remembers that they seemed to float through space in slow motion, so that he could read the name on top of each one. Lesce jumped up, jolted out of denial and into deliberation. He didn't know anyone very well in the office, since he'd been teaching there only for a few months. But he immediately flew into the hallway in search of companions.

In a disaster, strangers are not strangers anymore. John Drury, a social psychologist at the University of Sussex in the United Kingdom, has analyzed group behavior in a wide range of disasters—from sinking ships to stadium stampedes. He had assumed that crowds with a common connection (like soccer fans) would behave very differently than anonymous strangers. But it turned out that the disaster itself created an instant bond between people. "Even if they started out quite fragmented, they came together and showed an enormous amount of solidarity," Drury says.

Lesce's floor was relatively empty on the morning of 9/11, but he did find five others. They walked through another door toward the elevators and ran into black smoke. They turned back, moved into an office, sat on the floor, and started caucusing. "What's going on? What are we supposed to do?" Lesce asked.

"An airplane hit the building," someone said, after getting a cell phone call. "Remember in 1948?" Lesce interjected. "A B-25 bomber crashed into the forty-second floor of the Empire State Building."

The smoke was getting worse. "Maybe we should break a window," someone else suggested.

Lesce wasn't sure. "Are we going to be sucked out?" But he seemed to be in the minority, so he backed down. This is the very definition of groupthink: human beings do not generally like to go against the consensus of the group. So group members will work hard to minimize conflict. Dissent is uncomfortable. "If anyone wants to break the window, be my guest," he said.

"How do we break it?" someone else asked.

"We could throw this flowerpot through the window. That should do it."

Again, Lesce was worried. "Well, we could hurt someone down below," he said.

Someone else noticed a ball-peen hammer in the room. "We could use this."

Lesce and the rest of the group stepped back into the hallway while one man smashed the window. There was a whooshing sound, but no one was sucked out.

Now there were new problems, however. Smoke from outside seemed to be channeling in through the window. Hot shrapnel flew into the room, burning people's skin. Still, the group kept exchanging theories and ideas. No one discussed looking for a staircase, according to Lesce's recollection. "It was odd," he says. After about a half hour, a man knocked on the door to the floor and yelled, "Anyone in there?" Lesce's group followed the voice to the stairs and started descending, at last.

The stairway was dark and crowded, but people kept treating each other like old friends. "You know, you look kind of tired, buddy," one man said to Lesce. "Let me hold your jacket." Another man offered to carry his briefcase. Lesce had had a quadruple bypass, so he was grateful. As they made their way down, people passed bottles of water through the crowd. "I never saw so much drinking water. Bottles just kept coming up." Finally, they made it out of the tower. Lesce remembers looking at the shattered windows of a Gap store and thinking there would be a hell of a sale the next day. "Geez, I wish I could fit into those clothes," he said to himself. But then a massive explosion of soot and concrete threw him to the ground. The first tower had collapsed. Everything went black.

A man, another stranger, helped Lesce up and directed him toward the light, out of the shopping concourse. Finally, he emerged onto Nassau Street and tried to call his wife. At that moment, there was another explosion and the second tower fell. Once again, Lesce was slammed onto the ground. And once again, a stranger helped him up.

Eventually, with the help of still more people, Lesce made his way to a hospital. When he got home, he had a message on his answering machine. "Hi, my name is Peter. I'm a survivor; I hope you're a survivor too." The man had found Lesce's briefcase in the stairway of the Trade Center and wanted to return it.

From beginning to end, Lesce was held up by the people around him. When I ask him what he would have done if he had been alone on the eighty-sixth floor, he says he doubts he would have made it out. "If no one had been there, I would've wet my pants. I would've yelled. I would've done whatever I possibly could to communicate with somebody. Then I would have sat there and waited to die."

The Sociology of the Beverly Hills Fire

At 8:45 P.M., a waitress had opened the door to the Zebra Room in the Beverly Hills Supper Club. Thick black smoke roared out at her. But she did not call the fire department or try to fight the fire. She ran to find the club managers. Like the office workers in the World Trade Center on 9/11, she followed the preexisting chain of command. As word of the fire slowly spread, people reacted like actors in play, each according to role.

Servers warned their tables to leave. Hostesses evacuated people that they had seated, but bypassed other sections. Cooks and busboys, perhaps accustomed to physical work, rushed to fight the fire. In general, male employees were slightly more likely to help than female employees, maybe because society expects women to be saved and men to do the saving. Age mattered too. The younger cocktail waitresses seemed more confused. But the banquet waitresses, who tended to be older, were calm and reassuring.

And what of the guests? Most remained guests to the end. Some even continued celebrating, in defiance of the smoke seeping into the room. One man ordered a rum and Coke to go. When the first reporter arrived at the fire, he saw guests sipping their cocktails in the driveway, laughing about whether they would get to leave without paying their bills. Most people became surprisingly passive. The newspapers the next day would proclaim mass hysteria. MANY TRAPPED IN PANIC, read the headline of the Associated Press story. But later investigations would show that the vast majority of people were well behaved. In fact, children, wives, and the elderly were among the most likely to survive.

As the smoke intensified, Wayne Dammert, a banquet captain at the club, stumbled into a hallway jammed with a hundred guests, of all ages, from all different parties. The lights flickered off and on, and the smoke started to get heavy. But what he remembers most about that crowded hallway is the silence. "Man, there wasn't a sound in there. Not a scream, nothing," he says now. Standing there in the dark, the crowd was waiting to be led.

The Beverly Hills employees had received no emergency training, but they performed magnificently anyway. Dammert directed the crowd out through a service hallway into the kitchen. There were too few exits in the club, and they were hard to find. The place was like a maze, actually. He remembers having to repeatedly scream at certain patrons to "get the hell out!" He risked his life because he felt obligated to do so. "My thought was that I'm responsible for these people. I think most of the employees felt that way."

At the time of the fire, Norris Johnson and William Feinberg were sociology professors nearby at the University of Cincinnati. They were riveted by the news of the fire, like everyone else in the area. As sociologists, they were particularly curious to know how a group of strangers in tuxes and ball gowns had behaved during a sudden and merciless fire. Eventually, they managed to get access to the police interviews with hundreds of survivors—a rare and valuable database. "We were just overwhelmed with what was there," remembers Feinberg, now retired. People were remarkably loyal to their identities. An estimated 60 percent of the employees tried to help in some way—either by directing guests to safety or fighting the fire. By comparison, only 17 percent of the guests helped. But even among the guests, identity influenced behavior. The doctors who had been dining at the club acted as doctors, administering CPR and dressing wounds on the grounds of the club like battlefield medics. Nurses did the same thing. There was even one hospital administrator there who—naturally—began to organize the doctors and the nurses.

The sociologists expected to see evidence of pushing or selfish behavior. But that's not what they found. "People kept talking about the orderliness of it all. It was really striking," says Feinberg. "People used what they had learned in grade school fire drills. 'Stay in line, don't push, we'll all get out.' People were queuing up! It was just absolutely incredible."

Safety in Numbers

Life is simpler when lived alone. That may be why far more creatures roam the planet alone than in groups. Male elephants, which have no real predators, do not bother with other elephants except to mate. They stomp across the land unburdened by others.

Humans are not so self-sufficient. We mingle in groups our whole lives, and we cling to one another in disasters. After the terrorist bombings on the London transit system on July 7, 2005, which killed fifty-two and wounded hundreds, some victims actually resisted leaving the tube station. "I needed the [others] for comfort," one victim explained to U.K. psychologist Drury. "I felt better knowing that I was surrounded by people."

When children are involved, the reason for solidarity is plain. A species' survival depends upon protecting its young, and human babies are more vulnerable longer than any other animal offspring. But we see the same behavior among adult groups. One study of mining disasters found that miners tended to follow their groups even if they disagreed with the group's decisions. Grown men trapped underground would rather make a potentially fatal decision than be left alone.

Why is that? Morality aside, is there any practical reason to value camaraderie as much as we do? Why don't we behave like animals in these situations? Or do we? I called primatologist Frans de Waal to see if other mammals behave the same way in life-or-death situations. Maybe our own behavior is just a by-product of civilization—a charming but unnatural bit of gallantry.

De Waal has written eight books on chimpanzees and spent decades observing them in captivity. Chimps and humans share about 99.5 percent of their evolutionary history, so the comparison can be instructive. When chimpanzees see a possible enemy, de Waal says, they gather close and start to touch each other. They might even embrace. In other words, they act a lot like humans. "A common threat has a unifying effect," he says.

Why do chimps band together? For one thing, de Waal says, the show of affection might intimidate the enemy. If the predator wants one of them, he will have to deal with all of them. Companionship also calms the chimps, making them better able to handle the stress of the threat. The same is true in humans. In laboratory experiments, people who are asked to complete tasks with a friend at their side exhibit lower heart and blood pressure rates than when they go through the tasks alone.

Even before a challenge materializes, camaraderie has clear benefits. In the early 1980s, primatologist Carel van Schaik went to Indonesia to try to understand monkey groups. Van Schaik studied two communities of long-tailed macaques—one on the island of Simeulue, a blissful macaque paradise with no cat predators, and one in Sumatra, a far scarier place populated by tigers, golden cats, and clouded leopards. After watching both communities, van Schaik found a significant difference. On Sumatra, where there were more predators, the macaques traveled in much larger groups. The bigger the threat, in other words, the bigger the posse—and the more eyes, ears, and nostrils with which to detect a predator. On Simeulue, the monkeys traveled in very small groups—the smallest groups of virtually any macaque community ever studied. They simply didn't need one another the way the Sumatra macaques did.

Even lower-order animals band together in times of danger. Fish cluster in tight schools, and birds call to each other to warn of an approaching hawk. But they don't do it to be nice. As evolutionary biologist Richard Dawkins has noted, "Anything that has evolved by natural selection should be selfish." We help one another because we get benefits from doing so, if not immediately and directly, then eventually or indirectly. Evolutionary biologists call this "reciprocity." And, in evolutionary terms, it means that an animal does something to improve its odds of passing on its genes—either by reproducing or by protecting its relatives.

If I carry Lou Lesce's briefcase down the stairs of the World Trade Center, I might not get anything tangible in exchange, but I might still get something. "Evolutionary biology has a hypothesis to account for small conspicuous acts of kindness," says animal behavior expert John Alcock. "My guess is that the people who assisted others in the World Trade Center knew that others were observing. They were not calculating, but their desire to commit some nice act—commiserating, directing, guiding others to safety, might have had a substantial payoff in terms of improved reputation." There may have also been something calming about helping others that day; it lent a sense of normalcy and orderliness to the abnormal and disorderly.

Until about a fraction of a second ago, in terms of human history, we lived in small, extended-family bands. We all knew one another, from birth to death. So by aiding one another, we could build a reputation for being generous and helpful, which would encourage others to cooperate with us—which would in turn boost our chances of reproductive success. "I know this sounds cold and analytical to the average layperson," says Alcock. "I'm not saying that people who do this are not motivated by impulses that are moral, ethical, and desirable. I'm saying that it's precisely because these impulses are adaptive that we admire them as moral and ethical."

Sometimes what looks like altruism is actually quite the opposite. In an elegant paper published in 1971, biologist W. D. Hamilton described what he called the "geometry for the selfish herd." When a dog runs after a herd of sheep, the sheep at the back of the pack will butt or jump his way into the ranks ahead of him—leading the herd to become more and more tightly packed together. From afar, it may appear that the sheep are banding together in a grand show of unity. In fact, each is just trying to avoid being eaten, by reducing his "domain of danger," as Hamilton puts it. The animals on the edge of the herd are the easiest to pick off. So no one wants to be on the edge. Genes that help us avoid the edge are genes that are likely to endure through natural selection. So a human who feels compelled to stick with a group of strangers in a sinking ship may be doing it for all kinds of reasons—including, perhaps, a long-ago, deeply subconscious desire to avoid being eviscerated by a passing hyena.

It's difficult to know for sure whether humans had enough predators to need to form selfish herds. After all, humans' greatest predators have always been other humans. But we make formidable predators, and our best chances of survival are usually improved by sticking together. Groupthink, then, is the adaptive strategy of prioritizing group harmony. Dissent is uncomfortable for the group because it can be dangerous to the individual. Sometimes, when we appear to value the group ahead of our own skin, we are actually doing something else altogether.

The Wedding Party

At the Beverly Hills, the waitress told McCollister, the young bride, that her party had to leave. There was a small fire, but they could come back as soon as it was extinguished, she said. Hearing the news, McCollister turned to find her mother. As she turned, she noticed another waitress opening a folding wall in the center of the room. The opened partition revealed a wall behind it, entirely in flames. Then McCollister looked down the hallway and saw smoke flooding in like water. She felt a clarity of purpose, all of a sudden. "'Everybody out, now,'" she said, ushering the guests out the French doors to the garden. "I put my arms out and was pushing people out the door, kind of like cattle, to show them where to go." People were obedient and calm, she says, remarkably so. She felt filled with responsibility for her guests. "This is my party. They were there because of me."

A woman in an adjoining room appeared to be trapped. So one of her guests lifted up a chair to throw it against the glass and rescue the woman. McCollister's brother-in-law stopped the man. "Don't throw the chair. They will sue you," he said. But then another man threw the chair anyway, and the woman ran out.

McCollister was one of the last to leave the room. It seemed like a quarter of an hour had passed since they had learned of the fire, but it was probably just a couple of minutes. She and her guests got about seven feet into the garden when the room exploded behind them. The back of her dress was blackened. She turned around and stared at the inferno. "Most of us just sat there in shock," she says. "I think this is where the group-think happened. It looked like a movie. We just stood in disbelief."

But not everyone stayed with the herd. The band members reached into the room and began throwing instruments out of the fire. McCollister's cousin ran back in and rescued a wedding gift, a Baccarat crystal jelly jar that McCollister still has. One bridesmaid, Kathy, sprang into action. She was training to be a nurse, so she started helping the medics who arrived. Then she jumped in the ambulance and kept helping, shuttling back and forth between the fire and the hospital. "I remember seeing her carry IV bags back and forth. I was so amazed. She just picked up and went at it," McCollister says. "Her dress got torn, she lost her shoes, and finally she just took her dress off and wore a hospital smock. She was awesome, absolutely awesome."

McCollister herself picked up the train of her dress and wrapped it around her waist. She put her aunt and uncle in a jeep that was taking people away from the scene. Out of the corner of her eye, she saw one of her other friends leave with her husband. They had medical training, but they left. She was appalled. "You just don't leave." The women had been close friends, and McCollister was supposed to be in the woman's wedding shortly after her own. But she never spoke to her again. The woman had abandoned the group.

Along with her new husband, McCollister joined a human chain that had formed to pull people out of the Cabaret Room, just off the garden.

This room in particular seemed to have no end of victims. Most of them were dead or dying when they came out. One stranger died in her husband's arms. Finally a firefighter decided to close the doors to contain the fire.

The Science of Evacuation

For a long time, engineers assumed people would move out of a building like water. They would fill the space they had, coursing down the staircases and flowing out to safety like a river of humanity. Buildings were constructed accordingly. The problem is, people don't move like water.

Ed Galea has spent his career trying to understand crowd behavior in fires. He manages a team of mathematical modelers, behavioral psychologists, and engineers at the University of Greenwich, Old Royal Navy College Campus, in London. In his office in an ancient building alongside the river Thames, he has three framed photos of the burning World Trade Center. Another wall is decorated with eight pictures of train wrecks, plane crashes, and other assorted tragedies. If another man worked here, such a display might seem odd, even callous. But when I meet Galea here on a summer morning, it quickly becomes clear that he takes every disaster personally. I sit down amid the piles of videotapes and books, and we speak without interruption for four hours. Galea's intensity is contagious. He knows more about human behavior in fires than almost anyone in the world, and he agonizes over the needless loss of lives.

Galea is from Australia, where he trained as an astrophysicist. His specialty was using computer models to describe how magnetic stars are born. But not many people would pay him for this service. So he took a rather dull job as an industrial mathematician in the steel industry. He moved to the United Kingdom in the mid-1980s, and, not long afterward, an airplane caught fire during takeoff in Manchester, England. It was a bizarre accident. The Boeing 737 never became airborne, and firefighters quickly doused the plane in foam. There was no crash, just a fire. The last survivor was pulled out five minutes after the plane had come to a stop. And yet fifty-five people still died. Why hadn't they gotten out? In standard evacuation tests, this type of plane had been evacuated in just seventy-five seconds. What had gone wrong? "I couldn't understand how fifty-five people could have died. That caught my attention."

Fire modeling had only just begun, and the United Kingdom led the world. After London burned down twice—in 1212 and 1666—the country became a world model for fire safety. The first seminar on human behavior in fire was held at the University of Surrey in 1977. Galea managed to talk his way onto a project studying the crash at the University of Greenwich in London. But most of the early models were based on how fire moves in relatively small square rooms. And none could explain what happened on the Manchester flight. When Galea and his colleagues modeled the crash, they were amazed at how fast the fire could spread from one of the engines to the fuselage and then inside the cabin, filling the plane with black, toxic smoke. But that still didn't explain the casualty rate on the flight. "We understood the fire, but why did so many people die? Why couldn't they get out?"

So Galea decided to create a model to explain not the fire but the people. It was a revolutionary idea. He took the idea to the U.K. Civil Aviation Authority, which had funded his original model. They turned him down. "They said, 'This is impossible. You might be able to model fire but you can't model people.' To me, that was like waving a red flag in front of a bull."

Galea is a confident man. His website features nine photos of himself, including several of him receiving a prize for his work from Queen Elizabeth II in 2003. There are also pictures of his desk, from multiple vantage points. This is not a man to be easily put off. So Galea did what desperate professors do: he got some graduate students to work for free. For one year, they constructed a very crude model based on the scant research available into human behavior. It was called EXODUS. When Galea showed U.K. aviation officials what he'd come up with, they agreed to give him funding—and have been doing so ever since.

The problem with treating people like water is that water molecules do not experience pain or fear. Water molecules don't make decisions, and they don't stumble or fall. Human beings, on the other hand, fill a space unevenly, in clusters. They take shortcuts and pause to rest when they can. Once committed to a path, they don't easily change course. Groupthink has a momentum of its own.

EXODUS tries to treat people like people. Each evacuee receives a specific age, name, sex, breathing rate, and running speed, among other characteristics. Then EXODUS gives individuals behavioral capacities "so they can make decisions." For instance, until EXODUS, models assumed that people would begin to evacuate as soon as an alarm went off. Of course, anyone who has ever heard a fire alarm knows this is not what happens. With EXODUS, evacuees have lives and brains. Before leaving, each performs certain tasks—like grabbing a briefcase or searching for a child. And they have the ability to see an exit sign—and follow it—or not. (In experiments with real human beings, Galea has found that many people simply fail to see exit signs, even when they are in plain view. It remains unclear why.)

Most important, the newest version of EXODUS recognizes that people move in groups. That is a difficult behavior to model, which is partly why so few models have ever tried to do it. But it is essential. Galea and his colleagues have analyzed a database of 1,295 survivor accounts from plane accidents. About half of the survivors said they were traveling with someone else at the time of the accident.

EXODUS helped Galea understand that passengers on the Manchester flight had not reacted like synchronized swimmers. Some remained frozen in their seats. Others climbed frantically over seat backs, while still others piled up at an overly narrow exit row, slowing the evacuation to a standstill. One passenger tried to open the exit door beside her, not realizing that she was actually yanking on her armrest. Human behavior, combined with the noxious mix of smoke, heat, and gases, meant that the passengers had very poor odds of getting out.

Today, Galea's software is used in thirty-five countries. Galea would prefer that it be used before a fire—before a structure is even built. But it is often used as a forensic tool during investigations. The country with the most licenses—and a history shot through with disasters—is Korea. The United States has been "very backward in adopting this kind of technology in the design stage," he says. "It's very dangerous." Before

9/11, most U.S. buildings were constructed without the help of any evacuation modeling at all, he says. Now, models are in vogue, but they vary dramatically in quality. Many of them still treat people like water.

I ask Galea when most architects, engineers, and regulators started taking human behavior seriously. "They're still not," he says. "We're sometimes still told that EXODUS is too complex and has too much human behavior. They want to know, 'If I have someone here, how long will it take to get out?' They don't want to know how they move or if they move in groups. These guys who build buildings don't want to know about this."

Smoke Gets in Your Eyes

To get a better idea of what it might feel like to be in a fire, I visited the burn tower at the training academy of the Kansas City Fire Department. Kansas City has just under 450,000 people, and the fire department is the first responder for every emergency call. Each year, Kansas City fire-fighters respond to nearly sixty thousand requests—or 164 calls a day.

Tommy Walker, the Kansas City Fire Department's chief of training, insists on picking me up from the airport in a typical display of fire-fighter hospitality. He is a rail-thin man with a salt-and-pepper mustache and a gee-whiz manner who nevertheless swears like a truck driver. He's also one of the friendliest, most patient men you'll ever meet, so it's a little startling every time he calls someone a "piece of shit" or a "sonofabitch," which is often. "If I say someone's a 'piece of shit,' that's a compliment," he explains in his Mr. Rogers voice. "I hope I don't offend you with my language."

Like all good fire chiefs, Walker gets evangelical when he talks about training. After eight weeks of classroom work, his cadets spend ten weeks enduring every kind of simulated hell he can invent. He makes them climb stairs through thick smoke on their hands and knees, stand next to a live fire until they can't take the heat anymore, and crawl through a maze blindfolded until they get tangled in wires and have to cut their way out. He has seen every kind of human fear reaction, and he wants to evoke them all before a firefighter gets into a real fire. "You would be surprised at the number of people who are utterly panicked by a loss of vision," he says. "So we find that out before we get them hot." In every class of cadets, about 10–14 percent don't make it through the training. "Some people just don't take to it. I'd like to be a brain surgeon, too, but not everybody's supposed to be a brain surgeon." Nationwide, fire departments lose about two people a year to training accidents. But the training is so important that the risk is considered worthwhile.

To find out if I would get panicked, Walker took me out back. The burn tower is a six-story concrete, fiber, and sheet-metal structure full of old furniture and kindling. Charred La-Z-Boys, broken lamps, and worn sofas are scattered about, making the place look like a frat house that devolved into a crack house. The furniture is donated by the firefighters and their relatives, and the kindling comes from old pallets contributed by the local warehouses. The floors and ceilings are coated in black soot, and the air is acrid from thousands of training burns.

To simulate a fire, Walker's instructors turn on the smoke. The artificial smoke is made from banana oil, which is cheap to buy and turns into thick, gray nontoxic smoke when it is atomized. Before we go in, they take me to the storeroom and dress me up in full firefighter gear, which I have to confess is totally cool. (They really do wear suspenders.) But then we go into the tower and the metal door clangs behind us. And for a moment, I actually think I might turn and run right out the door.

One thing most people don't understand about fires is that the smoke is the main event. It is what makes it nearly impossible to find your way out. Your eyes literally close to protect you from the smoke, and you can't get them open again. It's an involuntary defense mechanism. Smoke is also by far the thing most likely to kill you. Firefighters rarely see a burned body. Toxic smoke from a smoldering fire can kill you in your sleep before any flames are even visible. That's why it's so important to have a smoke detector with a working battery.

Inside the tower, in the utter blackness, I turn on a flashlight. It doesn't help much, since the light just reflects off the smoke like headlights in fog. In this case, my firefighter escort has an infrared imaging camera that helps identify living bodies and offers a glimpse of the terrain. We can see ourselves, ghostly silhouettes on the screen. But normal people, of course, won't have any such help in a real fire. We creep along the wall, groping our way to the staircase and then counting the steps so that we can remember the number on our way back down. It is hard to imagine getting out of any unfamiliar structure in this darkness, especially in intense heat. In this case, there is no heat, but once we go through a few rooms, I still do not think I could get out in under two hours if I were on my own. I am in a group of two, but it is clear, even in a simulation, that it would be insane to leave my group. Two groping blind people are better than one.

Noise is the other thing most people do not expect in fires. In general, noise dramatically increases stress, and stress, as we know, makes it much harder to think and make decisions. Firefighters have learned to listen to the roar of a fire. "Sometimes you go in a fire, and it's hot all around you. Your knees are hot, your ears are hot, the walls are hot. But you can't see the fire," Walker says. "You stop. You turn to the other guys with you and you say, 'Shut the fuck up.' And you can hear where the fire is coming from. It snaps and pops, and usually in that situation it's right below you or adjacent to you."

Just to make things even more challenging, fires grow exponentially. Every ninety seconds, a fire roughly doubles in size. Flashover, when the flammable smoke in the air ignites, thereby igniting everything in the room, usually occurs five to eight minutes after the flames appear. At that point, the environment can no longer support human life.

Firefighting technology has improved in quantum leaps over the past fifty years. Today, smoke detectors and sprinkler systems save thousands of lives. But fires have gotten hotter at the same time. Construction materials are far less fire-resistant today than they were just twenty-five years ago. Lightweight roof trusses can collapse after just five minutes in direct flames. Plastic furnishings serve as fuel. So a fire in a modern house requires far more water, applied sooner, than the same fire in a hundred-year-old structure.

Richard Gist, a psychologist with the fire department, has had to notify hundreds of Kansas City residents that a family member has died in

a fire. Over and over again, they ask him why their loved one didn't simply walk out the door or climb out the window. They have no concept of
what it would be like to be in a fire. "I very frequently find myself standing with the survivors in a burned home explaining how their loved one
died. They say, 'Why didn't they just . . . ?' You have to explain to them
that it was 2:00 A.M., and they woke up out of a dead sleep." If you wake
up in heavy, hot smoke and stand up, you're already dead from scorched
lungs. You have to roll out of bed and crawl to an exit, not an easy thing
to remember. That's why Gist spends much of his time trying to get
people to put batteries in their smoke detectors and practice evacuating
before a fire, so that escaping becomes automatic. Echoing every disaster expert I've ever met, Gist says, "If you have to stop and think it
through, then you will not have time to survive."

Follow the Busboy

Walter Bailey was an eighteen-year-old busboy at the Beverly Hills Supper Club. On the night of the fire, he had asked to work the Cabaret
Room so that he could catch some of the act. The last group to hear of
the fire was the more than twelve hundred people in that ballroom.

Bailey was what they called a "party busboy." That meant he helped
prep mass quantities of food—two hundred butter bowls or one hundred salads with croutons. In the club hierarchy, party busboys ranked
down at the bottom, right above dishwashers. Unlike the waiters, who
wore jackets and ties, he had to wear a gold sort of smock. "It looked like
something a monkey would wear—a monkey that cranks music," says
Bailey. On May 28, he had worked at the club for only a little over a year.
The month before, he'd been there as a guest for his senior prom.

Shortly after 8:30 P.M., Bailey left the Cabaret Room to help out in
another dining room. On his way down the hallway, he ran into a waitress. She asked him if he knew where the club's owners were. He
pointed her toward the kitchen. She whispered into his ear: "There's a
fire in the Zebra Room," and then she headed toward the kitchen.

At first, Bailey did not believe the waitress. "She must be exaggerating," he thought. So he went to the Zebra Room to see for himself. When he got there, everything looked normal, at first. He walked over to the doors to open them, but then he stopped. Just as he approached, smoke started curling out from the cracks at the top of the door. The smoke was actually puffing out in little bursts, as he recalls. "That indicated there was pressure behind the doors," he says, then adding, by way of explanation, "Science was one of my favorite subjects in high school." As he watched, the smoke started leaking out through the center of the doors as well. He wisely decided not to open the doors. Instead, he did something remarkable, something many other people would not do. He went into the bar next to the Zebra Room and shouted, "Everyone out! There's a fire." The patrons got up and started moving. Then Bailey thought of the Cabaret Room. It was clear across the building, the show was now in progress, and no one had any way to know about the fire. There were no smoke detectors, fire alarms, or sprinklers in the Beverly Hills.

When Bailey got to the Cabaret Room, he walked up to a supervisor and told him there was a fire. "We have to clear the room," he said. The man just stared blankly at him. Then Bailey turned to find the club's owners. But then he stopped himself. "This is stupid," he told himself. "I'm wasting time. Either he has to clear this room or I will." So he went back to his supervisor and told him, again, to clear the room. The supervisor walked off. Bailey assumed he was going to start the evacuation. In the meantime, he decided to start moving a line of about seventy people who were still waiting to enter the show. "Everyone, follow me," Bailey said. And they did. Without a word of explanation, he led them down the hallway and out into the garden. "OK, everyone stay here," he said. To his amazement, they didn't ask any questions.

When he came back to the Cabaret Room, he was stunned to see that nothing had changed. The opening act was still in progress, the comedians were still chortling their way through their bit. "This isn't going to do," he told himself. "This room has to be cleared out, and it has to be cleared out soon. I'm probably going to lose my job, but I'm just going to do it." Then he walked right down the middle of the room, through the VIP seats in the pit and up the steps to the stage. He reached over to one of the comedians and took the microphone. The crowd stared up at him, confused. "I want everyone to look to my right," he said. "There is an exit in the right corner of the room. And look to my left. There's an exit on the left. And now look to the back. There's an exit in the back. I want everyone to leave the room calmly. There's a fire at the front of the building." Then he walked back off the stage.

Thirty years later, Bailey still has a flat, calm voice. He still uses words like *super* and *neat*. Back then, he was a quiet teenage boy who didn't have too many friends at the club. He had recently discovered at school that he had stage fright, so he was terrified when he climbed the stairs to take the microphone. But he did it anyway, saving hundreds of lives.

How did Bailey do it? Why didn't he stay within the narrow confines of his role, like most people that night? When I ask Bailey about this, he explains that his identity was actually a little more complicated than it appeared. Unlike a lot of the Beverly Hills employees, who loved working there, he was not particularly attached to his job or the club. He had lived all over the country as part of a military family and had worked at construction jobs that paid a lot more money. The busboy job paid just $1.10 an hour. "I put in my time and left," he says. So when it came time to react to the fire, Bailey had less to lose. He was not as impressed by the club's hierarchy, and he could easily imagine life without the smock. "When I decided to clear the room, my first thought was, 'I'm going to get fired.' But I wanted to do the right thing." Heroism is the subject of another chapter, and there is much to say. But suffice it to say that Bailey was, in some ways, a classic case.

After Bailey told everyone in the Cabaret Room to leave, he went outside. Then he circled around to check on another exit. He saw smoke coming out and headed back in. As soon as he got inside, he realized that he was witnessing a catastrophe. He couldn't see anything, but he could hear people—so many people—crying out for help. He started reaching into the depths, grabbing people by the collar and dragging them out the door. He went back and forth this way about ten times, pulling someone out each time. "I was afraid. I don't want to die, just like most people," Bailey says. "Maybe I was stupid." The smoke started burning his throat, so he began holding his breath on each trip back in. He had a high level of confidence in his lungs. "I was on the swim team in high school," he explains. "I could swim almost two lengths of the pool without taking a breath." On one trip, he made it all the way back to the Cabaret Room door. The voices in the blackness, moaning for help, seemed to be coming from all directions. As he groped into the smoke, he realized he was feeling a pile of bodies, jammed in the doorway. His lungs bursting, he grabbed whomever he could find lying on the perimeter of the pile. "I remember pulling one guy by his necktie. That's the only thing I could get."

Outside, Bailey decided to recruit more help. Several other men— mostly employees—were already helping, but the number of casualties was overwhelming. Rows of bodies were lined up on the grass. The victims had died from smoke inhalation, not fire, so their bodies looked strangely untouched, lying peacefully in their best dresses and suits. All around, guests who had become separated from their parties were searching for their loved ones, crying out the names of the missing like so many wretched ghosts.

Bailey ran up to the hillside, where several hundred patrons had gathered, and called out: "Can anyone help us? We need some help at that exit!" The guests, who had been comforting one another and staring at the fire, watched him. No one volunteered. They were guests, and guests aren't generally expected to go back into burning buildings. "I just figured I'd get a bunch of big guys," he says. "But no. They just looked at me."

So Bailey ran back to the club alone. Each time he went into the smoke, the voices were quieter. "You could tell people were dying in there. People were breathing heavy. They were reaching out from the pile. I remember thinking, 'These people are going to grab me, and I'm going to get stuck in here and die.'" On one trip in, Bailey didn't hear any voices at all. After that, he didn't go back inside anymore. He wandered around outside, placing napkins over the faces of corpses, before finally getting a ride home, where his mother was sitting in the kitchen waiting in dread for news of her son the busboy.

After the fire, Bailey did a handful of media interviews. But then he withdrew and refused to talk about the fire for decades. Like a lot of survivors, he felt shadowed by guilt. "I'm a perfectionist," he explains. "It was ripping me apart, having all those people dead. I thought a lot of people had died because I didn't do a good job." Thirty years after the fire, he agreed to be interviewed for this book, partly, he says, because so much time had gone by.

The Submissive Crowd

If disasters breed groups, then groups need leaders. In a study of three mine fires published by the U.S. government in 2000, the eight groups that escaped each had a leader. The leaders had some things in common. They did not bully their way into power, but they got respect because they seemed calm and credible. They were, like Bailey, knowledgeable, aware of details, and decisive. They were also open to other opinions; in many of the escape groups, a sort of second lieutenant emerged to help the leader.

But what about the followers? Why did so many people abandon expensive seats in order to follow a teenager in a gold smock? Again, we see the same tendencies in our primate ancestors. Chimpanzees always follow an elaborate hierarchy, with an alpha male on top. When facing an enemy, they become even more militaristic. They have a better chance of surviving if they obey without hesitation, says chimp expert Frans de Waal. A strong leader can make decisions fast, which is what you need in a crisis. "Hierarchy," says de Waal, "is more efficient than democracy."

Jim Cline, a retired New York City Fire Department captain, remembers when he discovered the human herd instinct himself. It was a bright Friday afternoon in Manhattan, the kind of day when the city actually sparkles through its layer of grit. The financial district was full of workers on their lunch hour. He was in the fire truck headed up Fulton Street when he heard a massive explosion. About two hundred feet in front of him, a gas tank had exploded on an ice cream truck, injuring 106 people and blowing out windows all around. People were screaming. Some were covered in blood. But no one yet knew what had happened, and it was impossible to see anything. "Wall Street was absolutely packed with cars and people. We couldn't even see where a hydrant was." The firefighters flipped on the lights and siren to try to clear a path. Hundreds of people, suddenly noticing the truck, started running toward it, away from the fire.

Then something strange happened: when the people got to the truck, they turned and started running alongside it—as it headed directly for the explosion. "It was a very strange phenomenon," Cline says, chuckling. "People will follow you, even when they don't know why they're following you." As the firefighters stretched the first hose line toward the fire, they had to navigate through the throng of onlookers. It was only after enough police arrived on the scene that the crowd could be pushed back to safety.

Now Cline trains firefighters and rescue workers to beware the herd instinct: "I tell them, 'If something goes wrong, people will tend to follow you—which is not what we want. We want them to go the other way!'" He advises officials to use loud, clear warnings and gestures to preempt the herd instinct.

"What you actually look for in these circumstances is someone who can tell you what to do," Ian, a victim of the 2005 London transit bombings, later told investigators. "Even if it is a basic 'Stay here' or 'Move there,' you just need guidance, because you are a bit all over the place, as you can imagine." Ian suffered severe burns to the chest and legs when the blast hurled him onto electrified cables in the train tunnel. After briefly losing consciousness, he heard the voice of the train driver, who told him to make his way out of the tunnel. This instruction, Ian told investigators, was enormously reassuring.

Our obedience to authority in a disaster can be an asset, if the people in charge understand it. For years, aviation safety experts could not understand why passengers did so little to save themselves in plane crashes. They would sit in their seats instead of going to an exit. Those who did get up had an infuriating tendency to reach for their carry-on baggage before leaving. Then, once they made it to the exit door, they would pause for a dangerous amount of time before jumping down the slide. And in plane crashes, remember, you usually have a matter of seconds, not minutes, to get out.

In a series of experiments, safety officials ran regular people through mock evacuations from planes. The trials weren't nearly as stressful as real evacuations, of course, but it didn't matter. People, especially women, hesitated for a surprisingly long time before jumping onto the slide. That pause slowed the evacuation for everyone. But there was a way to get people to move faster. If a flight attendant stood at the exit and screamed at people to jump, the pause all but disappeared, the researchers found. In fact, if flight attendants did *not* aggressively direct the evacuation, they might as well have not been there at all. A study by the Cranfield University Aviation Safety Centre found that people moved just as slowly for polite and calm flight attendants as they did when there were no flight attendants present.

On August 2, 2005, Air France Flight 358 skidded off the runway in Toronto, Canada, during a violent storm. The plane, arriving from Paris and full of passengers, slid into a gully at a speed of 92 mph. The fire was immediate and intense. Half the exits of the Airbus A340 were either blocked or unusable due to malfunctioning slides. Cable TV broadcast live images of the smoking hulk of metal. But all 297 passengers and 12 crew members got out alive. The passengers moved fast and deliberately. Some jumped from more than fifteen feet above ground. Then they ran fifty to hundred yards away from the plane. One man carried a passenger with a broken leg up to the highway. By the time the airport fire department arrived, fifty-two seconds after the crash, three-quarters of the passengers had already evacuated. Before three minutes, everyone was off. When the plane exploded in flames, no passengers were in the immediate vicinity.

It was called a miracle, but it was also a tribute to good training. On the Air France flight, the crew gave loud, clear directions from the moment the plane crashed. The copilot came over the intercom system and told the passengers to calmly exit the plane. The flight attendants screamed at the passengers, just as they'd been trained: "Everyone out the exits at the back! Do not go forward. Move out now!" They did not snuff out all misbehavior; some passengers still insisted on taking heavy carry-on baggage with them. But the plane emptied in remarkably little time. Afterward, passengers told reporters that the crew's orders had saved lives.

Maria Cojocaru, an Ontario resident who escaped with her two small children, remembers the crew guiding her, even as the cabin filled with thick black smoke. "All the time they speak to us and tell us, 'Move, move, move,'" she told the *Canadian Press*. "At the end, they saved our lives."

Leadership can save the life of the rescue worker, too. In river rescues, members of the Kansas City Fire Department rescue squad yell profanity-laced threats at victims before they get to them. If they don't, the victim will grab on to them and push them under the water in a mad scramble to stay afloat. "We try to get their attention. And we don't always use the prettiest language," says Larry Young, a captain in the rescue division. "I hope I don't offend you by saying this. But if I approach Mrs. Suburban Housewife and say, 'When I get to you, do not fucking touch me! I will leave you if you touch me!' she tends to listen."

As the Beverly Hills burned to the ground, Bailey gave the guests in the Cabaret Room clear directions, accompanied by hand gestures, showing them how to get out. He did exactly the right thing. But even so, there were some people who did not leave. Perhaps they didn't hear the warning. Or maybe they did, but they didn't believe it. Quite possibly, like so many disaster victims, they were in denial. Or maybe they couldn't get out, so they decided to wait until the crowd had thinned. Whatever the case, not everyone got up to leave. When firefighters finally got the blaze under control and entered the Cabaret Room the next day, they found one table with six burned corpses still sitting in their chairs. All told, 167 people died from the fire at the Beverly Hills. It was one of the deadliest fires in U.S. history.

The bride, McCollister, stayed on the hillside until 1:00 A.M., trying to help. She finally walked to a nearby hotel, still wearing her charred dress and holding her bouquet. "People did weird things," she says, remembering how someone had rescued her veil for her that night. The next day, she had to call everyone on her guest list to see if they had survived. That, she says, was the most excruciating part of the whole ordeal. "It was gut-wrenching. You didn't know what you were going to get hit with. Someone hysterical, someone angry." One woman, the wife of a family friend, died of smoke inhalation, and McCollister was devastated by guilt. "You feel like a real schmuck. I knew I had nothing to do with her dying, but you cannot look yourself in the mirror and say you're not accountable." After the fire, she says, her new husband was never the same. They got divorced four years later.

McCollister declined to discuss the fire with reporters until 2007. That spring, on the thirtieth anniversary of the fire, some of the survivors and relatives of the victims gathered for a ceremony at the site of the Beverly Hills Supper Club. The grounds were overgrown with weeds and honeysuckle, so it was hard to imagine what had once been there. One by one, people got up to speak and remember those who had died. One woman stood at the microphone and cried and cried. McCollister recognized her. It was the singer from the band that had played on her wedding night. After the ceremony, the former bride walked up to the former singer and gave her a long hug.

The Grand Bayou Model

Just as individuals can be more or less resilient, so can groups. Groups perform as well during a disaster as they performed before it. The healthier an office culture or family, the better it can absorb stress and recover. High-functioning groups know how to communicate and help one another, and they have the resources to do it. Even at the cellular level, camaraderie promotes survival. Multiple studies have found that people with supportive social networks tend to have stronger immune systems.

Recently, psychologists and disaster researchers have become obsessed with this idea of group resilience. Where does it come from and how can we make more of it? Instead of just studying people who are traumatized by disasters, psychologists have turned their attention to the healthy majority—the people who don't need their help. There are even software applications designed to create resilience through social networks. If every town had a sort of emergency MySpace community, the reasoning goes, then everyone would fare better in an actual emergency. And, in fact, during the 2007 wildfires in southern California, some of the best information came from neighborhood blogs—and photos taken with cell phones. "This is a neighbor-helping-neighbor situation," San Diego mayor Jerry Sanders told a crowd of evacuees at Qualcomm Stadium.

In 2005, the citizens of Grand Bayou, a remote Louisiana coastal town, had very little advanced technology. What they had were long traditions, close relationships, and a culture of self-sufficiency. For three hundred years, this Native American and Cajun fishing community had occupied a treacherous stretch of the Gulf, accessible only by water. Grand Bayou was there before the levees, before the oil tankers, before the National Weather Service.

In all that time, Grand Bayou never lost anyone to a hurricane. Rosina Philippe grew up in Grand Bayou. When storms approached, no one waited for an official evacuation order. "We know how to get ourselves out of harm's way, announcement or not," says Philippe. Residents would talk with one another and decide when it was time to leave. All of them would pile onto about twelve oyster, fishing, and work boats, hitching them all together in a long convoy. They had done it many times before. Grand Bayou was not an affluent community, but the connections between the people who lived there were strong. "Everyone has family," Philippe says. "If someone didn't want to go, we would make them go." The children of Grand Bayou loved evacuating. It was like a big slumber party. "You're going out on a big ol' boat ride with all your friends," says Philippe's teenage daughter, Anisor Philippe Cortez.

Grand Bayou's 125 residents evacuated two days before Hurricane Katrina made landfall, before the mayor of New Orleans had called for a mandatory evacuation. Philippe, her daughter, her sister, and her sister's family, along with a few friends, piled onto a work boat with plenty of provisions. Then they hooked onto the rest of the Grand Bayou convoy and headed out. The trip to a safe harbor took about two hours, and no one was left behind.

The citizens of Grand Bayou had the resilience to survive Katrina. They had maintained the ties that keep groups strong—the kind of ties many Americans have lost. But over the previous fifty years, builders and oil companies had changed the landscape around Grand Bayou, destroying the wetlands that normally protected it. The town's residents had fought against this development for years, to no avail. They had elevated their houses above flood level, only to see their houses sink again as the development marched on. In 1980, you could walk on land from one house to the next in Grand Bayou. By the end of the twentieth century, the land was gone. Grand Bayou, like Venice, was gradually sinking.

When Katrina came, it swept all of Grand Bayou away. There was literally nothing left but battered boats and scraps of metal—the ruins of a fine civilization. Since then Philippe has moved nine times. Now she lives about an hour and a half from her old home, hoping to one day go back. Ironically, she is now in more danger than she ever was. The community has scattered across many states, and Philippe and her daughter live in a FEMA trailer.

But the citizens of Grand Bayou intend to come back. The first house was finished in July 2007. All the houses will be "soft-build"—simple wooden structures that are cheap to rebuild. The community is still fighting to restore the wetlands and create a more sustainable civilization. But in the meantime, they plan to evacuate with each storm and then clean up the mess, as they always have. "We try to protect life, that's the most important thing," says Philippe. She now thinks that the population of Grand Bayou will be bigger after Katrina than it was before. "I know that we're going to survive," she says. "We've learned to depend upon each other."

A Tale of Two Cities

Places like Grand Bayou are models of resilience because the residents proactively help one another survive. They value their community more than their possessions, and they also trust the group's collective decisions. But that is a rare accomplishment in the modern era of large cities and anonymous neighbors. It is certainly the goal, but it is not the only option.

There are smaller, simpler forms of resilience. Sometimes the groups that survive disasters are the ones that preserve a single piece of vital information. One lesson, widely shared, can make all the difference, a fact both heartbreaking and hopeful. Life and death shouldn't be determined based on the preservation of one fact. But if it is, at least we know it is eminently possible to do better.

The 2004 tsunami in Southeast Asia killed an estimated two hundred thousand people. The real number is bigger or smaller; it was literally too big to count. The missing pictures in local newspapers went on for pages and pages, on and on, until it seemed there must have been some kind of printing mistake.

A crushing wall of seawater seems like one situation in which death is nonnegotiable. And it's true: for many of the victims, there was literally no chance of avoiding death—barring a sophisticated, multinational warning system, which the Indian Ocean did not have. But for thousands of people, the best warning system was old and homemade.

Consider two cities, both very close to the epicenter of the earthquake that set off the 2004 tsunami. Jantang was a coastal village on the northern coast of Sumatra. The residents felt the ground shake, and about twenty minutes later, a roaring wave swept their lives away. The water reached heights of forty-five to sixty feet. All of the village's structures were destroyed. Over 50 percent of the people were killed.

Langi, on the island of Simeulue, was even closer to the quake. Islanders had just eight minutes after the ground shook to get to high ground—the shortest interval between earthquake and tsunami anywhere and too fast for a buoy-based warning system, had there been one. Waves there reached thirty to forty-five feet—slightly less than the height in Jantang, but still decidedly deadly. As in Jantang, all the town's buildings were decimated.

But in Langi, 100 percent of the eight-hundred-person population survived. No one—not a child, not a grandmother—was lost, as Lori Dengler, a geology professor from Humboldt State University in Arcata, California, discovered when she visited in April of 2005. Why? In Langi, when the ground shook, everyone left for higher ground—and stayed there for a while. That was the tradition, no matter what. In 1907, the island had experienced a tsunami, which locals say killed about 70 percent of the population. And the survivors had passed this lesson on through the generations in Langi and other towns. Everyone knew the word *smong,* the word for tsunami in the Simeulue language.

When Dengler asked the locals where they went when the ground shook, they pointed to a nearby hill, about a hundred feet high, or, says Dengler, "right about where I would have told them to go." They seemed proud of their devotion to evacuating and said they never considered a false evacuation a waste of time. (Interestingly, on the entire island of Simeulue, only seven people out of seventy-eight thousand died from the tsunami. And they all died, Dengler says, because they were trying to save their belongings. They were gathering, a tendency that is, as we have seen, common in disasters.)

When Dengler's team visited Jantang, however, they found a totally different skill set. Before the disaster, "No one had ever heard anything about tsunami," she said. When residents heard what sounded like explosions coming from the ocean, many locked themselves in their houses, fearing gunfights between rebels and the Indonesian military.

Long before guns, there were tsunami. Human beings have dealt with killer waves for thousands of years, as have animals. Hours before the 2004 tsunami, a dozen elephants being ridden by tourists started suddenly trumpeting. One hour before the wave hit, the elephants headed to high ground—some of them even breaking their chains to get there. After the tsunami, wildlife officials at Sri Lanka's Yala National Park were shocked to find that hundreds of elephants, monkeys, tigers, and deer had survived unharmed. But people don't seem to have retained these survival skills as well as other mammals.

We have the ability to do better, and in some places, we clearly have. That is very good news. In communities with survival traditions, like Grand Bayou and Langi, precious time spent in the deliberation zone can be extremely productive. And it must be. Because now we are out of time. We have passed through the denial and deliberation phases, and there is nothing left to do but act. What happens next will be, as we will see, very hard to undo. The decisive moments are the cumulative results of the delay and dread, of the influences of fear, resilience, and group-think. They can be years in the making, and they can play out in a flash.

The devastated Port of Halifax, Nova Scotia, one of the busiest in the world, seen after a ship carrying explosives blew up on December 6, 1917. The blast killed 1,963 people. *Credit: U.S. Army Signal Corps*

In 1917, Reverend Samuel Prince opened up his church to treat the injured in Halifax. Later, he wrote the first serious study of human behavior in disasters. *Credit: Alan Ruffman Collection*

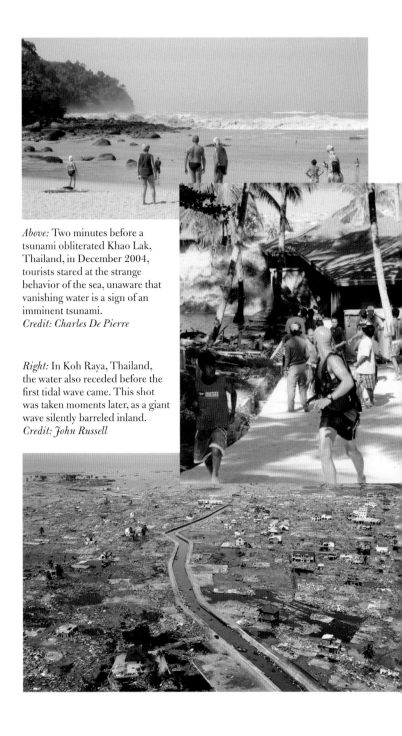

Above: Two minutes before a tsunami obliterated Khao Lak, Thailand, in December 2004, tourists stared at the strange behavior of the sea, unaware that vanishing water is a sign of an imminent tsunami.
Credit: Charles De Pierre

Right: In Koh Raya, Thailand, the water also receded before the first tidal wave came. This shot was taken moments later, as a giant wave silently barreled inland.
Credit: John Russell

Left: Before Hurricane Katrina in 2005, elderly people were among the least likely to evacuate—partly because the brain values experiences over official warnings, and older people had survived many storms. Here a Coast Guard rescue swimmer helps load survivors into a helicopter. *Credit: U.S. Coast Guard*

Below: A view of the Louisiana Superdome taken two days after Hurricane Katrina devastated the Gulf Coast. *Credit: U.S. Navy photo by Photographer's Mate Airman Jeremy L. Grisham*

Opposite: Taken ten days after the tsunami, this shot of the coast of Banda Aceh in Indonesia shows the epic reach of the disaster. *Credit: Choo Youn-Kong, Pool/AP*

The first phase of the survival arc is the reckoning stage, which takes precious time. On 9/11, people in the World Trade Center took twice as long to descend as safety engineers had predicted. Firefighter Mike Kehoe, who survived, was in the stairwell of Tower 1. *Credit: John Labriola/AP*

Deliberation is the second phase of the survival arc. As we contemplate our options, fear alters the way our brain works. Former U.S. Ambassador Diego Asencio was taken hostage in Bogotá, Colombia. He remembers feeling time speed up and then slow down—and thinking about a Norman Mailer book he'd once read. *Credit: © The Washington Post. Photo by Harry Naltchayan. Reprinted with permission.*

Some people, like Brigadier General Nisso Shacham, the police commander in the southern half of Israel, seem unusually resilient in the face of extreme stress. *Credit: Samantha Appleton/Noor*

To understand resilience, military psychiatrists have studied U.S. Special Forces soldiers. Even their blood chemistry is different from that of other soldiers. *Credit: David Bohrer*

Groups are just as important as individuals in a disaster. In 1977, a ferocious fire destroyed the glamorous Beverly Hills Supper Club outside Cincinnati, Ohio, killing 167 people. A study of the crowd behavior showed that most people performed according to their assigned role that night. *Credit: Dave Horn Collection*

The last phase of the survival arc is the decisive moment. Given the right mix of conditions, catastrophes like a stampede can happen. Since 1990, more than 2,500 people have been killed in crowd crushes during the annual Muslim pilgrimage to Islam's holy places in Saudi Arabia. This picture shows the normally peaceful crowd outside Mecca. *Credit: Khalil Hamra/AP*

Saudi security officers and rescue workers gather by the dead bodies after a stampede in Mina on January 12, 2006. At least 346 people were killed, and nearly 1,000 were injured. *Credit: Muhammed Muheisen/AP*

The most common reaction to a life-or-death situation is to do nothing. A kind of involuntary paralysis sets in, as experienced by a young man trapped in a classroom during the massacre at Virginia Tech in 2007. Here, students console each other at a campus vigil the night of the shootings. *Credit: Stephen Voss/WpN*

Sometimes people will take seemingly inexplicable risks to save total strangers. After Air Florida Flight 90 crashed into the frozen Potomac River in Washington, DC, on January 13, 1982, dozens of people watched from the banks as the survivors clung to the wreckage. Eventually, three men jumped in to help, and a U.S. Park Police helicopter pulled the survivors to safety. *Credit: Charles Pereira/U.S. Park Police*

What causes heroism? Roger Olian jumped into the freezing water the day of the Potomac River disaster because he had something to lose if he didn't, he says. "If you didn't get anything out of it, I mean flat-out nothing, you wouldn't do it." He is pictured here beside the Air Florida crash site, twenty-five years later. *Credit: Katie Ellsworth*

Every disaster holds evidence of the human capacity to do better. On 9/11, Rick Rescorla, head of security for Morgan Stanley and a decorated Vietnam veteran, sang songs into a bullhorn to keep people moving. He had spent years training the company's 2,700 employees to get out fast in an emergency. *Credit: Eileen Maher Hillock*

Part Three
The Decisive Moment

6

Panic

A Stampede on
Holy Ground

FOR MORE THAN fourteen hundred years, Muslims have journeyed to Mecca, the birthplace of Muhammad. The pilgrimage, or hajj, is required of every Muslim who can manage it. So the ritual has become one of the largest annual mass movements of human beings in history. People leave their homes with their life's savings in their pockets, anxious about the adventure ahead, and they return with stories of finding peace in the most unlikely of places: in the middle of a scorched desert, deep inside an undulating crowd of strangers from all over the world.

But over the past two decades, something awful has happened to the hajj. In 1990, a stampede in a pedestrian tunnel killed 1,426 people in minutes. The list of dead included Egyptians, Indians, Pakistanis, Indonesians, Malaysians, Turks, and Saudis. Four years later, another stampede killed more than 270 pilgrims. After that, the tragedies began to follow a sickening rhythm, coming closer and closer together. In 1998, the count was at least 118. In 2001, at least 35 pilgrims were killed in a crush. In 2004, the body count rose to 251. In 2006, the crowd took more than 346 lives. All of the past five tragedies happened in the same area, called "jamarat," around three pillars that all pilgrims must stone as a required ritual of the hajj. Somehow, a beautiful holy place became, for more than 2,500 people, a killing field.

What happened to the hajj? Why were people getting crushed and asphyxiated, year after year, when they had come to pray? What was causing what appeared to be mass panic?

Panic is one of those words that change shape depending on the moment. Like *heroism,* it is defined in retrospect, often in ways that reflect more about the rest of us than about the facts on the ground. The word comes from mythology, which is appropriate. The Greek god Pan had a human torso and the legs, horns, and beard of goat. During the day, he roamed the forests and meadows, tending to flocks and playing songs on his flute. At night, he devoted much of his energy to the conquest of various nymphs. But from time to time, he amused himself by playing tricks on human travelers. As people passed through the lonely mountain slopes between the Greek city-states, Pan made those strange, creeping noises that slither from the darkness, never to be fully explained. He rustled the underbrush, and people quickened their pace; he did it again, and people ran for their lives. Fear at such harmless noises came to be known as "panic."

Sometimes we use panic to mean a rippling kind of terror that robs us of self-control. But it can also be a reason for fear. There is panic, the emotion, and then there is panic, the behavior—the irrational shrieking and clamoring and shoving that can jeopardize the survival of ourselves and those around us. Both meanings get conflated in one short word, overloaded with implications. This chapter is about panic, the behavior, as manifested in a stampede—one of the most frightening and extreme versions of panic.

This chapter also marks the beginning of the end—the final phase of the survival arc. After denial and deliberation comes what I will call the decisive moment. This is a phrase borrowed from Henri Cartier-Bresson, the French photographer who may be the father of modern photojournalism. For him, the decisive moment was, among other things, "the simultaneous recognition, in a fraction of a second, of the significance of an event." It happened when his camera managed to capture the essence of a thing or a person in a single frame.

Likewise, the last stage in the survival arc is over in a flash. It is the sudden distillation of everything that has come before, and it determines what, if anything, will come after. As in photography, what happens in this single moment depends on many things: timing, experience, sensibility—and, perhaps most of all, luck. What happens once we have accepted the fact that something terrible is upon us and deliberated our options? Panic is the worst-case scenario in the human imagination. All norms of behavior, all the things that make us human, dissolve, and all that remains is chaos. If we think back to the dread equation, panic scores high on every metric: uncontrollability, unfamiliarity, imaginability, suffering, scale of destruction, and unfairness. The only thing as dreadful as panic might be terrorism.

The current fashion in disaster research is to deny that panic ever happens. But one exaggeration doesn't fix another exaggeration. Yes, people rarely do hysterical things that violate basic social mores. The vast majority of the time, as we have seen, panic does not occur. Doing nothing at all is in fact a much more common reaction to a disaster, as we'll see in the next chapter. Afterward, people may say they "panicked," and the media may report a "panic," but in truth almost no one misbehaved. They felt their breath quicken and their heart pound. They felt afraid, in other words, and it was an uncomfortable sensation. But they didn't actually become wilding maniacs, because to do so was not in their interest.

When you think about it, panic is not a very adaptive behavior. We probably could not have evolved to this point by doing it very often. But the enduring expectation that regular people *will* panic leads to all kinds of distrust on the part of neighbors, politicians, and police officers. The idea of panic, like the Greek god for which it is named, grips the imagination. The fear of panic may be more dangerous than panic itself.

But just because panic is rare doesn't mean we shouldn't speak of it. Panic does happen. This chapter is a cautious exploration of the exception: What is panic? When does it happen, and why? How can you make it stop?

A Woman Down

At the end of 2005, Ali Hussain, a driving instructor from Huddersfield, England, went on the hajj with his wife, Belquis Sadiq, a social worker for the elderly. The couple had been married for seventeen years and had four children, the youngest of whom was eight years old. Both Hussain and Sadiq had been on the pilgrimage before separately, and Islam requires only one hajj per lifetime. But they had always wanted to have the experience together. So on December 29, Hussain and his wife left for Saudi Arabia with an organized tour group of 135 other Muslims from their area.

On January 12, Hussain and Sadiq gathered their pebbles together and left their hotel for jamarat, the location of the previous four stampedes. Jamarat is a stretch of land surrounding three stone pillars, which are required stops on the hajj. In a ritual known as the "stoning of the devil," pilgrims must pelt the pillars with pebbles three separate times. It is a cleansing ritual, meant to commemorate the way Abraham, in the Islamic version of the story, repelled Satan each time he tried to stop him from sacrificing his son Ishmael. In the 1970s, the Saudis built an overpass to allow two levels of pilgrims to participate in the stoning at once. As the crowds grew, jamarat became the most dangerous bottleneck in the world.

Hussain and Sadiq knew they were entering the most perilous part of the hajj. But it was a matter of degree. They had been in intense crowds since their arrival. For Westerners, it can be especially unnerving to be so close to so many strangers. The men's bare shoulders touch, and the women's scarves can get entangled. If a shoe falls off, you don't dare try to salvage it. At the pillars themselves, it can be hard to even find the space to raise your arms and toss the pebbles. As the crowd pushed onward, Hussain and Sadiq clasped each other's hands tightly. They knew they needed to stay together.

That morning, the crowd approaching the pillars was extremely dense. Some of the participants had brought their luggage on rolling carts, in violation of the rules. But the throng was flowing fairly smoothly.

At 11:53 A.M., however, something changed. The crowd began to lurch in stop-and-go waves, a pattern visible on the video footage. Hussain and Sadiq began to feel a surge of pressure from behind. The crowd was so tight that they began to have trouble breathing normally. But there was no way to turn back. They just had to make it to the pillars, throw the pebbles, and then get back to the hotel safely.

At about 12:19 P.M., the situation became untenable. People began to be violently pushed in random directions by this amorphous force called the crowd. People stumbled, and then became obstacles for everyone else. Hussain's wife gripped his arm tightly. The heat from the other bodies wrapped around them like a woolen shroud. Breathing became even harder. Then, suddenly, Hussain tripped over a luggage cart. He felt his wife lose her grip. Down on the ground, he saw bodies and heard screaming. People scrambled over his back, injuring his shoulder. He managed to pull himself upright, and he started yelling his wife's name. It had been only a few seconds since he fell. She could not have gone far. But he could not see her anywhere in the thicket of humanity. It was 12:30 P.M. Soon Saudi soldiers arrived and cordoned off the area where the stampede had occurred. They'd gotten adept at cleaning up the carnage quickly. Hussain made his way to the entrance of jamarat and looked for his wife there. "I thought that perhaps Belquis had managed to get away," he later told the *Huddersfield Daily Examiner*, "but she did not come. So I walked back to our hotel, thinking she may be there." By 8:30 P.M., she still had not returned.

That night, the hotel operator took Hussain on the back of his motorbike to the two local hospitals. At the second one, Hussain found a photograph of his wife posted on the wall. She was wearing bangle bracelets in the photograph, just as he remembered. Sadiq, forty-seven, had been killed in the crush. Days later, a distraught Hussain tried to distill his wife's essence into one sentence in an interview with the *Yorkshire Post*. "She was a brilliant girl, very hard-working, a really good wife and a very lovely lady who was always pleased to see people and happy to help people where she could." Sadiq was buried in Saudi Arabia, along with more than 345 other victims.

The Physics of Crowds

After the stampede, Saudi Interior Ministry spokesman Mansour al-Turki blamed the victims. "Some of the pilgrims were undisciplined and hasty to finish the ritual as soon as possible," he said. From the vantage point of the pilgrims themselves, specific nationalities seemed responsible. The Indonesians had held hands, rupturing the crowd like earthquake fault lines; the Nigerians were pushing; and on and on. It wasn't hard to place blame. "You have all of these people from all these different places, people who may have never left their villages before, who don't know how to line up, and they are moving simultaneously," says Mohammed Abdul Aleem, CEO of Islamicity.com, an Islamic web portal run out of California. Aleem last went on hajj in 1999, and he remembers being lifted off his feet at one point, which was terrifying.

But here's the puzzle: the crowd at the hajj is not a crowd of hooligans. It is, overall, better behaved than the vast majority of crowds. Imagine a million people seeking enlightenment. As frightening as the sheer density of the crowd could be, Aleem remembers, the crowd could also be surprisingly soothing: "You are in this sea of humanity, and when it is not threatening, and people are just moving calmly, it is one of the greatest feelings of being connected."

That human connection, literally the opposite of panic, is what makes people want to go back to hajj, even after they've completed their required one trip. "Everyone is aligned, and the alignment creates harmony," says John Kenneth Hautman, a Muslim in Washington, D.C. Hautman came to the hajj with few points of reference. He was a white, Catholic lawyer from Ohio before he met his future wife, a Muslim woman, on Match.com in 2005. Later that year, they got married, and Hautman converted, quit his job as a partner at Hogan & Hartson, a major law firm in town, and began to offer spiritual and legal advice on his own. Months later, he went on the hajj, and it was unlike anything he had experienced.

I met Hautman in May 2007 at the National Islamic Center, the main mosque in D.C., after Friday prayers. Over lunch outside the imam's office, Hautman explained that he does not, in general, like crowds. If asked to watch the Fourth of July fireworks celebration on the National Mall, he would politely decline. But the hajj feels radically different, he says. There was a noticeable absence of rage, he remembers, despite the heat, despite the long waits, despite everything. "This was a colossal traffic jam, but I never heard anyone yelling." He learned to just let the crowd carry him along, something he'd never done before.

So what happens to suddenly transform this wave of believers into a stampede? Why does the crowd coexist peacefully most of the time, only to devolve suddenly on certain occasions?

G. Keith Still is a Scottish mathematician who has spent years studying the hajj crowds and advising Saudi safety officials. His own obsession with crowds began in 1992, when he was waiting in line with some ten thousand people to get into an AIDS awareness concert in London's Wembley Stadium. He had hours to watch the crowd move. "My friends were getting very angry, and I thought it was just fascinating," he says now. He went to graduate school and wrote his thesis on crowd dynamics.

Because he is Christian, Still is not allowed to actually attend the hajj. But he has spent many months in Saudi Arabia, working with Muslim engineers and watching thousands of hours of video footage from some three hundred cameras poised over the pilgrims' heads. The more he learned, the more he realized the crowd crush had more to do with physics than psychology.

As long as human beings have at least one square yard of space each, they can control their own movements. With less than one square yard of space per person, people lose the ability to counter the jostling of others. Small lurches get amplified. After 11:53 that morning, Hussain and Sadiq felt shock waves pulse through the crowd. At that point, the crowd became unstable. It would have been surprising if no one had gotten hurt.

Ironically, people can actually cause more problems at this point by trying to help one another. Eddies are created when people try to form protective rings around women, the injured, or the elderly. The same thing happens when groups of people link arms. In 2004, Farid Currimbhoy, a businessman from Minnesota, and his wife, a Montessori teacher, got caught in a crush in jamarat. When another man from their American tour group fell to the ground, Currimbhoy and the man's wife began frantically trying to rescue him. They found that the only way they could do it was by force. "We were pushing and shoving trying to prevent people from trampling on him."

One of the big problems in a crowd is the lack of communication. The people in the back have no way of knowing that someone in the front has fallen; all they see is a small space open up, where the person used to be, and so they push forward, putting more pressure on the fallen. That's what happened in 1990. Seven people walking across an overcrowded bridge fell when a railing collapsed. They landed at the mouth of a pedestrian tunnel leading to jamarat. The pileup caused the crowd to come to a standstill, but no one at the other end of the tunnel knew about the problem. So they kept trudging forward, strangling more than fourteen hundred people.

People who die in stampedes do not usually die from trampling. They die from asphyxiation. The pressure from all sides makes it impossible to breathe, much like getting squeezed in a trash compactor. Their lungs get compressed, and their blood runs out of oxygen. The compounded force of just five people is enough to kill a person. Pressure builds exponentially, so a crowd quickly picks up the same amount of force as a Mack truck. Humans can lose consciousness after being compressed for just thirty seconds. They become brain dead after about six minutes. They can die without ever falling down.

Once you are in a crowd crush, there is little you can do to save yourself. If possible, Still recommends gradually working your way to the outside of the crowd by stepping sideways as the crowd moves backward.

Panic can happen even without a crowd, in wide open space, as we'll see. But in almost every case, it is a symptom of a larger problem. In fact, the reason that so many disaster researchers are loath to talk about panic is that the word is a conversation killer. The crowd panicked, end of story. But there is a problem underneath the panic. But the problem was almost always preventable. Just like hurricanes don't have to kill people, crowds don't have to crush.

The closer you look at the crowd, the less irrational the behavior looks. If caught in a suffocating crush of humanity, is it irrational to try to survive, even if the only way to do that is by clawing on top of people? Certainly not. So does this mean that the crowd's behavior is irrelevant? Is a stampede simply inevitable at a certain crowd density? Is panic a myth after all?

Stampedes are primarily a function of time, space, and density. But there is an X factor. If a high-density crowd is moving through jamarat, a fatal crush may result. But it won't *necessarily*. As with a herd of cattle, something else has to happen to start the stampede.

The Prerequisites of Panic

One way to solve the panic riddle is to consider when panic does *not* happen. Before Britain entered World War II, there was a long period of anticipation in London. Evacuations of children began. Sandbags lined the roads. People carried gas masks, and movie theaters closed down. British military planes droned above the populace, day after day. Authorities worried that German attacks on civilians, when they came, would cause widespread panic. In the *Lancet*, the editor of the *British Journal of Medical Psychology* wrote: "Since air raids may produce panic in the civilian population it is well to consider the factors that facilitate or diminish panic, and what steps, if any, may be taken against it."

But when the bombs finally started falling, people behaved unexpectedly. In her captivating dispatches from London to the *New Yorker* after the war began, Mollie Panter-Downes described the public's defiant stoicism: "The British are either the calmest or the stupidest people in the world," she wrote. Appealing to the national sense of humor and identity, the Ministry of Information launched a clever series of advertisements depicting "correct British behavior" under stress: "What do I do in an air raid? I do not panic. I say to myself, 'Our chaps are dealing with them,' etc." (Note the wonderfully blasé use of the word *etc.*) After the first major raid killed four hundred people, train commuters bragged to one another about the size of the bomb craters in their neighbor-hoods, Panter-Downes wrote, "as in a more peaceful summer they would have bragged about their roses and squash."

Forty years later, the expectation of panic consumed U.S. authorities after a nuclear power plant accident at Three Mile Island in Pennsylvania. It was an unprecedented event, and good information was slow in coming. It was not even clear who was in charge. If ever a situation was ripe for panic, this would presumably qualify. At first, the governor advised everyone in a ten-mile radius to stay inside with their doors closed. Later, the governor announced that pregnant women and preschool children within a five-mile radius should evacuate. The National Guard was readied. Air-raid sirens sounded in the downtown area of the state capital. But the evacuation turned out to look a lot like any evacuation before a hurricane. The elderly were the least likely to evacuate. And the people who did leave did so in an orderly manner. The predicted anarchy from panicking drivers did not materialize.

What kept people calm? Ed Galea, the evacuation expert in the United Kingdom, had long wondered if culture influenced a public response to an emergency. The English are notoriously self-possessed, after all, and for all the countries' differences, American culture is closely linked to that of Britain. Perhaps public reasonableness was a matter of nationality.

In January of 2005, Galea ran an experiment to try to find out. Would Brazilians respond the same way as Brits to a surprise fire alarm? Before running the experiment, Galea took bets among his British colleagues about what would happen. Half said the Brazilians would never move as quickly as the Brits. They would sit, finish their coffees, and then consider, *just consider*, making an exit. The other half of his colleagues had an even less attractive view of Brazilians: they predicted they would break into some kind of Latin American hysteria dance—panicking and running in all directions.

First he tested the Brits. He ran an unannounced drill in the beginning of the school year at the library at the University of Greenwich, which proceeded in a very orderly fashion. Then Galea flew to Brazil. When he got there, he found that the Brazilian authorities had about as little respect for their own people as his colleagues. They were convinced the drill (an unusual event in Brazil, unlike in fire-safety-conscious Great Britain) would cause a panic. They were so distraught that Galea almost had to cancel the experiment. One high-ranking official actually said he was worried that people would bite their tongues off. And how would that look? Dozens of tongueless innocents fleeing from a library—all for the sake of research! Finally, Galea got approval to go ahead with the drill at a library.

The Brazilians, as it turns out, were just as orderly and rational as the Brits. He found no statistically significant difference in their response times. And miraculously, no one bit his or her tongue off in either hemisphere.

In 1954, a young sociology PhD candidate at the University of Chicago named Enrico L. Quarantelli pushed aside all the conventional wisdom and painstakingly mapped out when panic occurred and when it didn't. His resulting paper, published in the *American Journal of Sociology*, was dry but groundbreaking. Through 150 interviews following three different disasters, Quarantelli drew up a sort of recipe for panic.

Panic occurs if and only if three other conditions are present, Quarantelli concluded. First, people must feel that they may be trapped. Knowing they are definitely trapped is not the same thing. In fact, in submarine disasters, such as the horrific sinking of the Russian submarine *Kursk* in 2000, humans are not likely to panic. The crew knows there is no way out. At submarine depths, even if they were to swim out of the hatch, they would not survive.

But if people worry that they *might* be trapped, that is a trigger for panic—even in wide open spaces. "War refugees caught in the open by strafing planes can develop as acute a sense of potential entrapment as individuals in a building during an earthquake who see all exits becoming blocked by debris," Quarantelli wrote.

Second, panic requires a sensation of great helplessness—which often grows from interaction with others. What starts as an individual sense of impotence escalates when people see their feelings reflected around them. One person caught in explosions in a factory explained it this way to Quarantelli: "I can truthfully say that when I heard the

moaning and crying of the others, I did get quite panicky." Perhaps the
Blitz and the Three Mile Island accident, like most disasters, did not
cause panic because people did not feel very helpless. They could take
shelter or evacuate, after all. And following the Lake Wobegon effect,
the psychological phenomenon named after Garrison Keillor's above-
average town, most people probably suspected that they would be
among the lucky ones.

The final prerequisite to panic is a sense of profound isolation, Quarantelli found. Surrounded by others, all of whom feel utterly powerless,
we realize we are exquisitely alone. We understand that we could be
saved—but no one is going to do it. Panic is, in a way, what happens
when human beings glimpse their own impending mortality—and know
that it didn't have to be so.

Quarantelli's analysis is unsatisfying in some ways. "A sense of helplessness" is hard to define or measure. "A sense of isolation" is even
more nebulous. As we've seen, most people feel a strong sense of solidarity in a disaster. Hajj pilgrims feel an overwhelming sense of unity. So
if Quarantelli is correct, what causes a sudden sense of isolation?

Laboratory Panic

To find out, I returned to the aviation experts, people who understand
human behavior better than almost anyone else—largely because the
government requires them to do so. The crowd crush behavior seen on
the hajj is, once in a rare while, seen on planes as well. Remember the
Manchester plane disaster from Chapter 5, the mysterious 1985 accident modeled by Galea? A Boeing 737 carrying 131 passengers on a
charter flight to Greece began its takeoff out of Manchester. The crew
heard a thud and, thinking they had blown a tire or hit a bird, abandoned takeoff immediately. Nine seconds later, as they were cruising
down the tarmac, the crew got a warning of a fire in the left engine. At the
same time, a gust of wind carried the fire into the fuselage. Flames and
thick, black smoke began pouring into the cabin.

But the situation still did not look catastrophic. After all, the plane had stopped moving and the pilot had called for an evacuation. There were no injuries from any kind of crash impact. Airport fire and rescue trucks had already arrived and begun spraying foam all over the plane.

The problems began at the exit in the middle of the plane, over the wing. A young woman seated in 10F, just beside the exit, had trouble opening the hatch. She was unfamiliar with how it worked, and her amygdala was in charge. She spent precious seconds pulling on what turned out to be her armrest. Finally, her female friend in the next seat stood up and pulled at the release handle. The hatch, which weighed forty-eight pounds, fell into the plane across the chest of the original passenger, trapping her in her seat. The other passengers then intervened, lifting the hatch off of her. Finally, forty-five seconds after the plane had come to a halt, the door was opened, according to the investigation report issued by the British government.

The passengers still had at least a couple of minutes to get out. But then the situation deteriorated further. Alarmed by the smoke and intense heat, many passengers rushed toward the exits and stumbled, falling onto the floor of the aisle. Others then started climbing over the seat backs to get past the pileup. One passenger standing farther up in the plane looked back and saw a tangle of human bodies in the center section. It appeared no one could move forward in the chaos. "People were howling and screaming," he later told investigators.

This is the deadly "faster-is-slower" effect, as crowd experts call it. Above a certain speed, people moving for an exit will actually get out much later than if they had moved more slowly. An arch of bodies is created around an exit as everyone tries to get out at the same time. The friction leads to a clog, which slows down the entire evacuation. Imagine trying to walk out a narrow door moving shoulder to shoulder with five other people. You would knock into one another as you tried to gain access to the opening, spending time and energy squeezing past the other bodies before even getting to the door. If one of you tripped, the jam would become exponentially worse. The faster you tried to leave, in other words, the smaller the doorway would essentially become.

In the Manchester crash, the area by the overwing exit was not yet engulfed in flames, but it nevertheless became a death trap. People clogged the path, with some bodies half out of the exit. The last passenger to leave the plane was a young boy, who was pulled from the exit by a firefighter, five minutes after the plane had stopped. Fifty-five people died that day. Another fifteen were seriously injured.

A better word for panic might be *overreaction,* says G. Keith Still, the expert on hajj crowds. Something happens, some sudden stimulus, to cause a dangerously dense crowd to overreact. In the Manchester crash, it might have been the rush of heat or the slowdown caused by the confusion at the exit. In some cases, all it takes is one or two people to panic, dooming everyone. In a survey of 457 U.S. passengers involved in serious evacuations in the late 1990s, a large number of people reported misbehavior by a few. Twenty percent saw other people climbing over seats; 29 percent saw people pushing. Just over 10 percent said they saw passengers arguing with other passengers. And 6 percent actually admitted pushing someone else. At dusk on February 1, 1991, a Skywest plane collided with a USAir Boeing 737 plane at Los Angeles International Airport. Everyone on the Skywest plane died immediately. On the USAir plane, nineteen passengers died from inhaling smoke—ten of them while waiting in line to use the right overwing exit. The investigation found that the delay was caused in part by a scuffle between two passengers.

In the hajj, a stampede can be caused by people suddenly changing direction. Like a loud noise or a rumor of a bomb, a sudden surge of pressure can cause an overwhelming sensation of isolation and helplessness. Likewise, in a herd of animals, a stampede can be caused by something as legitimate as a flash of lightning—or as trivial as a cigarette lighter flicked by a foolish cowboy. So psychology matters, even though physics matter more.

Firefighter Tommy Walker found himself inside a ministampede most unexpectedly one Sunday afternoon in Kansas City, Missouri. He and a friend were off duty, sitting in a booth eating lunch at a busy pizzeria when a water heater blew up in the basement. No one knew what had happened. They had just heard an explosion, louder than fireworks, which shook the building. People started heading for the door. At first, the crowd was quiet, Walker remembers. There was no smoke or fire, no other threat aside from the initial noise. But very quickly, as the crowd clogged up at the small doorway and the exit slowed, the dynamics shifted. Walker watched from his seat as people started trampling over one another in their rush to get out. He could have been watching the Manchester evacuation. "People started yelling. People tripped over chairs, and they were just walked over. Good God, I kind of liken it to a cow going down in a cattle truck," he says. "Those cows usually perish."

Suddenly, Walker's friend, a fellow firefighter, got up to leave too. The aisle was jammed with people, so his friend started walking over the table. Walker couldn't believe what he was seeing. He grabbed his friend. "Sit the fuck down!" he told him. "There is no smoke, there is no fire, and that crowd is a lot more dangerous than anything else here." His friend sat down.

The crowd thinned out a few moments later. There was still no actual fire, smoke, or any threat at all. Walker and his friend walked outside. There, on the sidewalk, were the wounded. Ambulances began to arrive. A handful of people had broken bones and sustained other injuries— not from the explosion, which turned out to be minor, but from the crowd. Says Walker: "Literally it was a nothing incident that turned into complete chaos in five seconds."

It is hard to re-create panic in a laboratory without violating basic ethical principles. But after the Manchester crash, aviation safety researchers tried their best. In a series of experiments, they ran volunteers through evacuation drills in a mock-up of the plane. They couldn't do it. People remained fairly calm, as they do in most evacuations.

But then something amazing happened. The researchers offered the volunteers $10 if they were among the first to get out of the plane. Things changed. This time, people began tripping and falling as they raced off the plane, piling up in the doorway and halting the evacuation—just as the Manchester passengers had done! So even without the threat of death, people could become their own worst enemy. The volunteers thought they might not make it out in time to get the money; perhaps they also started to feel helpless as the line out the door slowed; and then they may have felt the isolation that accompanies an every-man-for-himself rampage. The prize injected competition into the crowd, just as fire creates competition for air and space. The competition motivated people to move faster, which increased the density of the crowd. Then physics took over.

Tragedy at IKEA

Money, as it turns out, often has deadly consequences for crowds. The list of fatal crowd crushes over the past twenty years is stacked with events that should have been frivolous—giveaways, sales, store openings. On September 2, 2004, three people were killed at the opening of a new IKEA store in Saudi Arabia. In England, just four months later, a man was stabbed in a crowd crush at the opening of another IKEA. Some six thousand customers had shown up for the midnight opening of the largest IKEA in the country. Witnesses reported people punching each other in the face to get a sofa. The chaos finally ended when IKEA shut down the store and riot police dispersed the crowd. "I think it's fair to say we misjudged it, and maybe were a bit naive," an IKEA spokesperson told the *Guardian*. "But some shoppers behaved like animals and started shoving and pushing everyone else. There's not much we can do to stop that."

Is it true that there is not much IKEA can do about customers who behave "like animals"? There is a reason stampedes happen over and over again in the same locations, says crowd expert Still. The problem lies in the design of the space and the management of the crowd. Simply put: too many people are moving through too small a space too quickly. There are plenty of practical solutions for these problems, at jamarat or at IKEA, says Still. One of the easiest fixes is to allow more time for the crowd to pass through. Also, traffic should be one-way, to avoid the turmoil of counterflow. Putting a column in front of an exit is an elegant way to help prevent clogging. In every case, communication between organizers and with the crowd is critical. Officials need to constantly monitor the crowd's movement and quickly relieve pressure points. The New Year's Eve celebration in Times Square in New York City is a model event, Still says. Police funnel over half a million revelers into separate viewing pens. Once people leave a pen, they cannot come back. That rule reduces the amount of traffic flow. At police headquarters, meanwhile, about seventy officers monitor live feeds of the crowd from dozens of cameras.

We understand how to prevent crowd crushes. That's not the problem. The problem is convincing the people in charge to make the changes. In 1971, at the Ibrox stadium in Glasgow, Scotland, sixty-six people were killed in a grisly scene in a stairway after a soccer game. But the very same stairway, which was dangerously long and steep, had been the scene of major accidents in 1961, 1967, and 1969, which had left two people dead and dozens injured. It was only after the fourth disaster in 1971 that the stairway was removed.

Panic has been used too many times as a way of blaming the victims. The tradition of negligence has been particularly acute in Saudi Arabia, where officials tend to alternately blame the crowd or God for the disasters. After the 1990 stampede, King Fahd called the catastrophe "God's will." Of the 1,426 victims, he said: "Had they not died there, they would have died elsewhere."

Even before a disaster occurs, the people in charge—of the hajj or the U.S. Department of Homeland Security—use panic as an excuse to discount the public. People will panic, the legend says, so we can't trust them with the information or the training—the basic tools of their own survival. When John Sorensen, director of the Emergency Management Center at the federal government's Oak Ridge National Laboratory in Tennessee, offered to develop easy-to-understand brochures to help people prepare for chemical and biological attacks in the late 1990s, the Federal Emergency Management Agency told him, "We're not in the business of terrifying the public," Sorensen says. It is a perverse cycle. "Do you know how many Americans have died because someone thought they would panic if they gave them a warning?" says disaster expert Dennis Mileti. "A lot."

In some ways, the hajj is uniquely, unintentionally designed for failure. To begin with, the pilgrimage is an inherently populist event. All men, rich or poor, wear two white sheets. A prince prays next to a peasant. That is part of the appeal. So the hajj must be made available to as many people as possible. Saudi officials restrict the number of visas permitted to each country, but, under pressure to keep the event accessible, not nearly enough to make it safe.

Until relatively recently, almost no one but princes could afford to travel to Mecca for the pilgrimage. In the 1930s, the crowds numbered approximately seventy thousand. Then, in the last half of the twentieth century, air travel became much cheaper. At the same time, Saudi rulers began to encourage more pilgrims to come. The government dropped its normal tax on pilgrims and spent millions to increase the capacity of the holy sites. In 1965, 1.2 million pilgrims arrived. Today, 2 to 3 million people descend upon Saudi Arabia for the hajj. In less than a week, they move en masse through the same twenty-five-mile course, all with the same itinerary, following in the steps of Muhammad: first, the Grand Mosque in Mecca, a city of just eight hundred thousand people. Then, after a side trip to Medina, they proceed to Mina. The rest of the year, Mina is a quiet desert valley. During the hajj, it becomes a teeming tent city, organized by country. The pilgrims use the tent city as a staging ground for their obligatory trips to the three granite pillars.

The hajj is also merciless on the body. Hundreds of people die on the hajj every year, whether the crowd kills them or not. In 2007, no one died in a crowd accident, but 431 Indonesians (of the 205,000 who came) died from pneumonia, heart attacks, and other "natural" causes. Most people catch vicious fevers or colds, and the poor endure the harshest conditions of all. Days of waiting in exhaust fumes and sleeping in crowded tents try the patience of even the most devout. But believers have embraced the suffering as part of the challenge of the hajj, and so the crowds keep growing. Each day of the hajj, the Saudi police bring the new corpses into the Grand Mosque on gurneys for funeral prayers. Those who die on the hajj are said to be guaranteed a place in heaven. So the hajj tragedies become cruelly self-perpetuating.

In their defense, Saudi officials have made many costly attempts to prevent crowd disasters over the years. If they cannot manage Islam's holiest places, after all, then the legitimacy of the entire government is in question. After a fire in the tent city of Mina killed three hundred people in 1997, the government equipped the tents with sprinklers. After the 2004 stampede, officials widened the pillars into walls, giving pilgrims a wider target for the stoning ritual and spreading the crowds. But after the 2006 disaster, Interior spokesperson al-Turki fell back on the usual rhetoric. "This was fate" he said, "destined by God."

Crowd expert Still has spent years wrestling the Saudi status quo. "You're dealing with a culture where God is the final arbiter, and only he can decide to take or give life." He would warn authorities about new bottlenecks and then watch as his predictions came true, he says. Over the past few years, however, he believes the Saudis have made tremendous progress. The design, management, and scheduling teams have been working together at last. The Saudis have invested $1.2 billion in rebuilding the jamarat bridge, creating a much bigger, four-story complex with many more entrances and exits. Today, when pilgrims arrive in the airports, officials hand them pamphlets instructing them how to behave safely in the crowd. The warning urges people to be patient and, above all, not to push. Perhaps most important, after the 2006 disaster, some Islamic clerics issued fatwas, or religious edicts, declaring that pilgrims do not have to wait until noon to carry out the stoning ritual. That way the crowd can be spread out over the entire day.

In the last hajj in 2007, no one was killed in a crowd crush. With that, Still's job advising the Saudis officially ended, he says. "Unless of course there is another accident."

The Panic of One

If we think of panic as an overreaction, it starts to make more sense. The way to avoid a panic, then, is to reduce the causes of overreaction—by reducing the density or turbulence of the crowd or by giving the crowd better information. But sometimes panic happens to just one person, all alone, and no one else. Sometimes a single exception is enough to change history. So what causes this kind of overreaction?

Early in the morning on Memorial Day in 1993, a scuba club gathered to go diving off Singer Island in Florida. The divers wanted to be among the first to check out a brand-new artificial reef, the largest in Palm Beach County. The week before, local officials had sunk the *Princess Anne,* an old, 340-foot ferry, hoping to attract tourists.

One of the divers exploring the *Princess Anne* that day was Scott Stich, thirty-four. Stich was a healthy, experienced diver. He had graduated from the U.S. Military Academy at West Point. Then he had gone to law school and started practicing real-estate law at a firm in West Palm Beach, where he lived with his wife. With the rest of the group, named The Scuba Club, Stich descended into the water to check out the hulking wreck of the *Princess Anne.*

Each year, about a hundred people die in scuba accidents in North America. That is not a big number, when you consider that there are at least a million divers in all. But the deaths are complicated in interesting ways. Scuba diving is a uniquely claustrophobic experience: the diver's nose is covered and he or she cannot breathe into it, which can, in some people, feel very similar to suffocation. In one survey of 254 scuba divers, 54 percent said they had experienced panic at least once while diving. Dive sites become a laboratory for human behavior under stress.

At about 9:00 A.M., with no warning, the other divers saw Stich—then about seventy feet underwater—rip his air regulator out of his mouth for no apparent reason. The regulator contains the mouthpiece, air gauges, and tubes that connect with the air tank. It is essential. Another diver frantically tried to push the regulator back into his mouth. But Stich wouldn't take it. He seemed adamant that he'd made the right decision, even as his face began to turn blue. Then, unable to breathe, he slipped into unconsciousness in the dark water. The dive master raised him to the surface and performed CPR. But he was pronounced dead shortly afterward. The regulator was found to be in fine working condition. At such a shallow depth, it was extremely unlikely that Stich had suffered from nitrogen narcosis—a state of mental impairment also called "rapture of the deep." The Palm Beach County medical examiner found that Stich died as a result of drowning. There was no evidence of equipment failure or malfunction, nor of any other natural disease, traumatic injury, or alcohol or drug use. Stich had been diving since he was twelve, and his equipment was less than six months old.

Why would any human being willfully abandon his oxygen source at the bottom of the ocean? Deep in the darkness of the sea, an equipment malfunction can, needless to say, rapidly escalate into terror. But sometimes there doesn't even need to be an equipment malfunction. Every so often, all over the world, divers are found dead with plenty of air in their tanks.

At the exercise-psychology lab at the University of Wisconsin at Madison, William Morgan spent decades studying diving deaths. About 60 percent were attributed to health, environmental, or equipment problems. But the remaining 40 percent were usually classified as "unexplained." The more he looked, the more mysteries Morgan found. Sometimes divers didn't stop at ripping out their own regulator; sometimes they also forcibly grabbed the regulator out of the mouth of the person next to them.

It turns out that similar "freak" accidents occur among firefighters, who are on occasion found dead with their oxygen tanks in good working order. In Kansas City, Missouri, one firefighter crawled into a burning room just as the fire rolled across the ceiling. In the midst of this inferno, the firefighter stood up and ripped off his respirator, searing his lungs. His captain tackled him and dragged him out of the fire. The firefighter suffered severe burns but survived.

Panic is the leading cause of deaths among divers overall. Certain people experience an intense feeling of suffocation when their noses are covered. They respond to that overwhelming sensation by relying on their instinct, which is to rip out whatever is covering their airway. For the vast majority of human experiences, that would work. For scuba divers and firefighters, unfortunately, it is their oxygen source.

So which people tend to rip out their oxygen source? Is there any way to predict this behavior? Morgan invited twenty-five firefighters to his lab and tested them himself. He had each man run at high speed on a treadmill for ten minutes while wearing a breathing apparatus. Sure enough, some of them suddenly ripped off the masks in distress and complained that they weren't getting enough air—even though the masks were working normally. Morgan had predicted in advance which six men would rip off their masks. He was wrong; only five of them did. But it was a pretty good guess.

How did he know? Before he put the men on the treadmill, Morgan had given them a common psychological test measuring their anxiety levels. Generally speaking, anxiety comes in two flavors: the first is "state anxiety," which describes how a person reacts to stressful situations, like a big exam or a traffic jam. The other kind is "trait anxiety," which refers to a person's general tendency to see things as stressful to begin with. Trait anxiety, in other words, is your resting level of anxiety on any given day.

As it turns out, people with higher trait anxiety are more likely to rip out their air supply, Morgan found. Luckily, most people who become scuba divers or firefighters have low trait anxiety to begin with. But not all of them. After running the same tests on scuba divers, Morgan found he could predict who would panic with 83 percent accuracy. Essentially, he found that certain people are slightly more likely to lose touch with their reality when under physical stress. Their brains, overwhelmed by the situation, sort through their database of responses—and choose the wrong one. They may not cause a stampede or a mass panic, but they will likely put themselves, at least, in sudden and intense jeopardy. They have overreacted, in the purest form of panic.

Panic may be the most frightening kind of disaster reaction, at least in the popular imagination. But the more I learned about it, the less diabolical it seemed to be. Panic is a tragedy—but one of errors, not malice. It can of course be catastrophic. But it is one of the more preventable human mistakes in the disaster portfolio. If mass gathering places are designed with physics in mind, then the prerequisites to panic should never develop. People will not feel potentially trapped, helpless, and alone. They will just feel crowded. Then, if something goes terribly wrong, they will be much more likely, as we will see next, to default to a far more common disaster response—which is to say, they will do nothing at all.

7

Paralysis

Playing Dead in French Class

THE NOISE STARTED about halfway through intermediate French on April 16, 2007. An insistent, popping sound. The students stopped their conversation. "It's probably construction," one said. Then the banging got louder. A moan came from the classroom next door. The teacher, Jocelyne Couture-Nowak, had long gray hair and was known for her generous smile. But now she stiffened and said, "That's not what I think it is, is it?"

With that, Clay Violand, a junior in her class at Virginia Tech in Blacksburg, Virginia, stood up. He felt certain of what needed to happen, but he suddenly could not remember his teacher's name. It was strange, but it didn't slow him down. "You," he said, "put that desk against the door." Couture-Nowak did exactly as he said. Then Violand turned toward the window. He knew he had to get out.

Violand saw the gun first. As he turned, he saw the semiautomatic weapon appear in the doorway. The shooter, Seung-Hui Cho, a rage-filled, silent young man, who would kill thirty-two people and himself that day, making it the deadliest shooting rampage in U.S. history, strode into the room. He easily shoved the desk aside. Seeing this, Violand automatically changed course. "I wanted to go to the window; it was only two stories. But as soon as I saw the gun come in, I just froze."

Then Violand, an international studies major with a music minor, crumpled onto the floor underneath his desk. He didn't curl up into a ball or cover his head; he lay down on his side, in a relatively vulnerable position, with his arm slightly, unnaturally twisted. Then he lay very still. "My mind just went into this mode. I remember thinking, 'He's going to shoot the moving people first.' I remember movement was the key."

As Violand lay under his desk, his arm flung across his face, Cho started firing. "He began methodically and calmly shooting people. It sounded rhythmic, like he took his time between each shot, moving from person to person. After every shot, I thought, 'OK, the next one is for me.' Shot after shot went off. I tried to look as lifeless as possible. Sometimes after a shot, I would hear a quick moan, or a slow one, or a grunt, or a quiet yell from one of the girls."

Like most disaster victims, Violand has no sense of how long the ordeal lasted. "I couldn't tell you if it was five minutes or two hours," he told me when we spoke five weeks after the shootings. But eventually, Cho left the room, and the shots continued, at a distance. With the same certainty he'd had when he'd fallen to the floor, Violand knew Cho would come back. He doesn't know how he knew; he'd never been in any situation like this before. He wasn't a hunter or a soldier. He was a twenty-year-old from Potomac, Maryland, a posh suburb of Washington, D.C. He had long, fashionably messy brown hair and played in a band. But this voice inside his head seemed to have experienced all of this before.

Hypnosis

Under certain conditions, on burning planes, sinking ships, or even impromptu battlefields, many people cease moving altogether. The decisive moment arrives, and they do nothing. They shut down, becoming suddenly limp and still. This stillness descends involuntarily, and it is one of the most important and intriguing behaviors in the disaster repertoire. It happens far more often than, say, panic. (Some researchers actually call this paralysis "negative panic," since it is in some ways the opposite of panic.) It is also vastly more common than the subject of the next chapter, heroism. If you are curious about what you might do in a disaster, this chapter might be the most illuminating part of this book. Because if it is the most common behavior in the survival arc, paralysis is also among the most misunderstood.

In the early 1980s, a young assistant psychology professor named Gordon Gallup Jr. was raising chickens in his laboratory at Tulane University for use in basic learning experiments. Then one day an undergraduate student poked his head in the lab and asked Gallup a question that would redirect his research for the next twenty-five years: "Hey, have you ever seen a hypnotized chicken?"

Gallup invited him in. The young man showed him a trick he'd learned as a child: he grabbed the chicken and held its head down on the table. At first, the chicken fought back, a hysterical blur of feathers and squawks. Gallup got a little nervous. But then, five or ten seconds later, the chicken became suddenly calm and quiet. The student lifted his hand off the bird and it stayed there, unmoving but still breathing. "Lo and behold, the chicken appeared to be hypnotized," Gallup remembers. "It was in what appeared to be a catatonic state. I could not believe my eyes."

From there, Gallup went directly to the library to research "animal hypnosis." It turned out to have been a fascination of humans for several hundred years. Medieval monks used to "bewitch" blackbirds, owls, eagles, and peacocks this way. One of the first academic references to the topic was made in 1646, in a paper by a Jesuit priest and scholar. But it remained primarily a parlor trick. In the nineteenth century, boys in the south of France used to bewitch turkeys to irritate local farmers. The little hooligans would stick the turkeys' heads under their wings and swing them to and fro a few times, and then leave them in the poultry yard, a still life in terror.

Gallup found that paralysis could be induced in all kinds of creatures—in every single one he tested, in fact. "In a nutshell, it's been documented in crustaceans, amphibians, frogs, lizards, snakes, birds, even mammals—wild boars to cows to primates to rats to rabbits." Every animal seemed to have a powerful instinct to utterly shut down under extreme fear. All you had to do was make sure the animal was afraid and trapped. The more fear the animal felt, the longer it would stay "frozen." The question was why?

These days, Gallup works at the State University of New York in Albany, where he does research and teaches evolutionary psychology. I visited him there in the spring of 2007, two days after the Virginia Tech shootings. He wore a black T-shirt, jeans, and white sneakers. He set up an old slide projector to show me a picture of one of his early immobilized chickens and one of his son with an immobilized cow. Slide after slide, of a paralyzed gecko, a rabbit, a Mississippi Gulf Coast blue crab, flashed by on the screen.

Here is what we know about an animal in paralysis: the heart rate drops, as does body temperature; respiration goes up; and the body becomes numb to pain. The eyes tend to close intermittently, but when they are open, they stare ahead in an unfocused gaze. The pupils are dilated. Sometimes the body shakes with occasional, Parkinsonian-like tremors. But all the while, the brain is consciously taking in all kinds of information about what is happening around it.

In his writings, Scottish missionary David Livingstone described what it is like to be paralyzed: on a hunting trip in South Africa in the mid-1800s, he had fired at a lion about thirty yards away and hit him. As he was reloading, the lion lunged at him, clamping his shoulder in his jaw and knocking him to the ground:

> *Growling horribly close to my ear, he shook me as a terrier dog does a rat. The shock produced a stupor similar to that which seems to be felt by a mouse after the first shake of the cat. It caused a sort of dreaminess, in which there was no sense of pain nor feeling of terror, though quite conscious of all that was happening.*

The other hunters drew the lion away, and it soon collapsed from its injuries. Livingstone was left with a broken bone and eleven neat teeth wounds on his upper arm.

It might seem like a bad idea to go limp and calm while a lion is mauling you like a chew toy. To an observer, paralysis can look a lot like a failure—as if the paralyzed animal has simply gone into shock or given up. But that would give the victim too little credit. After decades of study, Gallup has come to have enormous respect for the paralysis strategy.

Animals that go into paralysis have a better chance of surviving certain kinds of attacks. But why? Why would surrender lead to survival? Wouldn't it tend to lead to certain death? Well, the explanation, as with all of our fear reactions, goes back to evolutionary adaptation. A lion is more likely to survive to pass on its genes if it avoids eating sick or rotten prey. Many predators lose interest in prey that is not struggling. No fight, no appetite. It's an ancient way of avoiding food poisoning. And, in turn, prey animals have evolved to try to exploit this opening—by simulating death or illness when they are trapped. It's not a sure thing; many animals will still get killed this way. But when there are no other options for escape, it's a reasonable strategy. Paralysis, like heroism, may be more adaptive than it seems.

The Disaster Default

After Cho left the Virginia Tech classroom, Violand noticed that his whole body felt numb, as if all his limbs had fallen asleep. This feeling likely came from the natural painkiller that his body produced as part of the paralysis reaction. But Violand had no way to know this. So he figured he must have been shot. "I didn't know how it felt to get shot. I remember saying to myself, 'Man, this isn't as bad as I thought it would be.'" But he kept trying to move and eventually found that he could break through the numbness. "I kind of wiggled around, and I thought, 'OK, I guess I didn't get shot.'"

The classroom was quiet except for some muffled crying. Someone muttered, "It's OK. It's going to be OK. They will be here soon." But Violand wasn't confident of a rescue. He lifted his head off the ground just enough to let that voice inside his brain address the students around him. "Play dead," he said. "If he thinks you're dead, he won't kill you."

Rape victims sometimes undergo something similar. About 10 percent of female sexual assault victims later report that they experienced extreme immobility during the attack, according to multiple studies by Gallup and his colleagues. A stunning 40 percent said they remembered having some kind of symptoms of paralysis—feeling "frozen," or oddly impervious to pain or cold, among other symptoms. That's actually slightly higher than the percentage of sexual assault victims who report that they tried to fight back or flee their attackers. In other words, paralysis may be a more common response to rape than fight or flight. Unfortunately, rape victims do not usually understand what they did. Many go on to experience extreme remorse because they think they simply surrendered to their attacker, Gallup has found. "They don't realize that what they did may have been a very adaptive reaction." Paralysis can also make prosecution of the rapist much more difficult, since the lack of struggle may look a lot like consent.

Strangely, we have tended to dismiss our own paralysis as a kind of embarrassing meltdown, while ascribing all kinds of more interesting motives to birds. But everything we have learned from animal research suggests that it is a hardwired, adaptive response that serves a very specific purpose.

In researching this book, I kept stumbling across anecdotes about human paralysis in unexpected places. Everyone, from firefighters to police officers to driving instructors, seemed to have a story about a frightened person who froze. They didn't always understand the behavior, but they had all seen it. Even Nassim Taleb, the trader and risk expert, told me he has seen stock traders freeze—while they are losing all of their money. "They just stand there, doing nothing," he says.

I met "U.," the commander of an elite Israeli undercover operations unit, at a rest stop outside of Jerusalem. For security reasons, he liked to arrange meetings at anonymous places. He requested that I identify him only by the initial U. because of his undercover status. Like most professional killers, he didn't look like the part. He was slightly built and wore a black T-shirt and jeans. He had a kind smile and spoke fluent Arabic. It wasn't hard to imagine him melting into the Palestinian territories. We talked over sodas about the six years he had spent running hundreds of operations under extreme stress. Sure enough, when I asked him if he had ever seen anyone freeze, he had a story too.

In 2002, U.'s unit was following two suspects from Nablus, a city under Palestinian control in the West Bank, to Jerusalem. The men were suicide bombers, and they were believed to be carrying a bomb with them. Along the way, they stopped at a crowded parking lot. From a nearby vehicle, U. watched them through video surveillance from a drone device. Although the area was crowded, he decided that a better opportunity might not present itself. He gave the order to take the men out. The operation lasted just seconds. Four of U.'s men, dressed as Palestinians, descended upon the suspects, wounding one and killing another. A bomb was found in one of their bags, U. says.

Among the innocent bystanders in the parking lot, U. noticed two distinct responses. As the gunfire and shouting broke out, a small number of mostly younger people started to run. But there wasn't an obvious escape route, since the parking lot was surrounded by large piles of dirt. So what did everyone else do? The rest of the crowd dropped to the ground and froze exactly where they were. They did not move, even after the danger had receded. One hour later, U. remembers, many were still there, uninjured but not moving.

It's always possible, of course, that these bystanders were suffering from shock or despair. But the lines between these experiences are not distinct. We don't either go into shock or freeze. These behaviors are most likely connected. Much more research needs to be done, but we can say that it is a mistake to underestimate the complexity of doing nothing.

"I Wasn't a Human Being"

Cho came back to the French classroom, just as Violand had expected. When he returned, Violand lay perfectly still once again. But this time, the gun fired too many times. "He began unloading what seemed like a second round into everyone again. It had to be the same people. There were way more gunshots than there were people in that room. I think I heard him reload maybe three times." Violand waited to discover what it would feel like to have a bullet tear through his body. He thought about his parents. At one point, as the shots kept coming, he locked eyes with a girl lying in front of him. He didn't know her name, but they stared at each other, unflinching, under the desks.

Finally the gunshots stopped. Cho had killed himself last. The police pounded on the door, shouting directions that Violand does not remember very well. He remembers getting up and going directly to the door, with his hands up. He doesn't remember seeing his teacher, dead on the ground, or anyone outside of the immediate vicinity of his desk. Later, Violand would learn a startling fact. Of all the students in the French classroom that day, the only person not to be shot was Clay Violand.

After Violand answered my questions, he had some questions for me. "Do you know what makes one person respond one way and another a different way? I mean, is it your personality or what? Do they know why some people do this?" I told him I didn't know for sure, and then I gave him one of those true but unsatisfying answers. I told him that our behavior is almost always a product of our genetics and our experience. He politely disagreed. "I don't see how life experience has anything to do with this situation. You're not a person with experiences anymore. You're just surviving," he said. "I wasn't a human being when that was happening." I asked him what he meant. He had a hard time explaining it. "I don't even know what emotion I was feeling. I wasn't crying."

Human beings think, reflect, and make decisions. We don't always realize how much other work our brain is also doing all the time, with or without us. In retrospect, Violand has created a narrative, as all survivors do, about what he did. "If I had to sum it up in one word, it was all about movement. I wasn't really playing dead to convince him that I was dead so much, but just so that I wasn't moving." But at the time, he adds, it didn't feel like he was making any choices at all. "Only now that I think about it a month later, I guess I had a strategy. The week after, I would have said it was chaotic, I didn't know what I was doing." When I asked Gallup if Violand's story resembled all the thousands of paralysis cases he has studied in animals and humans, he said, "It sounds like a textbook case." Violand was attacked by a lethal predator, and he experi-

enced a radical and involuntary survival response. It may or may not
have been the reason he survived.

The summer after the shootings, Violand decided to stay in Blacksburg, Virginia, where the university is located. When we spoke, he said he
was doing well so far. He found himself crying about once a week, but
otherwise he felt OK. His friends seemed to expect him to be doing worse
than he was. Three survivors of the World Trade Center had e-mailed
him, for which he was grateful. They warned him that he might go
through a more difficult period six months or a year from now. He didn't
know what to do with that information, so he decided to stick to his original plans. He spent the summer break playing in his band and working.
Then he planned to spend the fall semester studying in Paris, speaking
French in a place where no one knows what happened to him.

A Cigarette Break on a Sinking Ship

Certain kinds of disasters, like shootings or rape, closely resemble the
predator-prey encounters we evolved to survive. In those situations,
paralysis may effectively deter a predator. There is always that chance. In
other cases, paralysis becomes a tragedy unto itself.

The sinking of the *MV Estonia* ferry in the Baltic Sea on the night of
September 28, 1994, was the worst sea disaster in modern European
history. It was followed by years of official reports, conspiracy theories,
and recrimination. But one mystery has received relatively little attention: in the horrific final moments aboard the ferry, witnesses reported
later, a surprising number of passengers did exactly nothing.

The *Estonia* had left its home port in Tallinn, Estonia, on a routine
fifteen-hour trip to Stockholm, Sweden. The massive roll-on, roll-off
automobile ferry was fancier than most. It had a pool, sauna, casino, and
three restaurants. It was a symbol of the newly independent, free-market
nation of Estonia. Almost all 989 people onboard had sleeping cabins.
Although the weather had been stormy all night, the crew did not expect
serious problems. A band was playing in the Baltic Bar, and the ten-deck
vessel churned through the inky waters as it had for fourteen years. It had

passed two inspections earlier that month. And it carried the required number of lifeboats and life jackets.

Kent Härstedt, now a member of Sweden's parliament, was a passenger on the boat that night. He was then twenty-nine, and he was there because he had helped to organize a "peace conference" to bring together businesspeople from around the Baltic Sea. In the aftermath of the cold war, the conference, sponsored by the Swedish government, was meant to foster peace through economic codependence. "The idea was that if we had more trade, more business, we wouldn't so easily want to have war," he says now. The conference was going well. It had started in Estonia and then continued on the sea onboard the giant ferry. During a break in the itinerary that afternoon, Härstedt took a sauna on the ship. It was then that he noticed the water in the pool sloshing back and forth. "Normally, these ferries are so huge that you can barely notice that the boat is rocking," Härstedt says. "But to see that in the pool, that was the first [clue]."

Later, Härstedt went to dinner, but he felt seasick. He left to take a nap in his cabin. He woke up around 10:30 P.M. to the sound of a slamming noise. Later, he would wonder if this was the beginning of the disaster. But at the time, he figured that some piece of cargo must have been improperly secured. Feeling rejuvenated from his nap, he went back to the restaurant to join his colleagues. He sat down and ordered a Coke. This particular restaurant had a band and a dance floor, and Härstedt remembers how he and his colleagues amused themselves by watching people try to dance on the tottering boat. "They had to hold each other and run from one side to the next, with the waves. It looked really quite funny. I started to joke with my friends. I said, 'This is almost like the *Titanic*. Soon they will give us champagne.'" Once dancing became impossible, and people started to leave the restaurant, Härstedt and a colleague moved to a bar in another part of the ship. The bar was full of about fifty people, he remembers. "All the people were having quite a good time. There was karaoke music. My friend and I sat down on two stools at the bar. We were in a good mood. Everybody was laughing and singing."

Just after 1:00 A.M., the *Estonia* suddenly listed starboard a full thirty degrees, hurling passengers, vending machines, and flowerpots across its passageways. In the bar, almost everyone fell violently against the side of the boat. Härstedt managed to grab on to the iron bar railing and hold on, hanging above everyone else. "In just one second, everything went from a loud, happy, wonderful moment to total silence. Every brain, I guess, was working like a computer trying to realize what had happened." Then came the screaming and crying. People had been badly hurt in the fall, and the tilt of the ship made it extremely difficult to move.

Though no one knew it, everyone onboard the *Estonia* had just ten minutes before the starboard side of the vessel would be submerged and the tilt would become almost impossible to negotiate. Härstedt began to strategize. "I started to react very differently from normal, a little bit like I'd learned in my military service. I started to say, 'OK, there is option one, option two. Decide. Act.' I didn't say, 'Oh, the boat is sinking.' I didn't even think about the wider perspective." Like Zedeño in the World Trade Center, Härstedt experienced the illusion of centrality. "I just saw my very small world." Härstedt considered trying to crawl through a window before noticing that it was bolted shut. Then he decided to make his way into the corridor.

But as Härstedt worked through the deliberation phase, he noticed something strange about some of the other passengers. They weren't doing what he was doing. "Some people didn't seem to realize what had happened. They were just sitting there, totally apathetic." Not just one or two people, but entire groups of people seemed to be immobilized. They were conscious, but they were not reacting.

Härstedt climbed up the stairwell, fighting against gravity. Out on the deck, the ship's lights were on and the moon was shining. The full range of human capacities was on display. One man stood to the side, smoking a cigarette, Härstedt remembers. Most people strained to hold on to the rolling ship and, at the same time, find life jackets and lifeboats. Some re-assured each other. Härstedt helped an injured woman find a life jacket. Others grabbed life jackets off the backs of fellow passengers, survivors would later tell investigators. To complete the nightmare, the passengers and crew had severe problems unhooking the lifeboats. They could not find directions for the automatic releases nor could they force the rusted manual parts to work. The life jackets—mandatory in fifty-degree water with waves up to twenty-eight feet high—were also maddeningly hard to use. The straps were too short—or at least it seemed that way. Many were tied together in bundles of three, further slowing the process. As the ship continued to capsize, the water around it filled with floating, empty life jackets.

But here, too, there were people who did nothing. In the middle of this frenzy, certain people seemed petrified. British passenger Paul Barney remembers groups of people standing still like statues. "I kept saying to myself, 'Why don't they try to get out of here?'" he later told the *Observer*. "They just sat there . . . being swamped by the water when it came in," one passenger said. Another passenger saw about ten people lying on the deck near the bulkhead. He threw life jackets to them, but they did not react. One passenger was seen entering a lifeboat, which was still secured in place, and then calmly lying down inside, making no effort to launch it.

Later, when interviewed by the police, some survivors would say they understood this behavior. At some point, they, too, had felt an overwhelming urge to stop moving. They only snapped out of this stupor, they said, by thinking of their loved ones, especially their children.

At 1:50 A.M., just thirty minutes after its first "Mayday" call, the *Estonia* vanished altogether, sinking upside down into the sea. Moments beforehand, Härstedt had jumped off the ship and into the sea. He climbed onto a life raft and held on. He would stay there for five hours, waiting to be rescued. At the start, there were about twenty other people on the raft. By the time the helicopter arrived, only seven, including Härstedt, were still alive.

All told, only 137 people survived the disaster. Investigators would conclude that the ship sunk because the bow door to the car deck had come unlocked, and the Baltic Sea had come gushing into the ship. Most of the 852 victims were entombed in the *Estonia*, where most of their bodies remain to this day.

What did the immobilized people on the *Estonia* have in common with Clay Violand at Virginia Tech? They were all under attack and felt trapped. They were also extremely frightened, more frightened than most of us have ever been. But in the case of the *Estonia*, the freezing response may have been a natural and horrific mistake. "What we may be witnessing is a situation in which a previously adaptive response has now become maladaptive as a consequence of technological changes," says Gallup, the expert on paralysis in animals. In more modern disasters, in which the threat is not actually another animal, paralysis may be a misfire. Our brains search, under extreme stress, for an appropriate survival response and choose the wrong one, like divers who rip their respirators out of their mouths deep underwater. Or like deer who freeze in the headlights of a car. Of the twenty-three people on board with Härstedt for the conference, only one other survived.

Some people, like some animals, are clearly more likely to freeze. The behavior is built into their fear response. No one knows exactly why. Genetics are undoubtedly important. Gallup has bred chickens that tend to stay frozen for longer periods of time and found that their offspring show the same behavior. This makes sense, says brain expert Joseph LeDoux. The amygdala, the part of the brain that handles fear, is made up of two key parts. The lateral nucleus handles input, and the central handles output. "You can imagine individual differences, for either genetic or experiential reasons, in the wiring of the lateral nucleus that makes one person more sensitive to input," LeDoux says. "So the same terrifying stimulus might make the more sensitive person freeze."

The more important point, perhaps, is that the brain is plastic. It can be trained to respond more appropriately. More fear, on the other hand, makes paralysis stronger. Animals injected with adrenaline are more likely to freeze, for example. Less fear, then, makes paralysis less likely. A rat with damage to its amygdala will not freeze at all—even if it encounters a cat. House pets also tend not to freeze when they are restrained, Gallup has found. They seem to think the exercise is a game. They might fight back, but they won't freeze. They are not frightened enough. So it makes sense that if we can reduce our own fear and adrenaline, even a little bit, we might be able to override paralysis when we need to.

Breaking Out of the Stupor

On March 27, 1977, a Pan Am 747 awaiting takeoff at the Tenerife airport in the Canary Islands was sliced open without warning by a Dutch

KLM jet that had come hurtling out of the fog at 160 mph. The collision left twisted metal, along with comic books and toothbrushes, strewn along a half-mile stretch of tarmac. Everyone on the KLM jet was killed instantly. But many of the Pan Am passengers had survived. They could live if they got up and walked off the fiery plane.

Floy Heck, then seventy, was sitting on the Pan Am jet between her husband and her friends, en route from their California retirement residence to a Mediterranean cruise. When the KLM jet sheared off the top of their plane, the impact did not feel too severe. The Hecks were thrown forward and to the right, but their safety belts held them down. Still, Floy Heck found that she could not speak or move. "My mind was almost blank. I didn't even hear what was going on," she told an *Orange County Register* reporter years later. But her husband, Paul Heck, sixty-five, reacted immediately. He unbuckled his seat belt and started toward the exit. "Follow me!" he told his wife. Hearing him, Floy snapped out of her daze and followed him through the smoke "like a zombie," she said.

Just before they jumped out of a hole in the left side of the craft, Floy looked back at her friend Lorraine Larson, who was just sitting there, looking straight ahead, her mouth slightly open, hands folded in her lap. Like dozens of others, she would die not from the collision but from the fire that came afterward.

Unlike tall buildings, planes are meant to be emptied fast. All passengers are supposed to be able to get out within ninety seconds, even if only half the exits are available and bags are strewn in the aisles. As it turns out, the people on the Pan Am 747 had at least sixty seconds to flee before fire engulfed the plane. But 326 of the 396 people onboard were killed. Including the KLM victims, 583 people ultimately perished. Tenerife remains the deadliest accidental plane crash in history.

At the time of the Tenerife crash, psychologist Daniel Johnson was working on safety research for McDonnell Douglas. He became fascinated by this paralysis behavior, which had been observed in other plane crashes as well. Floy and Paul Heck are both deceased now. But a few months after the accident, Johnson interviewed them both. He made an important discovery. Before the crash, Paul had done something highly unusual. During the long delay before takeoff, Heck had studied the

747's safety diagram. He even walked around the aircraft with his wife, pointing out the nearest exits. He had been in a theater fire as an eight-year-old boy, and ever since, he had always checked for the exits in an unfamiliar environment. Maybe this is a coincidence. But it is also possible that when the planes collided, Heck's brain had the data it needed to take action.

The National Transportation Safety Board has found that passengers who read the safety information card are less likely to get hurt in an emergency. In a plane crash at Pago Pago three years before the Tenerife accident, all but 5 of the 101 passengers died. All the survivors reported that they had read the safety information cards and listened to the briefing. They exited over the wing, while other passengers went toward other, more dangerous but traditional exits and died.

After preparation, the next best hope is leadership. That's one reason that well-trained flight attendants now shriek at passengers in evacuations—to break into their stupor, just as Paul Heck did for his wife. Otherwise, the amygdala works like a positive feedback loop: fear leads to more fear. Cortisol and other stress hormones go back to the amygdala and make the fear stronger. The more intense the fear, the less likely the hippocampus and other parts of the brain can intervene and readjust the response. "The amygdala will keep firing away," says brain expert LeDoux. "Unless you have some way to overcome that, you're going to be sort of locked in."

The easiest way to get a paralyzed animal to snap out of its daze is to make a loud noise, Gallup found. The sound of a door slamming shut will do the trick. An animal will start suddenly and try to flee. Sometimes this would happen in the lab by accident: if a researcher sneezed or a car backfired. "Any sudden change will terminate the response," he says. Otherwise, animals can stay in their trance for hours. They can even die that way. (Gallup has found that about 30 to 40 percent of mice actually die while paralyzed, presumably of cardiac arrest.) The paralysis response is so powerful that "playing dead" can turn into being dead.

Paralysis seems to happen on the steepest slope of the survival arc—when almost all hope is lost, when escape seems impossible, and when the situation is unfamiliar to the extreme. Sometimes it works. But paralysis remains mostly a mystery. Aside from Gallup, very few people have researched it seriously, which is a shame. In a way, the paralysis response is so good that it has had us all fooled. Victims appear motionless, overwhelmed, and useless, so researchers move on to the next subject. But there, trapped in a still life, might be one of the most interesting and problematic defense mechanisms in the animal kingdom.

8

Heroism

A Suicide Attempt on the
Potomac River

THE SNOW STARTED out lovely, blurring the edges of Washington's hard buildings and bleaching the memorials storybook white. But by midafternoon on January 13, 1982, it had turned unforgiving. Great groaning piles of snow fell from the sky like mud. Government employees were liberated early, stacking the city's streets with traffic. Normally, it took Roger Olian, a sheet-metal worker at St. Elizabeth's Hospital, half an hour to get home. On this day, after driving for two hours, he was only halfway there. It would have been faster to walk.

By the time he got to the Fourteenth Street Bridge, which crosses over the Potomac River from D.C. into Virginia, Olian's old red Datsun pickup truck was protesting. It had needed a new battery for a while and now it was desperately low on gas, too. Worried the car might stall and never start again, Olian kept the radio and the windshield wipers off.

When the Boeing 737 sliced into the bridge span next to him at 4:01 P.M., Olian didn't even see it. Encased in his snow-covered truck, he didn't hear or feel the crash. It was only when the car in front of him stopped that Olian had any indication that something strange had happened. The driver got out and walked back to his truck. Olian rolled down his window, and the man's shouts jangled through the snow-bound quiet.

"Did you see that?"

"What's that?"

"A plane! A plane just crashed into the river!" the man screamed.

Olian dismissed him. "I thought, 'This guy is nuts.' All I wanted to do was to get out of there."

But the man kept yelling. "I think that plane might explode!"

"So get in your car and go!" Olian told him, rolling up his window.

The man did as he was told. But as Olian started to follow him, he noticed that the other cars were behaving oddly too. "It was as if you'd dropped food into the middle of an anthill and all of a sudden the ants started to move in weird ways. So I thought, 'Maybe that guy was right.'" Without thinking too much about what he was doing or how he would start his truck again, Olian eased over to the shoulder and parked. If a plane had gone down without him even noticing, he thought, it must have been a small private plane. "Well, maybe I could see what's going on," he said to himself. "Or maybe somebody needs help, maybe I could do something—some nominal thing, and it will be interesting."

"This Is Not a Small Plane"

What makes a person risk his or her life to save someone else? It's one thing to carry someone's briefcase as you evacuate a burning building, or to help a frightened stranger to her feet. Small acts of kindness don't cost very much, and they have clear evolutionary value, as we've seen. But how do we explain truly irrational acts of generosity? Heroism, much as we revere it, is rather incomprehensible. Isn't it exactly the kind of behavior that should get naturally selected for extinction?

This chapter is about exceptional grace. We have already dissected exceptional failure, known as panic. And we've explored the far more common default behavior called paralysis. But for almost every disaster, there is a hero. Sometimes there are hundreds. The following is not a celebration of heroes. That is the topic of many other worthy books.

This chapter is an attempt to understand, not applaud; to look the hero straight in the eye and ask: what the hell were you thinking?

As Olian jogged down toward the river, he could make out a dozen other people, drivers like him who'd emerged to investigate. They were clustered on the riverbank tying scarves and jumper cables together, trying to make a lifeline. In the water, about seventy-five to a hundred yards from shore, Olian saw the tail section of a passenger jet. "My first thought was, this is not a small plane," he remembers. "My second thought was, where is the rest of it?"

As he got closer, Olian saw something else. Six people were in the water, floating amid the pieces of airplane, trying to keep their heads above the slush. They were the passengers. Olian realized immediately that there was no obvious way to save them. The river was frozen over, so no boat could get through. The plane had shattered the ice between it and the shore, making it equally impossible to walk to safety. And the snowstorm was so bad that Olian couldn't imagine a helicopter making it out. As he approached the river, he could hear the survivors' calls for help. Their cries bounced across the frozen landscape. "You knew they knew they were in trouble," Olian says. But the bystanders on the river and on the bridge above could only watch.

As he reached the water, Olian didn't stop to talk with the people gathered there. He didn't take off his steel-toed boots or remove the five pounds of keys in his pockets. He just jumped in. He needed to let those people know someone was trying to save them, he said later. That was all. "They had to see someone right now. If I was ever confident of anything in my life, it was this," he says in his slow, methodical way. "Worst-case scenario, I would be totally ineffective in saving them, but at least I would give them hope."

Olian is bald now, with a white beard and wire-rimmed glasses that make him look like a man who likes to read classics and collect wine. But he actually spends most of the day outside doing hard physical work. He runs his own small tree service, a profession he took up in 2002 when he was laid off from his government sheet-metal job after twenty-eight years of service. He often works alone, climbing up into the treetops like an acrobat and cutting down unwanted branches. When we meet at his small red-brick home in Arlington, he is wearing a denim shirt, tan jeans, and the kind of earth-tone sneakers you see on people at technology start-ups in Seattle. His long arms hang languorously by his sides, like a basketball player's.

We sit in the living room, next to the woodstove, which Olian periodically feeds with wood from a symmetrically stacked pile of logs. As we talk, he gently pets Sandy, a miniature poodle and one of two small dogs that he and his wife dote over. For the first half hour or so, Olian doesn't meet my gaze very often. He stares down at the dog as he describes that strange, long-ago day on the Potomac. When Pumpkin, the other dog, comes over to lick Sandy's nose, Olian interrupts his story to fuss over them. "Oh, look, they're kissing!" he says. As he relaxes, Olian looks up more often. Eventually, the dogs move on to other things.

The Hero On Board

Air Florida Flight 90 had taken off that morning with ice and snow on its wings. The Boeing 737, en route to Fort Lauderdale, Florida, had been delayed almost two hours while snow was swept off the runways at D.C.'s National Airport. Shortly before 3:00 P.M., the airport had reopened. The flight crew had deiced Flight 90, but not as thoroughly as they should have. When the plane took off, it strained and stretched to reach up to the sky, but the armor of ice weighed it down.

Joe Stiley knew the plane was going to crash before it even left the runway. He traveled constantly for his job as an executive at GTE. He flew in 737s out of National Airport about once a week. Maybe because Stiley had also been a pilot himself, he noticed things that most people didn't. For one thing, the crew hadn't finished deicing the plane. He could see them through his window. And when the plane finally took off, he could tell it was going far too slowly. He got into the brace position and told his secretary, Patricia "Nikki" Felch, to do the same thing. "What I said was, 'Nikki, we're in deep shit. Do what I do.' I put my head right up next to my rear end."

Stiley looked up once more before the plane crashed. He saw through the window that the plane's left wing was slanted downward. He put his head back between his legs. That day, January 13, was his son's birthday. Before the plane slammed into the bridge, Stiley apologized to God for leaving on a business trip on that day. He ached to think that his son would forever remember his birthday as the anniversary of his father's death.

Just seconds after takeoff, less than half a mile from the airport, Flight 90 hit the Fourteenth Street Bridge like a wrecking ball, destroying seven cars, killing four people, and tearing away a section of the bridge wall. The plane broke into a dozen pieces on impact.

When the plane hit the bridge, Stiley remembers, it felt a lot like being rear-ended hard in a car. The impact rattled him down to his bones. Hitting the water, though, was much worse. "That impact was unbelievable." He could feel himself blacking out. "I didn't expect to wake up."

When Stiley came to, he was sitting upright in his seat with water up to his neck. Felch was still next to him. He could hear other people moaning around him. Then the plane started to sink. It slipped underwater and kept drifting downward for what seemed like a very long time, until it finally settled on the bottom of the river. While this was happening, Stiley made a checklist in his head. He had much to do. First, he needed to free his left leg, which was horribly broken and pinned in the wreckage. He also had to unbuckle his seat belt. Then he had to help Felch. Like many of the survivors in this book, his military training had taught him to always make a plan. It probably saved his life. "There is a tremendous benefit to having that training," he says. "You don't sit there wondering what to do. You do it."

Once the plane stopped falling, Stiley started working on the checklist. He wrenched his leg free, unbuckled his belt, and started to help Felch. He had to break her foot to get it free. Then the two of them swam over the other seats, past the college kids they had been chatting with on the runway. They couldn't stop to help anyone else. They'd been underwater for too long. Their lungs were throbbing. They kept swimming, clutching each other's hand, and groping through the black water.

Finally they broke through to the surface. As they sucked in the twenty-four-degree air, they saw the tail section of their plane sticking out of the water about ten yards away. It was the only thing to hold on to. They helped each other swim toward it. Then they saw Kelly Duncan, a twenty-two-year-old flight attendant, and the only member of the crew to survive. She came over to hold on to the tail too. Then Priscilla Tirado surfaced, screaming. "Where is my baby? Does anyone see my baby?" In less than five minutes, she had lost her two-month-old infant and her husband forever. Stiley swam over to Tirado and floated her over to the little group of survivors. She pulled so hard on his tie she almost choked him to death, he remembers.

Snow fell intermittently. The drops of water on Stiley's eyelashes froze into tiny icicles. Both of his legs were broken, as was one arm. All of the passengers were seriously injured. Stiley found a life vest floating in the water, but he couldn't open its plastic packaging because his hands were so cold. Finally Duncan ripped it open with her teeth. They put it on Felch, and Duncan pulled the inflation cord. Despite her injuries and her relative inexperience, Duncan performed masterfully that day, just as she had been trained to do.

By now, quite a crowd had gathered on the bridge above. They were staring down at the little band of survivors. Some dangled pieces of rope. But Stiley didn't think he could make it over to the bridge, especially not while dragging Felch. And he knew he couldn't make it to the riverbank, which was much farther away. So he stayed where he was, clinging to the steel fragments of airplane. He remembers looking up at the crowd at some point and seeing cameras staring back at him.

Stiley checked his watch to see how long they'd been in the water. Ten minutes. He remembered from his Navy training that people tend to go into cardiac arrest after about twenty minutes in extremely cold water. He tried to move the parts of his body that weren't broken, to generate heat. Finally, Stiley saw flashing red lights. Rescue workers raced down the riverbank with their gear. "Oh, they're here! Thank God," Stiley thought. "They showed up just like they were supposed to." But then he watched as the rescue workers ran to the water's edge and came to a stop. There was nothing they could do. "They became spectators like everyone else."

Until that moment, Stiley had been trying to reassure the other survivors. One man, who was pinned into his seat next to the tail, had been mumbling repeatedly, "I'm not going to make it out of here." Stiley had countered such talk with relentless optimism. He encouraged everyone who could move to try to do small exercises to stave off hypothermia. But now, watching the rescue workers watch them, he felt an emptiness open up in his chest. "I thought, 'Jesus Christ, I survive an airplane crash and I'm going to sit out here and freeze to death with ten thousand people watching.'"

Electric Cold

When Olian jumped into the water, he was wearing all his clothes, a jacket, and a wool cap, but no gloves. The water cut to the bone. "It was like getting electrocuted," he remembers. Someone on the shore shouted to him to take the makeshift lifeline. He grabbed it and tied it around him.

Human beings do not tolerate temperature extremes very well. Other animals—like rats and pigeons—do much better. If you stick one finger in sixty-four-degree Fahrenheit water, you will feel a deep ache after about one minute. With lower temperatures, the pain comes on faster and is more intense. The water Olian jumped into was thirty-four degrees.

Here's what it would feel like to jump into water that cold: first, your heart rate would spike. Your blood pressure would immediately shoot up. Your body would automatically reduce blood flow to the surface of the skin by constricting your blood vessels. Blood travels, so the cold blood on the surface of your skin would eventually make its way to your heart. The constriction of the blood vessels slows down that process, but it also hurts. At the same time, you may experience a sudden urge to urinate. That's your body's way of trying to reduce the total fluid volume in your system. Meanwhile, your heart rate would begin to fall, beating fewer times per minute until, without warming, it would eventually stop altogether.

As your skin temperature continues to cool, the pain would get worse. It would build up to an almost unbearable intensity. Then suddenly the pain would fade, and it would feel like the water had miraculously gotten warmer. In fact, in order to keep your skin supplied with oxygen, your blood vessels would have dilated, bringing a wave of blood back to the surface of your skin. That's why your cheeks and nose look red in cold temperatures. But then, just as you're getting more comfortable, the process would reverse itself again. The blood vessels constrict, and the pain returns. This opening and closing of the blood vessels would continue until the body becomes even colder, at which point the blood vessels would stop dilating altogether. Your blood would begin to abandon your extremities to frostbite, choosing to save your heart instead.

As soon as you entered the water, goose bumps would have popped up on your skin. Goose bumps are your hair follicles standing on end. The technical term for this is *horripilation* (from the Latin *horrere*, "to stand on end," and *pilus*, which means "hair"; *horrible* is a close relative of this word for obvious reasons). Like the rest of our survival response, it is an obvious descendant of evolution, and a classic example of how outdated our fear response can be. In animals with a lot of fur, goose bumps help to boost insulation in the cold. Or, when animals are afraid, goose bumps can bristle the animal's coat, creating a more intimidating silhouette. But of course, humans don't have enough hair to reap such benefits.

Meanwhile, as in any extreme situation, your abilities to reason and make decisions would deteriorate rapidly. So would your fine-motor skills. Humans lose manual dexterity in water less than fifty-four degrees. Swimming can help delay the onset of hypothermia. But as your body continued to cool you would start to shiver violently. Shivering is like involuntary calisthenics. It causes your muscles to contract, which creates heat.

Because humans have such a weakness for cold temperatures, it has been a subject of a sometimes perverse fascination for scientists for many years. In the 1930s, doctors tried treating schizophrenia and tumors with cold temperatures, under the theory that the cold might kill the diseased tissue. During World War II, Nazi scientists subjected prisoners at Dachau to atrocious experiments in temperature extremes. To this day, much of what we know about human responses to cold water comes from the suffering of these prisoners.

Like Stiley, Olian had formed an instant plan. He guessed that the water might be shallow enough that he could walk out to the survivors. Immediately, he realized he was wrong. The land dropped off dramatically, and he had to tread water as soon as he jumped in. Plan B was to walk on water. Maybe he could leapfrog from one floating ice slab to the next. He scrambled up on the nearest, dinner-table-sized ice block. But as soon as he stood up, the block flipped, tossing him back in the water. He tried again, but the ice was too unstable. He'd been in the water only a couple of minutes, but already he'd lost feeling in his hands. They felt like giant wooden clubs, and they were useless to him in this ridiculous dance he was doing in the water.

Next, Olian tried swimming between the ice blocks. He had been a powerful swimmer in high school and still swam several days a week. He plowed his arms through the water, but got nowhere. The plane had shattered the ice, but the fragments were still too close together to allow him to pass through. "It was like a jigsaw puzzle. Every piece was in exactly the right place."

Plans A, B, and C had all failed. "I'm getting into the Greek alphabet, and I'm beginning to think I'm in trouble." So Olian did the least elegant thing he could do. He threw himself up on an ice block, then crawled across it and fell back into the water. He did this over and over again, slowly working his way toward the wreckage. Every couple minutes, he yelled to the passengers: "Hold on. I'm coming!"

When Olian entered the water, his temperature was probably about 98.6 degrees, or normal. For a while, his body could keep his core at that temperature through the constriction of his blood vessels and the hard work of swimming. As he began to cool further, though, his temperature began to drop. The Potomac was one degree cooler than the coldest water used in the Dachau experiments. In general, doctors consider patients in need of treatment when their temperatures drop below 95 degrees—and in danger of dying below 90 degrees. Below 87 degrees, the rhythm of the heart becomes abnormal. At Dachau, the Nazis concluded that death becomes almost certain below 75 degrees.

Olian didn't know the people he was trying to rescue. I asked him if he experienced any feelings of doubt or regret as he thrashed about in the water, his body lacerated by cold. "I wondered vaguely if I would ever regain use of my hands," he says. "But some switch in my head said, 'It doesn't matter. Keep going.'" Olian admits he was not behaving logically. "If rational thought had entered my head at any point, I wouldn't have done it."

If you ask heroes why they did what they did, they invariably say they had no choice. How could they watch a man drown? Or starve? Or burn to death? Heroes are universally uncomfortable with the label. They attribute their actions to the situation, rather than their own profile. "I am just a guy who happened to be somewhere and do something," says Olian. "If it happened again next week, it might not work out so well."

But at the Flight 90 crash site, there was a control group. At least a couple dozen people did not jump in. That was a fair decision. If they had, there may have been even more casualties that day. But what was the difference between Olian and everyone else?

It's not, Olian assures me, that he is such a great guy. "A lot of people may not even like me," he says, laughing. "I'm always mad at someone for something." He is not particularly optimistic about his fellow humans. "Ordinary human behavior generally sucks." Had the crash not happened, he would have been stuck in traffic, he says, swearing at the people around him instead of trying to save them.

Profiling a Hero

Over the past twenty-five years, sociologist Samuel Oliner and his wife, Pearl Oliner, have interviewed more than four hundred documented heroes—all people who risked their lives to rescue Jews during the Holocaust. The Oliners also interviewed seventy-two other people who were living in the same countries at the same time and did not save anyone. They asked them every imaginable question: Did your father belong to any political party when you were growing up? What was your religious affiliation? Did any Jews attend your elementary school?

While most of us are content to marvel at the occasional beneficence of man, Oliner has spent his life systematically dissecting the hero. When he was twelve years old, the Nazis came for his family. They were living in a Jewish ghetto in Bobowa, Poland. His own mother had died of tuberculosis five years prior. But his stepmother was there, holding his baby sister, when the Germans pulled up their trucks and starting yelling for the Jews to get out. She met his little-boy eyes. And with the hollow clarity of a woman facing her own execution, she told him to run. "Run away so that you will stay alive!" She gave him a push.

Samuel Oliner ran. He went up to a rooftop and lay there, flat and still in his pajamas, for almost an entire day and night. He saw atrocious scenes no child should see—a child thrown from a window and another stabbed with a bayonet, he says. After the German voices faded, he crept into a house and scavenged for clothing. Then he slipped out of the ghetto and began wandering the streets. From a farmer, he learned that all the Jews in the ghetto had been shot and killed, their bodies shoved into a mass grave and covered with dirt.

And then he was saved. Fate scooped Oliner up and held him close, just as inexplicably as it had abandoned him. He walked to a nearby village and knocked on the door of a peasant woman. He did not know her well, but he knew she had gone to school with his father years ago. Balwina Piecuch fed him, gave him a new name, and taught him the Lord's Prayer and the Polish catechism. Then she arranged for him to work on a farm several miles away and sent her son to check up on him routinely.

Oliner has lived a long life because of this woman. He eventually came to the United States, fought in Korea, and attended college on the GI Bill. He became a professor at Humboldt State University in California. "I saw and understood the tragedy of evil," Oliner told me. But heroism . . . heroism was harder. He has devoted his life to unraveling the mystery this peasant woman presented. Why do some people risk their lives to save strangers while other people just watch?

What Oliner found was subtle. "There is no single explanation for why people act heroically. It's not absolutely genetic or personality or cultural." But first, consider what did *not* matter. Religious conviction didn't seem to make a difference. In the Oliners' study, about 90 percent of both rescuers and nonrescuers said they had been affiliated with a religious institution while growing up. (Most were Catholic.) More to the point, both groups reported similar levels of religious intensity among themselves and their parents.

Many individual heroes would disagree. Walter Bailey, the busboy who saved hundreds in the fire at the Beverly Hills Supper Club, believes his faith filled him with a sense of calm. "I generally feel that a person who knows where they're going to go when they die is less afraid of death." Roger Olian, the man who jumped into the Potomac River after the Flight 90 crash, on the other hand, does not have strong religious convictions. His values overlap with religious ideology, but he got them somewhere else, he says—from his family, the military, and any number of other influences.

Politics also do not predict behavior, the Oliner study found. Rescuers and nonrescuers alike were simply not all that concerned with politics. Rescuers were, however, more likely to support democratic, pluralistic ideologies in general.

Despite what so many heroes say, their acts were not simply products of chance, the study concluded. The rescuers were not just in the right place at the right time. People who knew more about what was happening to Jews were not more likely to help. Nor were people who faced less severe risks by helping. Rescuers were not wealthier than nonrescuers, and they hadn't known more Jews while they were growing up.

But there were important differences. Rescuers tended to have had healthier and closer relationships with their parents. They were also more likely to have had friends of different religions and classes. Their most important quality seemed to be empathy. It is tricky to say where empathy comes from, but Oliner believes the rescuers learned egalitarianism and justice from their parents. When they were disciplined as children, rescuers were more likely to have been reasoned with; nonrescuers were more likely to have been whipped.

For all these reasons, perhaps, heroes feel a nonnegotiable duty to help others when they can. "It's something in your heart, your soul, and your emotions that gets a hold of you and says, I gotta do something," Oliner says. This finding agrees with the results of other (albeit scant) research into heroism. People who perform heroic acts are very often those who are "helpers" in everyday life, be they firefighters or nurses or police officers.

Perhaps because of their training and experience, heroes also have confidence in their own abilities. In general, like almost all people who perform well under extreme stress, heroes believe they shape their own destinies. Psychologists call this an "internal locus of control." I asked Roger Olian if he felt in control of what happens to him. "There's no question in my mind. To a very large degree," he said. "Even if I couldn't control it, I would feel like I should."

Bystanders, on the other hand, tend to feel buffeted by forces beyond their control. "They pay scant attention to other people's problems. They will concentrate on their own need for survival," Oliner says. And bystanders, it's worth remembering, are what most of us are.

"He Just Kept Coming"

Stiley heard Olian before he saw him. "Hey, guys! Hold on! I'm coming!" Stiley looked toward the shore and saw a person, a tall, determined, and possibly crazy person hacking his way through the ice. Stiley felt a rush of gratitude. "I thought, 'That guy's a man.'" He and the other passengers said the Lord's Prayer as they waited. It wasn't clear what Olian could do for them if he ever got to them, but it would be better to die knowing someone had tried and failed to help than knowing no one had tried at all.

Twenty minutes came and went. None of the six survivors passed out. The cold was becoming unbearable, though, and they kept swallowing jet fuel in the water. Meanwhile, Olian slashed through the water, ever so slowly. The lifeline around his waist kept getting caught on the ice, so he tried to take it off. But his hands had turned into useless stumps from the cold. Then he heard shouts from the people on the bank; they'd run out of rope. He had to wait for them to find more. He thought to himself: "Good night nurse, I can't wait! This is hard enough." But soon they lengthened the rope, and he charged back into the slurry.

At that point, Olian was just halfway there. He'd been in the water for about fifteen minutes. If it took another fifteen minutes to get to them, and it would probably take more since he was exhausted now, what would he do next? If he somehow summoned the strength to carry even one of them back across the football-field length of water, it would take yet another thirty minutes at least. Realistically, there was no way his body—or the survivors—could last another forty-five minutes in that water. He remembers staring at the tail section of the plane and noticing how smooth it was. Even if he made it out there, there might be nothing to hold on to, he thought. "I was pretty sure I was gonna die," Olian says in a quiet voice. "But that was OK. I had an internal calm and good feeling about that. I was not going to turn my back on those folks."

Stiley and Olian both felt the helicopter before they saw it. The *whoomp, whoomp* of the blades broke through the sky like thunder. That afternoon, the Park Police helicopter had been grounded at its home base a few miles away. Chief pilot Donald Usher had ruled out flying in the storm conditions—until he got the call from the airport about a downed plane. He and rescue technician Melvin Windsor decided to lift off. Flying in a near whiteout with periods of freezing rain, Usher and Windsor found their way to the bridge by following the roadways below.

Olian watched the chopper get closer. "I knew instinctively that this was a Vietnam pilot," he says, smiling. "Because those guys, they were great. They would do anything." The windshield was iced over and the helicopter's downdraft was blowing debris dangerously close to the rotor system. But Usher, indeed a Vietnam veteran, delicately lowered the chopper toward the water.

First, the helicopter headed toward Olian, mistaking him for a passenger. He waved it off, and the bystanders began to reel him in toward the shore. He had done all he could do. "A helicopter was real help. I was an illusion," he says. When he got to the shore, he couldn't walk. When the body gets extremely cold, muscle rigidity sets in. Someone dragged him up the bank and into a heated truck. He started shaking violently, the body's way of generating heat through muscle friction.

The helicopter eventually plucked five of the survivors from the river, dragging them one by one over to the bank with a lifeline. After Priscilla Tirado, the woman who had lost her baby, repeatedly lost her grip on the line and dropped back into the water not far from shore, two other men—a firefighter and a government clerk—jumped into the water to drag her out and finish the job. The final crash survivor, the man whose legs had been trapped by the wreckage, died, just as he had predicted. He sunk into the water before the helicopter could reach him. Of the seventy-nine people on Flight 90, seventy-four died.

Olian rode in an ambulance with Stiley and other survivors to a nearby hospital. He was placed in a warm shower until his body temperature went up to ninety-four degrees. Then he went home to his wife.

The next day, the government was closed due to the blizzard. So Olian had the day off. He went to an impound lot to pick up his truck, which had been towed from the riverside. Sure enough, the battery was dead. Luckily he and his wife had brought jumper cables. When Olian went to pay the fine, he was a few dollars short. The money he took out of his wallet was still wet. He muttered an explanation to the cashier ("There was this plane crash, and I jumped in, and everything is still wet, see . . ."). The cashier let him take the truck.

One of the other men who had jumped in at the end of the ordeal, Lenny Skutnik, became an instant celebrity. His feat had been captured by the news cameras. Skutnik appeared at the State of the Union address at the invitation of President Ronald Reagan, the start of a new tradition at the speech. But no one knew about Olian until Stiley and the helicopter pilots told reporters they had to find him. "I was fascinated by this man. He just kept coming," Stiley would later tell *Life*. "It was he who saved my life."

A Hero Database

Olian and Skutnik, along with the helicopter crew, received something called the Carnegie Hero Medals. Over the past century, the little-known Carnegie Hero Fund Commission has doled out over nine thousand medals and cash assistance to people who voluntarily risk their lives to an extraordinary degree to try to save others.

Andrew Carnegie, even more than most people, was enchanted by the hero. In the winter of 1904, from his sixty-four-room mansion on Manhattan's Upper East Side, he heard about a horrible coal mine disaster outside of Pittsburgh. A massive explosion had killed 181 people. Within hours, a respected engineer who had designed the mine had arrived at the site and descended into the main shaft to help rescue survivors. Deep underground, he encountered toxic gas, a by-product of the explosion. He died soon afterward, leaving a widow and a stepson. Another volunteer, this one a coal miner, went searching for survivors the next day. He, too, died from the asphyxiating gases, leaving a widow and five children. Carnegie, not an easy man to impress, was moved to match the $40,000 in public donations for the victims' families. "I can't get the women and children of the disaster out of my mind," he wrote. He also arranged for two gold medals to commemorate the heroism of the dead volunteers.

A few months later, Carnegie, then the richest man in the world, established a $5 million trust and the Hero Fund Commission. Of all the charitable organizations he started, the Hero Fund was his favorite. "I don't believe there's a nobler fund in the world," he once said with characteristic immodesty. "It is the fund that may be considered my pet." Most of Carnegie's other philanthropies were someone else's idea. But Carnegie dreamed up the Hero Fund himself. For all his ruthlessness as a businessman, he had a soft spot for civility. He disdained football as a sport for savages, so he donated a lake to Princeton University to give athletes another outlet. He was a pacifist and railed against the traditional definition of heroes as warriors. "The false heroes of barbarous man are those who can only boast of the destruction of their fellows," he wrote. "The true heroes of civilization are those alone who save or greatly serve them."

The Hero Fund offers an unusual database of documented heroes. (The Commission does not award medals without thoroughly investigating each case to confirm the facts.) And the list of recipients is diverse. "They come from every conceivable occupation, every age group, every ethnic background," says Douglas Chambers, director of external affairs for the Commission. "I think our youngest was a seven-year-old girl. Our oldest was an eighty-six-year-old woman."

But some similarities do emerge. Of the 450 acts of heroism recognized by the Commission from 1989 to 1993, a whopping 91 percent were performed by males, according to a study by psychologist Ronald Johnson at the University of Hawaii. Of course, that could just be a bias of the sample. The Hero Fund is hardly comprehensive. The Commission learns about most of its heroes through media outlets, so perhaps the kinds of heroics that men perform are more likely to get coverage. Or maybe men are just more likely to be in high-risk situations where someone needs to be rescued. (After all, 61 percent of the victims who got rescued were also male.) Due to their occupations as well as their higher tolerance for risk, men are more likely to be caught in perilous situations. And men are stronger, on average, which could influence their willingness to walk into danger.

But the gender breakdown might also suggest something more nuanced. Men are probably far more likely to see themselves as rescuers—to believe they are not only capable of heroics but that such behavior is expected of them. A disproportionate number of Carnegie Heroes were also working-class men, like Olian. Of the 283 men who rescued someone other than a member of their family, only two had high-status jobs. Once again, it's possible that most of these men were doing what they thought was expected of them, given their roles in society. They tended to be truck drivers, laborers, welders, or factory workers—physical jobs that required taking some risk, just like rescuing.

A surprising number of the rescues occurred in rural or small-town America, the study found. About 80 percent of the heroic acts happened in places with populations less than one hundred thousand. Again, that could be a bias of the sample. But it's also true that in small towns, people tend to know one another. And, following the theory of reciprocal altruism, acts of kindness are recognized and remembered.

Samuel Oliner, the Holocaust survivor who has devoted his life to understanding heroism, has analyzed the Carnegie Heroes as well. He chose 214 of them at random and interviewed them about why they did what they did. As with the World War II rescuers, he found a range of explanations. But a full 78 percent cited the moral values and norms they had learned from their parents and the wider community. "Many talked about how they had been taught at some point in their lives that people are supposed to care for one another and felt that being a helper is intimately connected with their own sense of who they are," Oliner wrote. Roger Olian, the man who jumped into the frigid Potomac after the Flight 90 crash, did not live in a rural setting. But otherwise, he looks a lot like the other heroes in these studies: he is male, he had a working-class job, and he had a strong sense of duty to help others.

So we are coming around to a psychological explanation for heroism. A sense of empathy, combined with an identity as someone who helps and takes risks, may predispose one for heroism. But none of this explains how Olian's actions make any sense from an evolutionary point of view. When I ask animal behavior expert John Alcock about heroism, he is skeptical. Tales of heroics are probably "overblown," he says. After all, among other mammals, like lions, "Powerful predators will band together to defend themselves. [But] it's not a matter of one lion sacrificing himself for the good of the group. If that ever happens, it happens accidentally."

So are heroes accidental? Is Olian a mutation, genetically speaking? And what about cases of even more extreme risk-taking? There have been Carnegie Heroes who could not swim—but who jumped into bodies of water to save people anyway. Some of them died doing it. Is this not insanity, from a natural selection point of view?

Olian has thought a lot about this question since he nearly froze to death in the Potomac River. "I've always found it extremely interesting that people who treat each other so badly in everyday life can do tremendous things for each other in the worst of times," he says. He can't speak for other people, but in his case he's concluded that what he did *was* self-interested. "If you didn't get anything out of it, I mean flat-out nothing, you wouldn't do it," he says. "I wouldn't do it."

During the Holocaust, Alec Roslan rescued two young boys at great risk to himself and his family. Many years later, when he gave a speech at a temple in Los Angeles, Oliner served as his translator. Afterward,

Oliner remembers, journalists crowded around and asked Roslan the same question over and over. "Why did you do this? What made you risk your life? Why?" As usual, we seek out heroes with a religious fervor, and then we act incredulous when we find them. Finally Roslan turned to them in exasperation and said, "Why are you asking me why I did this? You mean there's another way to behave?"

Time after time, heroes explain their actions with the statement, "I couldn't have lived with myself if I hadn't done it." It's become a post-disaster cliché. But that doesn't mean it isn't the simple truth. The more heroes I interview, the more I realize that I've been asking them the wrong question. It's not a matter of why they did something; the better question is, "What were you afraid would happen if you did *not* do what you did?"

"Basically, you're doing it for yourself," Olian says, "because you wouldn't want to *not* do it and face the consequences internally." In his case, he was afraid of disappointing himself. His determination at the crash site grew out of confidence—and insecurity, he says. Confidence because he knew he had the strength and skill to try to swim to those passengers, and insecurity because he needed to prove to himself that he could do it. He didn't jump into the river to be a hero; he did it to avoid being a coward. Or, as he puts it: "It's more a feeling of an emptiness than adding to something that's already there."

Olian enlisted in the military during Vietnam for the same reason. He didn't particularly agree or disagree with the reasons for going to war. He went to Vietnam because he was scared not to go. "For that reason, I had to do it. I didn't want to spend the rest of my life wondering if I could've done it. Could I rise to the situation, whatever it was? I didn't know if I could survive, how I'd feel about killing people. I had a lot of questions."

In 1969, Olian was on patrol with a small group of soldiers in the Central Highlands of Vietnam during the rainy season. They crossed a river using a small footbridge one day, only to find in the morning that the rains had flooded out the bridge—leaving them no way back but to swim a hundred yards through the crushing current. They waited for hours, sending out calls for help over their barely functioning radio. No help arrived, and they were running out of food. Once again, faced with a river and a problem, Olian had just enough confidence—and just enough insecurity—to jump in. He made it across, and so he answered one of his questions.

Evolutionary psychologist Gordon Gallup Jr. does not hesitate to make a prediction about the average hero: "I would bet most heroes will be male, single, childless, and young." (Coincidence or not, Olian, while married, was male, childless, and young.) Gallup tosses off this prediction because he knows that evolutionary imperatives rule our lives. If we are going to do something, it is probably going to promote our genetic survival. Men are more likely to be heroes because they accrue reproductive benefits from doing so, Gallup says. If they don't already have children, heroism is a good way to ensure that they will one day have many. Heroes, put a different way, get all the girls. "Scratch an altruist, and you'll find a hedonist underneath," Gallup says. That might be a bit strong, but the point is taken. And if would-be heroes die trying? Well, then their sisters and brothers and parents—the other keepers of their genes—will benefit from being the grieving relative of a hero. Women, on the other hand, can most efficiently promote their genes by finding high-quality (not quantity) mates, evolutionary theory suggests, and by parenting—which, if done well, can be heroic, Carnegie Medal or no.

Reducing heroism to its evolutionary roots can at first be a bit deflating, like seeing the inside of a magic hat. But these are just the buried roots, remember. A giant, gnarled tree has grown up over millions of years of evolution, laden with cultural and psychological motivations. If evolutionary theory tells us that heroism can, at least genetically speaking, be selfish, then that need not be bad news. What it means is that we all have the potential to be heroes at some point in our lives. Grace, in other words, is good for you. If we all have the potential, then we can encourage that potential in our culture, and we'll see it more.

The Problem with Fantasy

It would be remiss to leave the subject of hero worship without visiting its dark side. The history of disasters is riddled with stories of heroism gone wrong. We admire heroism because we might need it ourselves one day. But sometimes the urge to find a hero or to be a hero can be powerful to the point of pathological.

The more atrocious the wrong, the more urgent the demand for a hero. After teenagers Dylan Klebold and Eric Harris killed twelve students and one teacher in Littleton, Colorado, in 1999, a story circulated about one of their victims. In the library, one of the shooters, the story went, had asked Cassie Bernall, seventeen, if she believed in God. She was reported to have answered yes. Then she was shot to death. This story appeared just days after the shootings. Already, Bernall had a label: the teenage martyr. She inspired several songs, including Michael W. Smith's "This Is Your Time" and Flyleaf's "Cassie." Bernall's mother, Misty Bernall, wrote a book titled *She Said Yes: The Unlikely Martyrdom of Cassie Bernall.* The book became a *New York Times* nonfiction bestseller.

But this conversation probably never happened, according to the local sheriff's official investigation into the shootings. What Harris most likely said when he saw Bernall hiding under a table was, "Peek-a-boo!" Then he shot and killed her. According to the report, Klebold had taunted someone else about believing in God. But that girl survived. The confusion quickly developed into lore, and it became more powerful than truth. Long after the official investigation came out, news articles continue to perpetuate the mistake.

"That idols have feet of clay is a banality; what is interesting is the question why, knowing it, we are still enthralled by them," writes Lucy Hallett-Hughes in the book *Heroes: A History of Hero Worship.* "Looking at heroes, we find what we seek." Stories of children killing other children at random are unbearable. If life really is as purposeless, unfair, and uncontrollable as it was that day at Columbine High School (or as it is every day, somewhere), then life is simply too terrifying to be managed. So we search for a redemptive narrative, and often we find it. That search is a survival mechanism unto itself.

Sometimes we need heroes so badly that we embellish them—often with no harm done, as in Littleton. But other times the quest for a hero can get ugly. It can become a vehicle for all sorts of other ambitions. After Air Florida passenger Joe Stiley was fished out of the Potomac, he woke up in a hospital bed with severe injuries. A hospital spokesperson appeared and told him he had some visitors, he says. Next thing he knew, a phalanx of ravenous reporters had surrounded him with microphones and cameras. They needed a hero by deadline. Then the bedside phone rang. The hospital operator said his mother was on the line. "OK, put her through," Stiley said through his haze. It was a newspaper reporter. He thought there had been some kind of mistake, until it happened again—with another reporter.

Peel open the history of any disaster aftermath and you will find a second, third, and fourth strata of heartbreak. Over the years, Skutnik, the other Flight 90 hero—who received dozens of awards and a standing ovation at the State of the Union address—became increasingly embittered by his interactions with reporters, Hollywood producers, and even the woman he had rescued, according to multiple news stories. "What I've found out is this: If you do something like that for people, they are not always as grateful as you'd think," he told the *Washington Times* in 1992. (Skutnik declined to be interviewed for this book unless he was paid for doing so. For more on why I did not pay him or anyone interviewed for this book, see the endnotes for this chapter.)

Disasters often bring out the worst in people, right after they bring out the best. Emergency vehicles frequently have problems getting to plane crashes because so many locals have piled into their cars to see the wreckage. At the scene, police have to be diverted just to control the spectators. Everyone wants to see a disaster site, sometimes to help but often for more complicated reasons.

Immediately after the attacks of 9/11, David Jersey, a homeless man, volunteered to search for victims in the smoking ruins of the Trade Center. He claimed at one point that he had heard the voices of survivors. Firefighters stopped what they were doing and conducted an anxious search. They found no one. When I interviewed him a year later, Jersey denied he had done anything wrong and insisted that he had heard voices. "He had no evil motive," said his attorney Brad Sage. "I think for the first time in his life he was part of something." But New York City juries showed little mercy in those days. He was convicted of reckless endangerment and sentenced to five years in prison.

Two days after the attacks, Sugeil Mejia, a twenty-four-year-old mother of two, told police that her husband was a Port Authority police officer who was trapped under the rubble of the Trade Center. He had just called her on his cell phone, she said. A police officer drove her down to Ground Zero while she appeared to take two more calls from her husband.

Rescue workers searched for the man, risking their lives in precarious rubble. Then Mejia disappeared. Officials checked the badge number she'd given for her husband and found no match. Four months later, when Mejia pleaded guilty to reckless endangerment in Manhattan Supreme Court, she wept openly. She was sentenced to three years in prison.

Israeli psychologist Hanoch Yerushalmi believes that most of us have "fantasies" about what we will do in a disaster. Some of us take them further than others. One of Yerushalmi's clients, a college student, was at a Jerusalem café when it was blown up by a suicide bomber, and although he was not hurt himself, he did help some of the wounded. He tore off his shirt and used it to help stop the bleeding. After that, he became consumed with the part. He started to bring first-aid supplies with him in his knapsack wherever he went, just in case. "His fantasy was to save. He got some kind of kick out of it, in a way," Yerushalmi says. "When [the victims] were lying there helpless, he felt like he was a little God. He could elect for life or death for people."

Finally, the young man's fantasy came true again. He happened to be nearby when a bomb went off on a bus. He rushed over and began helping the victims, just as he had planned. When the paramedics arrived, one of them mentioned that one victim should not be moved due to spinal injuries. But the young man had already moved the person. He was stricken by what he'd done. He contacted doctors later, trying to find out what had happened to the victim, to no avail. "He was in a terrible state of rage for a long time. He was left with a lot of guilt, a lot of damage and memories—the smell of burned hair and other things," Yerushalmi says. "He could not rest."

Today, the man is doing much better, after years of treatment. Yerushalmi asked that I not reveal too many details of the case in order to protect the man's anonymity. It's interesting to imagine what would have happened if he had moved a different victim at a different time. Maybe then I would be writing about him using his full name, telling you every detail of his life. He would be a hero, after all.

When I started this book, I resisted writing about heroism for this very reason. One disaster's hero is another's accomplice. So much depends on the situation—and luck, of course. But then I realized that this problem is true, to a degree, for most disaster behaviors. Denial helped Elia Zedeño get down the stairs of the Trade Center on 9/11, but for other people, denial may have led to fatal delay that day. Heroism is more nebulous than other behaviors, it's true. But it is also real, and, like so many of the other puzzling behaviors we have examined, a product of experience, aspiration, and fear. For certain people caught in rare circumstances, heroism may be just as much a survival strategy as freezing; it's a survival strategy not for the body, but for the mind.

Conclusion

Making New Instincts

IN EVERY DISASTER, buried under the rubble is evidence that we can do better. In the case of Hurricane Katrina, there was the story of the U.S. Coast Guard, which rescued thirty-four thousand people without waiting for orders from anyone. On 9/11, there was Rick Rescorla.

Rescorla was head of security for Morgan Stanley Dean Witter in the Trade Center. He was one of those thick-necked soldier types who spend the second halves of their lives patrolling the perimeters of marble lobbies the way they once patrolled a battlefield. You can find them in any high-end, landmark office building, whispering into walkie-talkies and nodding curtly to the executives who pass by in clicky shoes. They are generally overqualified for their jobs.

But Rescorla was the wisest investment Morgan Stanley has ever made. Born in England, Rescorla joined the American military because he wanted to fight the communists in Vietnam. When he got there, he earned a Silver Star, a Bronze Star, and a Purple Heart in battles memorialized in the 1992 book by Lieutenant General Harold G. Moore and Joseph L. Galloway, *We Were Soldiers Once . . . and Young*. The book is considered required reading for Army officers. That's a picture of

Rescorla on the cover, clutching an M-16 rifle and looking wary, ex-hausted, and most of all, young.

Although he eventually moved to New Jersey and settled down into the life of a security executive, Rescorla still acted, in some ways, like a man at war. Morgan Stanley occupied twenty-two floors of Tower 2 and several floors in a nearby building. After the 1988 bombing of Pan Am Flight 103 over Lockerbie, Scotland, Rescorla worried about a terrorist attack on the Trade Center. In 1990, he brought one of his old war bud-dies up to New York City to take a tour of the towers. He wanted to know how his friend, who had counterterrorism expertise, would attack the building if he were a terrorist. After his friend saw the Trade Cen-ter's garage, he pronounced the task "not even a challenge," as James B. Stewart writes in his 2002 biography of Rescorla, *Heart of a Soldier.* If he were going to attack the Trade Center, he would drive a truck full of explosives into the garage and walk out.

Rescorla and his friend wrote a report to the Port Authority explain-ing their concerns and insisting on the need for more security in the parking garage. Their recommendations, which would have been ex-pensive, were ignored, according to Stewart. (The Port Authority did not respond to repeated requests for comment for this book.)

Three years later, Ramzi Yousef drove a truck full of explosives into the underground parking garage of the World Trade Center, just as Rescorla had predicted. After the bomb went off, sending vibrations through the tower, Rescorla stood in Morgan Stanley's large, open trad-ing floor and shouted. Everyone ignored him, just as they had when he had tried to run fire drills before the bombing. So he stood on a desk and yelled, "Do I have to drop my trousers to get your attention?" The room quieted down, and he handed out flashlights and directed the employees down the darkened stairways.

After the 1993 bombing, Rescorla had the credibility he needed. Combined with his muscular personality, it was enough to get Morgan Stanley employees to take full responsibility for their own survival—something that happened almost nowhere else in the Trade Center. He understood the danger of denial, the importance of aggressively pushing through the denial period and getting to action. He had watched the employees wind down the staircase in 1993, and he knew it took too long. He had made sure he was the last one out that day, so he saw the stragglers and the procrastinators, the slow and the disabled.

Rescorla also had an unusually keen sense of dread. He knew that the risk of another terrorist attack did not diminish with each passing, normal day. And he knew it was foolish to rely on first responders to save his employees. His company was the largest tenant in the World Trade Center, a village nestled in the clouds. Morgan Stanley's employees would need to take care of one another.

From then on, no visitors were allowed in the office without an escort. Rescorla hired more security staff. He ordered employees not to listen to any instructions from the Port Authority in a real emergency. In his eyes, the Port Authority had lost all legitimacy after it failed to respond to his 1990 warnings.

Most impressive of all, Rescorla started running the entire company through frequent, surprise fire drills. He trained employees to meet in the hallway between the stairwells and, at his direction, go down the stairs, two by two, to the forty-fourth floor. Not only that, but he insisted that the highest floors evacuate first. As the last employees from one floor reached the floor below them, employees from that floor would fall in behind.

Only someone with an advanced understanding of human behavior in evacuations would know to do this. Without specific training, people become bizarrely courteous in an emergency, as we've seen. They let those from the floors below them enter the stairwell in front of them. The end result is that people from the upper floors—who have the farthest to walk and therefore face the most danger—will get out last. Training people to resist this gallantry was smart and wonderfully simple.

The radicalism of Rescorla's drills cannot be overstated. Remember, Morgan Stanley is an investment bank. Millionaire, high-performance bankers on the seventy-third floor chafed at Rescorla's evacuation regimen. They did not appreciate interrupting high-net-worth clients in the middle of a meeting. Each drill, which pulled the firm's brokers off their phones and away from their computers, cost the company money. But Rescorla did it anyway. He didn't care whether he was popular. His military training had taught him a simple rule of human nature, the core lesson of this book: the best way to get the brain to perform under extreme stress is to repeatedly run it through rehearsals beforehand. Or as the military puts it, the "Eight P's": "Proper prior planning and preparation prevents piss-poor performance."

After the first few drills, Rescorla chastised the employees for moving too slowly in the stairwell. He started timing them with a stopwatch, and they got faster. He also lectured employees about some of the basics of fire emergencies: they should always go down. Never go up to the roof. Ever.

Rescorla did not grant exceptions. When guests visited Morgan Stanley for training, Rescorla made sure they all knew how to get out too. Even though the chances were slim, Rescorla wanted them ready for an evacuation. He understood that they would need the help more than anyone else. Like the patrons in the Beverly Hills Supper Club fire, they would be passive guests in an unfamiliar environment—a very dangerous role to play.

After the 1993 bombing, Rescorla wrote another report, this one warning Morgan Stanley executives that terrorists would stop at nothing to take down the towers. He even sketched out another possible attack scenario: terrorists might fly a cargo plane full of explosives into the Trade Center. Rescorla had the imagination that the government lacked, and it stalked him with hypotheticals. Finally, Rescorla recommended that Morgan Stanley move its headquarters to a low-rise campus in New Jersey. But the firm's lease didn't end until 2006. Partly as a result of Rescorla's findings, Stewart writes, Morgan Stanley decided to sue the Port Authority to win damages from the bombing—and to be released from its lease. (The lawsuit was ultimately settled in April 2006 under terms that Morgan Stanley agreed to keep confidential.)

Rescorla's drills went on for eight years, even as the memory of the 1993 bombings faded. "He used to say, 'They're gonna get us again. By air or by the subway,'" remembers Stephen Engel, who, as facilities manager, worked closely with Rescorla. When he hired security staff, Rescorla looked for more-sophisticated candidates than Engel had seen in those kind of jobs before. "He got people with a computer background, rather than a retired beat cop looking to add to his pension."

Rescorla still relied upon fire marshals, but he had more of them, and he rotated the jobs often. "He was very serious about making sure everyone came out to the drills. We used to say, 'Well, it's the sergeant doing the drills again. It was kind of repetitive," remembers Bill McMahon, a Morgan Stanley executive. "There were times when I just sat in my office and the fire marshal would come by and say, 'No, you gotta go.'" Rescorla also made the fire marshals wear fluorescent orange vests and hats. "You'd make fun of the marshals: 'Oh, you got your hat? Where's your vest?'" remembers McMahon. "But in retrospect, thank God."

Meanwhile, Rescorla's own life changed dramatically. He fell in love with a woman he met while jogging in his neighborhood, and they got married. He was also diagnosed with cancer. He underwent painful treatments and gained weight. He didn't look like a soldier anymore. But he kept coming to work every day at 7:30 A.M. in a suit and tie, and he kept his people ready.

Rescorla was disciplined in everything he did, even his hobbies. He took up pottery and made a flowerpot for his friend Engel. "One day, he decided he was going to take up wood carving. A couple months later, he comes in with this duck. It was beautiful!" says Engel, laughing. Rescorla loved to watch old westerns, and he read voraciously. "If you mentioned something, martial arts or old movies, he would know something about it."

In 1998, Rescorla was interviewed by a filmmaker named Robert Edwards, whose father had fought alongside Rescorla in Vietnam. The documentary focused on the nature of warfare. Watching the footage now, it is clear that Rescorla thought about terrorism a lot—and not just the way it might impact his own office. He warned that the nature of war had changed, and America's leaders had not adapted. "Hunting down terrorists, this will be the nature of war in the future. Not great battlefields, not great tanks rolling," he said. "When you're talking about future wars, we're talking about engaging in Los Angeles. Terrorist forces can tie up conventional forces; they can bring them to their knees."

There were moments, truth be told, when Rescorla's job felt too small for his imagination. In a September 5, 2001, e-mail to an old friend, Rescorla spoke about *kairos*—a Greek word for an existential or cosmic moment that transcends linear time. "I have accepted the fact that there will never be a kairos moment for me, just an uneventful Miltonian plow-the-fields discipline," he wrote, "a few more cups of mocha grande at Starbucks, each one losing a little bit more of its flavor."

"A Voice Straight from Waterloo"

On the morning of 9/11, Rescorla heard an explosion and saw Tower 1 burning from his office window. A Port Authority official came over the public address system and urged everyone to remain at their desks. But Rescorla grabbed his bullhorn, his walkie-talkie, and his cell phone and began systematically ordering Morgan Stanley employees to get out. They already knew what to do, even the 250 visitors who were taking a stockbroker training class and had already been shown the nearest stairway. "Knowing where to go was the most important thing. Because your brain—at least mine—just shut down. When that happens, you need to know what to do next," McMahon says. "One thing you don't ever want to do is have to think in a disaster."

On 9/11, a handful of people might not have died if they had received Rescorla's warnings. But they did not work at Morgan Stanley. About 50 percent of Trade Center employees did not know that the roof would be locked, according to the Columbia survey of survivors. In the absence of other information, some remembered that victims had been evacuated from the roof in helicopters in 1993. So they used the last minutes of their lives to climb to the top of the towers—only to find the doors locked. They died there, wondering why.

As Rescorla stood directing people down the stairwell on the forty-fourth floor, the second plane hit—this time striking about thirty-eight floors above his head. The building lunged violently, and some Morgan Stanley employees were thrown to the floor. "Stop," Rescorla ordered through the bullhorn. "Be still. Be silent. Be calm." In response, "No one spoke or moved," Stewart writes. "It was as if Rescorla had cast a spell." Rescorla immediately shifted the evacuation to a different stairwell and kept everyone moving. "Everything's going to be OK," he said. "Remember," he repeated over and over, as if it were a tonic unto itself, "you're Americans."

Morgan Stanley employees had seen what had happened in the other tower after the first plane hit. They had a clear view of the flames scaling the building and people—people just like them—jumping out of windows, their ties flapping in the wind. So when the second plane hit, they knew exactly what was happening in the floors above them.

Rescorla had led soldiers through the night in the Vietcong-controlled Central Highlands of Vietnam. He knew the brain responded poorly to extreme fear. Back then, he had calmed his men by singing Cornish songs from his youth. Now, in the crowded stairwell, as his sweat leached through his suit jacket, Rescorla began to sing into the bullhorn. "Men of Cornwall stand ye steady; It cannot be ever said ye for the battle were not ready; Stand and never yield!" One of his security employees brought out a chair for him. But Rescorla chose to keep standing.

Later, U.S. Army Major Robert L. Bateman would write about Rescorla in *Vietnam* magazine. In this passage, he was describing Rescorla on the battlefield. But he could just as well have been writing about Rescorla in the Trade Center:

> Rescorla knew war. His men did not, yet. To steady them, to break their concentration away from the fear that may grip a man when he realizes there are hundreds of men very close by who want to kill him, Rescorla sang. Mostly he sang dirty songs that would make a sailor blush. Interspersed with the lyrics was the voice of command: "Fix bayonets . . . on liiiiine . . . reaaaa-dy . . . forward." It was a voice straight from Waterloo, from the Somme, implacable, impeccable, impossible to disobey. His men forgot their fear, concentrated on his orders, and marched forward as he led them straight into the pages of history.

On 9/11, between songs, Rescorla called his wife. "Stop crying," he said. "I have to get these people out safely. If something should happen to me, I want you to know I've never been happier. You made my life."

Moments later, Rescorla had successfully evacuated the vast majority of Morgan Stanley employees out of the burning tower. Then he turned around. He was last seen on the tenth floor, heading upward, shortly before the tower collapsed. Rescorla had his kairos moment. His remains have never been found.

People who knew Rescorla well knew he would not have left the towers until everyone else was out. "When the buildings went down, I never thought for a second that he wasn't inside," says Engel, the facilities manager. "Rick would want to go out in a blaze of glory." No one knows exactly what happened, but Engel believes that Rescorla heard about a few people who had been left behind. In particular, a Morgan Stanley senior vice president had not left his office. The executive was last seen talking on the phone, even as everyone else evacuated. "Knowing Rick," says Engel, "he'd go up and coldcock him and carry him over his shoulder."

Self-sufficiency was a religion for Rescorla. He once told a friend that every man should be able to be sent outside naked with nothing on him. By the end of the day, the man should be clothed and fed. By the end of the week, he should own a horse. And by the end of the year, he should have a business and a savings account.

Rescorla taught Morgan Stanley employees to save themselves. It's a lesson that had become, somehow, rare and precious. When the tower collapsed, only thirteen Morgan Stanley colleagues—including Rescorla and four of his security officers—were inside. The other 2,687 were safe.

Devolution

When people believe that survival is negotiable, they can be wonderfully creative. All it takes is the audacity to imagine that our behavior matters. It can happen in a moment, with a phone call or an idea muttered aloud.

In 1996, after a flood wiped out Parsons, West Virginia, for the second time in eleven years, Katie Little called up a couple of her friends and told them they needed to make some money. The three women, all in their eighties, started with a bake sale on the first Friday of every month, held at the local bank. Then they held gospel sings. They auctioned off a pig named Muddy Waters. At the end of the year, the women, known to all by then as "the cookie ladies," had $40,000, which they leveraged to get $1.5 million in state money. Then they used it to build a floodwall to protect their town, which it did.

"What I've always found," says James Lee Witt, FEMA director from 1993 to 2000, and the man who told me this story, "is that people will respond to meet a need in a crisis if they know what to do. You give people the opportunity to be part of something that will make a difference, and they will step up."

Why aren't there more evacuation drills and pig auctions? To understand how a country built on self-sufficiency could become so vulnerable, it helps to consider why people with the best of intentions miss opportunities to do better. In 2004, New York City passed Local Law 26, making the biggest changes to the building code in over thirty years. The new rules require more training for each building's fire-safety director and more elaborate emergency plans. But the rules still do not include serious evacuation drills like the ones run by Rescorla. "Unfortunately, this is one aspect where we met with some obstacles," says Captain Joseph Evangelista, who oversees planning for the Fire Department of New York. Just like the changes the Port Authority made after the 1993 bombings, the reforms focused on technological fixes and experts, not regular people. Why? Among other concerns, the city's Real Estate Board was worried that mandatory drills could lead to injuries that could lead to lawsuits, according to Joe McCormack, a fire and safety consultant involved in the rule-making process. So in the end, the rules just require people to descend at least four floors once every three years.

The story of New York City's missed opportunity is a reminder of the power of fear to distort our behavior. Like the fear of panic, the fear of litigation is a silent partner in emergency management. Two days before Hurricane Katrina made landfall in 2005, New Orleans mayor Ray Nagin delayed calling for a mandatory evacuation. He had to check with his lawyers, according to a *New Orleans Times-Picayune* story from that day, to make sure the city wouldn't be held liable by business owners forced to shutter their shops.

Like the fear of panic, this fear of being sued is not entirely irrational. Responding to a lawsuit, even a bogus one, can be punishingly expensive and stressful. It's also true that lawsuits have made the world a safer place in many cases. But that benefit comes at a great cost. "Fear of liability slows response. It can cost lives," says William Nicholson, the author of two books on emergency management law and a former general counsel for the emergency management office in Indiana.

Because of this fear, officials do not share vital information with the public, and uncertainty can stop good people from helping one another. The anxiety also poisons the relationship between the public and the people who are supposed to protect them. Every line of legalese breeds distrust. We start to confuse real safety warnings with legalistic nonsense. We lump fire drills and airline safety briefings together with the sticker on our new toaster warning against using it in the bathtub.

To make matters worse, the people in charge also routinely misunderstand liability. Ironically, after Hurricane Katrina, the government was sued anyway. One wrongful death lawsuit was filed by three families who had lost elderly relatives in the aftermath of the storm—including a man whose mother died in her wheelchair after waiting in intense heat for help to arrive at the Convention Center in New Orleans. The image of Ethel Mayo Freeman's slumped corpse became a symbol of America's tragedy around the world. But in the spring of 2007, the lawsuit was thrown out. The federal judge correctly noted that government officials enjoy immunity against many lawsuits—so that they can do their jobs without fear of lawsuits. "Fear of liability—like most fear—is, in my opinion, based largely on ignorance," Nicholson says. In fact, most government employees are protected from lawsuits if they are doing their jobs in good faith, according to sound training. But not enough people understand emergency management law. "The ignorance of public officials, from leaders of government to emergency managers, is compounded by the ignorance of the attorneys who advise them."

In New Orleans, the lawyers should have known what the liability risks were well before the hurricane even had a name. The evacuation decision never should have been delayed because the lawyers needed to get educated. "If it were a town of five thousand, I wouldn't have any complaints about that," says Nicholson. "But for a huge city like New Orleans, which had obvious hazards everyone knew about, [that] is scandalous, I think."

But fear of liability can be a convenient excuse, too, like fear of panic. Whether they are at an airline or at a command center, experts will err on the side of excluding the public, as we have seen. If they can avoid enrolling regular people in their emergency plans, they will. Life is easier that way, until something goes wrong.

In the 1990s, a committee of the British House of Commons suggested that aircraft cabin simulators be placed in airport waiting areas. That way, passengers would have a chance to practice actually doing some of the lifesaving tactics they are forever being told about. Instead of staring glumly at cable news TV while they wait to take off, people could be opening emergency exits, inflating life vests, and strapping on oxygen masks. What a clever idea! But the idea quietly died, remembers Frank Taylor, the former head of the Aviation Safety Centre at Cranfield University. "The U.K.'s Civil Aviation Authority threw it out without any proper consideration at all," he remembers. "They just don't seem to want to consider any change at all. They're understaffed, and they don't do things that they can't see an immediate advantage from."

Likewise, many U.S. high schools have dropped driver's education classes due to cost-cutting and litigation fears. Schools teach typing, but they no longer do anything to protect your children from the most likely cause of their accidental deaths. In many states, kids now learn to drive from their parents, which is a terrible idea. Teenagers taught by their parents are more than twice as likely to be involved in serious accidents than those taught by professionals, according to a 2007 study by the Texas Transportation Institute.

We're at risk of devolving, becoming worse at surviving one of the most dangerous things we do. Each year, over 6 million accidents get reported to police in the United States. About forty thousand people die, and about 2 million get hurt. Like all other disasters, car accidents are preventable tragedies. We could have fewer of them if we could train our brains the way Rescorla did. And this is not just an exercise in wishful thinking. There are more Rick Rescorlas out there, trying to teach us to do better. It is possible to speed up our own evolution for survival, even on the freeway.

"Imagine What We Can Practice!"

Late on the night of August 31, 1986, Ronn Langford was awakened by a call telling him his youngest daughter, Dorri, had been in an accident. She was riding in a car in a residential area of Colorado with her boyfriend. As they crossed through an intersection, another car going more than 55 mph ripped through a red light and crashed into the passenger side, T-boning the car. Dorri died instantly. The other car was driven by a nineteen-year-old man who had been drinking. He and everyone else involved survived.

Langford could visualize his daughter's death with iridescent clarity. He was at the time a race-car driver who had won a string of championships. He understood the power of a car to do harm. And he understood the limitations of the human driver. He knew that the brain had evolved to do many things, and driving was not among them. He had often marveled at the lack of training required of new drivers, and now he was left to suffer for it for the rest of his life.

When he got back from the hospital that morning, Langford remembers, he lay down on his bed. He told himself he had to make a choice: he could be bitter for the rest of his life. He could feel the bile building up in his throat, and he could imagine letting it fill his body and mind. He could picture dedicating his life to hating the idiot who killed his daughter. It was tempting.

Instead, Langford went on a crusade. "You lose your mind. Literally, you lose your mind for a while," he says now. He sold his share of a real-estate company, which he had started and which had been very successful. Then he opened a school called MasterDrive. He wanted to teach people that handling three thousand pounds of metal in motion is not intuitive. Like Rescorla, he wanted to make people better survivors by rewiring their brains for their modern age.

Langford can come across as a man carefully guarding a large store of anger. "Car-control skills, crash-avoidance maneuvers, the quality of decision making, all these skills are important skills for driving," he says, starting out quietly. "But nobody teaches it. Nobody learns it!" he says, shouting now. "People are just ignorant. They don't know what they don't know. Do SUVs have a different weight ratio than a new Honda Accord? Hell, yes. Of course they do. The problem is that Mrs. Smith driving an Expedition doesn't understand vehicle dynamics from a performance standpoint. You can't jerk one of those things sideways. The damn thing will roll. Crap, the car companies make cars with fantastic [safety] systems today. The problem is, guess who doesn't know how to use the systems?"

But Langford is a true believer in the brain, and it gives him enough hope to go on. "The brain is so powerful. Imagine what we can practice! Everything." We can all become excellent drivers, Langford insists, but we have to change our brain's programming. It's not productive to tell drivers how to get out of a skid—just like it's not useful to tell people to remain calm in case of an emergency. In a life-or-death situation, your brain needs subconscious programming, not just vague advisories.

So Langford takes students of all ages, some of whom have never driven before and some of whom have been traumatized by horrible car accidents, out on a course at MasterDrive and puts them into a skid, over and over again. In a safe environment, he re-creates the feeling of losing control and teaches the students to recover. MasterDrive students spend twenty-six hours behind the wheel of a car; in most states, the requirement is less than ten hours. They learn crash-avoidance techniques and how to dial up and dial down their personalities to cope with what's happening on the road. Five thousand kids come through the Colorado locations each year. Some wet their pants or freeze up behind the wheel, which, in Langford's mind, just means the training is sufficiently realistic.

Like Rescorla, Langford understands that realistic practice brings out our faults and then makes us stronger. As a young race-car driver, he read about the power of visualization techniques to improve performance. "So I started pretraining my brain to learn a track at the subconscious level." He would visualize going around the track again and again. Now he helps race-car drivers do the same thing, with the car jacked up so that they can turn and lean and brake at the right moments. Like the police and military trainers in Chapter 3, he teaches drivers to breathe, too, especially when they go through high-speed turns, the most dangerous part of the track.

To experience Langford's hands-on training, I visited the Master-Drive clinic outside of Denver, Colorado. Langford was wearing all white—white slacks and a white short-sleeved shirt with MASTERDRIVE over his heart. We sat in a small office overlooking the track, and Langford began to talk. "If you need water or anything, let me know," he said, "because I have a tendency to not stop." Then he stood up at a dry-erase board and sketched out a flowchart of how the human brain processes information. "Skill is my ability to do something automatically, at the subconscious level. I don't have to think about it. It is programmed. How do I get that? I do that by repetition, by practicing the right thing. The only way you learn it—on a response level—is to program it."

Langford has learned about how the mind works through formal and informal study of brain research. In the past decade, scientists have begun to understand just how malleable we are. "The ability for change is phenomenal," says Jay Giedd, chief of brain imaging at the child psychiatry branch of the National Institute of Mental Health. Throughout our lives, the geography of our brains literally changes depending on what we do.

Abilities we think are strictly innate almost never are. Most men, for example, tend to have slightly better spatial reasoning skills, and women have slightly better verbal skills. The stereotypes take over from there. But as with our fear responses, the room for improvement is bigger than the gaps. In an experiment at Temple University, women showed substantial progress in spatial reasoning after spending an hour a week playing the video game Tetris, of all things. The males improved with practice too. But the improvement for both sexes was far greater than the difference.

Without training, the brain falls back on its most basic fear responses in a crisis. "You put a kid in a car, take him out on an interstate at 60 mph during a snowstorm and the car goes out of control, I can tell you what his brain is going to do," says Langford. "It is going to totally disintegrate. There is no programming. So what does he do? Freezes. Closes his eyes. Does all the wrong things. Young people can respond in a nanosecond. The problem is, most of the time they do the wrong thing."

After lunch, we go out back to the track and get into a gray Corolla with racing stripes. I am behind the wheel and Langford is in the passenger seat. The sun is baking the course. We start out by doing a simple slalom course around orange cones, practicing braking and turning. First, I go too slowly, erring on the side of not humiliating myself. Langford starts working on my confidence. "Feel the rhythm of the car. That's it! You got it! Make it dance!" And after a few rounds, it works. I'm going faster, having more fun, and even boldly knocking over a few cones now and then.

Then we move to the skid pad, which is essentially a wet, slippery piece of asphalt. At Langford's direction, I drive onto the skid pad at about 20 mph. Then Langford yanks up on the parking brake in the middle of the car and, at the same time, leans over and yanks the steering wheel toward him. The reflex of most drivers at this point is to slam on the brakes and turn the car in the exact wrong direction. That's because their brains are programmed to look toward the threat. "Whatever you're looking at, the brain has a tendency to direct the hands toward it," Langford says. This is problematic on a highway. When people see an oncoming car swerving into their lane, they slam on the brakes and . . . steer directly toward it.

Langford calls this phenomenon "potholism": the more drivers stare at potholes, the more likely they are to drive into them. The hands follow the eyes. One of his clients was a woman who had seen a terrible accident. A car in front of her had hit a pedestrian, killing the man. From then on, the woman had become hypervigilant behind the wheel. She looked obsessively for pedestrians, and when she found them, she kept her eye on them. Soon she came to the sickening realization that she was steering directly toward the pedestrians. She hired Langford because she was afraid she was going to kill someone. He worked with her to help her learn to redirect her focus—away from watching pedestrians and toward controlling her car.

On the skid pad, the goal is to experience a skid enough times that your brain knows what to do: squeeze the brakes and steer where you want the car to go. After a while, I can pull the car out of each skid without any trouble, almost gracefully. I leave with an appreciation for the automobile. Like the brain, it is an amazing machine, fluid and adaptable, if the driver knows how to work it.

In Defiance of Dread

Terrorism is another hazard, like any other, except that it demands even more initiative from regular people. Civilians are the involuntary draftees, after all. We should not forget this after 9/11, says Stephen Flynn, a homeland security expert and former U.S. Coast Guard officer. "There were two narratives after 9/11. One narrative was, 'There are bad people coming to kill us, and we have to take the battle to them.'" That was the narrative deployed by President Bush as he sent American soldiers to fight overseas and told the American people to stay calm and keep shopping.

"The other narrative," Flynn says, "is the United Flight 93 narrative." There was one plane on 9/11 on which regular people were well informed. The passengers on Flight 93 had time to learn that the plane would be used as a missile if they did nothing. And what did they do? They pushed through the denial phase fast. Then they deliberated, whispering behind their seat backs and gathering information over their phones. They operated as a group. Then, in the decisive moment, they charged into the cockpit and changed the course of history.

If regular people got as panic-stricken in a crisis as most of us think they do, Flight 93 would have almost certainly destroyed the White House or the U.S. Capitol. "It's highly ironic," says Flynn, "that our elected representatives were protected on 9/11 by everyday people." Latent resilience is everywhere, and it is the only certain defense against terrorism. Not every attack can be prevented, but just enrolling regular people in the everyday counterattack is itself a victory. Because terrorism is not the same as the cold war; it is a psychological war more than a physical war, and in that distinction lies great opportunity. "Fear requires two things," Flynn says. "An awareness of a threat and a sense of being powerless to deal with that threat." Without the powerlessness, terrorism is far less destructive. If we understand dread, we can starve it.

After 9/11, small groups of employees at the Sears Tower in Chicago, Illinois, took their fate into their own hands and started arranging their own full-evacuation drills. The U.S. Department of Homeland Security, meanwhile, made some attempts to engage the public. It started a program called Citizen Corps, designed to train and organize volunteers. Some neighborhood chapters of Citizen Corps are amazing. Many are associated with outstanding Community Emergency Response Teams (or CERTs) that offer serious training to anyone willing to put in the time. In some towns, the CERT is written into local emergency plans. Thousands of citizens sandbag during floods, help evacuate people in wildfires, and map their neighborhoods' strengths and weaknesses before anything goes wrong.

But the groups are run locally, and their usefulness varies wildly. There are 2,300 Citizen Corps groups across the country, but the government keeps no tally of how many people have received training. (I signed up online to participate in D.C. and never got a response.)

In 2003, the government launched a public preparedness website, Ready.gov, which has received over 23 million unique visitors. But it was found to contain some errors and was generally uninspiring ("During a nuclear incident, it is important to avoid radioactive material, if possible"). So in 2006, an intern for the Federation of American Scientists took it upon herself to build a competing site, called ReallyReady.org, that is a bit smarter ("The cloud of dust and smoke from the explosion will be visible and will be carried by the wind. Walk across the direction of the wind, away from the dust cloud.").

These people have discovered that the more they learn about the things that scare them, the less scared they feel. The first and most important task is to get smart about risk. Depending on where you live, your most likely threat may be a hurricane or an earthquake, two very different problems. There's no need to prepare for everything.

Beware of warnings without data. It's important to rely on facts here, as opposed to emotion. Local TV news is a terrible way to judge actual risk, as we have seen. So whenever possible, look for actual risk data. What are the chances of a plane crash happening to me, given how often I fly? What are the chances of a terrorist attack affecting me, given where I live and work? These questions seem obvious, but they are very rarely part of our conversations about risk. Getting smarter requires an almost countercultural dedication to facts over emotion.

The website for this book (www.TheUnthinkable.com) has clear-eyed, specific advice based on relative risk—a thinking-person's survival guide. You can also look for your state's homeland-security or emergency preparedness website to get a list of the major threats for your region. Then systematically prepare for those risks. But do it holistically. Don't just stockpile water like an automaton; learn about the history and science of the risk and try to conduct a dress rehearsal for your brain. It doesn't need to be elaborate. It can just mean taking the stairs out of your office building once a week.

If possible, involve your whole office or your neighborhood in this exercise, not just your family. You will all be in this together, so it's wise to get to know one another in good times—not just bad. You'd be surprised how receptive people are if you give them a chance.

If you are, for whatever reason, particularly frightened of something that is not on your risk list, then prepare for it, too. The more control you feel you have, the less dread you will feel day to day. And the more control you feel, the better your performance will be, should the worst come to pass.

Disaster experts think about disasters for a living, but they don't feel powerless. They do tiny things to give their brains shortcuts in the unlikely event they need them. FAA human factor analysts always look for their nearest exit when they board planes, for example. And they read the safety briefing cards that most people think are useless. They do this because each plane model is different, and they know they may become functionally retarded in a plane crash.

Every time Robyn Gershon, who is leading a study of the World Trade Center evacuation, checks into a hotel, she takes the stairs down from her room. She knows that most hotel stairs take a confusing path through back rooms and empty onto unexpected streets. (I once did this in a hotel in Manhattan and ended up in the kitchen. A supervisor, assuming I was an employee leaving for a break, asked to search my bag. Apparently not very many guests took the stairs.)

Once a disaster begins, people who have some familiarity with their disaster personalities have an advantage. First, they know that if something does go terribly wrong, the odds favor their survival. Just knowing there is hope can help people muster the presence of mind to push past denial and deliberation and act. "The important thing is to recognize that you need to get out. Everything you've done to prepare yourself will help you," says Nora Marshall, who has spent twenty-one years studying survival factors at the National Transportation Safety Board. Knowledge also helps to self-correct. Now that you know you are likely to delay evacuating or to waste time grabbing your carry-on bags from the overhead bin, you have a chance to override your own worst instincts. Above all, it is essential to take the initiative—to remember that you and your neighbors must save yourselves. Now that you have glimpsed the survival arc, you might have a better chance of finding the shortcuts.

Teddy Bears and Wheelchairs

An old mill town called Samoa, 250 miles north of San Francisco, held the first tsunami evacuation drill in the history of California—on June 28, 2007. Samoa is located on 185 acres, right on the water. It has a town square and a restaurant, but it's not fancy. Samoa's one hundred houses were built by a logging company that used to own the town. Today, the logging company is gone, but Samoa's residents are still there, working in a nearby pulp mill as well as in construction and other service jobs.

Troy Nicolini is a National Weather Service meteorologist and a beauty salon owner in the area. Since the 2004 tsunami in Southeast Asia, he has been working on developing evacuation routes in at-risk areas like Samoa. But it occurred to him that it might make sense to ask regular people to tell him where the evacuation-route signs should be. So he made the signs portable for the time being and started planning a drill. The process was made much easier because Nicolini didn't have to worry about asking many property owners for permission to have people traipsing through their land. Samoa is one of the few towns in America that is still owned by a private company. The current owner is Danco, a construction and development company. And the company agreed to help with the drill. "We could just do whatever we wanted without having to worry about anything," Nicolini says. With that, Samoa became one of the first towns in America to take responsibility for improving its citizens' performance in a disaster. It's ironic that it was a company—not a government—that cleared the way.

That Thursday evening at 6:00 P.M., a tsunami siren attached to the firehouse whirled to life. Danco CEO and president Dan Johnson was there, and he had low expectations. "I wasn't even sure if people were going to come," he says. "This is a pretty working-class community. They're all blue collar, they're drinking their beer." But as he watched, the town's residents poured into the streets and up the evacuation route. Nearly two hundred people, or about 75 percent of the population, hustled up to a gathering spot forty-eight feet above sea level. Babies, cats, and dogs came too. Peggy Weatherbee pushed her mother, Delores, up the path in a wheelchair. On the steepest part of the trail, three large men stepped in to help.

CEO Johnson was stunned. "All of a sudden, all these people are walking with their dogs and a bird, and a little girl is dragging her teddy bear, which was bigger than she was. I couldn't believe it. These big gruff guys were walking up there with their backpacks full of all the stuff they wouldn't want to lose from their houses." As Nicolini headed up the trail, he saw a little girl carrying a backpack. "I said, 'Wow, is that your evacuation pack?'" he remembers. "She looked at me like, 'Look, buddy, this is serious, I got a mission here, don't bother me.'"

Everybody made it to the top in ten minutes, which is about all the warning they might have in real life. As each family arrived, they punched a time card so that they would know exactly how long the trip would take in a real tsunami—a fine souvenir from high land. Then Nicolini addressed the crowd: "I want to congratulate everyone and tell you that you're alive and well." He also reminded them all that the siren may not work, so if they ever were to feel the earth shake for more than twenty seconds, see the ocean recede, or hear a strange roar come from the horizon, they should make a break for it. He plans to do the drill every year and try to expand it to other towns. "You've got to practice stuff that's important," Nicolini says. "I hope this will allow people to think less about tsunami. You have a plan, and you don't have to worry."

After the drill ended, a strange thing happened. People didn't seem to want to leave. "It was like this whole community-building event," says Johnson, laughing. "People are giving me hugs, and saying, 'Thanks for doing this.' You see the appreciation."

There was one sheriff's deputy at the drill. A few people asked why there weren't more. Where was the fire department? Where were the thundering trucks and the flashing lights? It was an excellent question, and the answer might have been the most important part of the drill. The firefighters and police officers were absent by design. Because in a real tsunami, they will not be there. It will just be us, on our own, carrying one another to high ground.

So as you drive to work tomorrow, on top of long buried sewer pipes or across fault lines strained by the weight of our ambition, as you walk home tonight under low-flying airplanes and over frozen rivers, take a minute—just a minute—to contemplate your disaster personality. You've made each other's acquaintance, after all this time, by finishing this book. Now that you have, you should keep in touch. You might need each other one day.

Author's Note

Survivors offer our greatest hope for reconstructing disasters—not just the plot, but also the smells, the sounds, and the spontaneous acts of kindness. Their memories of the banal and the horrifying are portals into the unknown.

It is important to acknowledge, though, that memory is imperfect. I have in some cases interviewed five survivors from the same disaster and heard five very different sets of facts. These distortions of time and space happen for good reason, as other parts of this book explain. The passage of time also leads to revisions, as our minds work to create a narrative of the event that makes sense, and as media reports begin to congeal around a story line. Then there is also the simple problem of forgetting. Memory fades, of course, and in some cases, I've asked survivors to remember details from two or three decades ago.

I have tried to compensate for the frailties of memory in three ways. First, I checked and supplemented survivors' recollections with official investigations, books, and media reports. All told, I have consulted more than 1,000 articles from academic journals and mass-market media and at least 75 official reports on specific accidents from the plane crash in Tenerife to the sinking of the *Estonia*. I have also reviewed transcripts and video footage of incidents for which such material exists.

Second, wherever possible, I interviewed multiple survivors from the same disaster in order to identify and resolve major discrepancies. I traveled to several countries in order to talk to as many experts and survivors in person as possible. In each case, I tried to leave the questions open-ended, so as to avoid shaping the answer. Also, in the interest of transparency and accountability, no names in this book have been changed.

Last, I tried to complement the stories of survivors with the best available research. Admittedly, serious research into human behavior in disasters is spotty. The funding has been scarce, with a few exceptions during periods of heightened anxiety. But there is some very good and careful work that has been done—particularly in aviation and in the military—and I rely heavily on this material. It helps to put the anecdotes of survivors in perspective, and it also has the benefit of being extremely interesting.

But in the end, I have to ask the reader to keep in mind that the memories of survivors, like the findings of researchers, are fallible. A book about human behavior is not exempt from the complications it describes.

Anything that is right and true in this book, on the other hand, is the product of collaboration. I am first and last grateful to the survivors who have shared the details of their darkest hours with me—and then shared them again when I returned with follow-up questions and fact-checking queries. Their patience and generosity, even in response to what I am sure were some profoundly foolish questions, have been humbling.

This book relies on the knowledge of experts, from neuroscientists to pilot instructors to police psychologists, who have altogether taken hundreds of hours of time to explain to me what they have learned in words I can understand. I am particularly grateful to Mark Gilbertson, Gordon Gallup Jr., Robyn Gershon, Ronn Langford, the Kansas City Fire Department, Susan Cutter, Dennis Mileti, Kathleen Tierney, and everyone else affiliated with the Natural Hazards Center at the University of Colorado, Boulder.

But I never would have had the time to do this book right if I had not had the blessing of *Time* magazine and managing editors Jim Kelly and Rick Stengel. One of the distinctions about a magazine like *Time* is that there are (still) people there who recognize the importance of getting to know a story through and through before you dare to tell it.

For wisdom, phone numbers, and inspiration, thank you to my colleagues and friends Michael Duffy, Ta-Nehisi Coates, John Cloud, Nancy Gibbs, Priscilla Painton, Michele Orecklin, Eric Roston, Suzy Wagner, Adam Zagorin, Romesh Ratnesar, Daniella Alpher, Lisa Beyer, Aaron Klein, Jay Carney, Amy Sullivan, and Judith Stoler. *Time* photo editor Katie Ellsworth was exceedingly generous in helping me find (and in one case shoot) the pictures for this book. Thank you also to Ellen Charles and Frances Symes, my brilliant and kind research assistants who made no mistakes, except leaving me to get real jobs.

My agent Esmond Harmsworth has been an invaluable ally, counselor, and satirist in this endeavor from beginning to end. Thank you to everyone at Crown and to my editor, Rick Horgan, for "getting it" from the beginning—and for backing this book with resources, passion, and professionalism.

For reporting help, I am grateful to Jane Prendergast in Cincinnati and Sibylla Brodzinsky in Colombia. For help with editing and related magic-making, thank you to Stephen Hubbell, David Carr, Lisa Green, Becca Kornfeld, my PACE book club, Mike Schaffer, Dave Ripley, Louise Ripley, Ben Ripley, and Alan Greenblatt. For advice and encouragement on every single thing, from word choice to storytelling to font to web strategy, thank you to my husband, John Funge.

Appendix 1

How to Boost Your Survival Odds

By Amanda Ripley

This is not a book about how to build an emergency kit or make a plan. The world has more than enough pamphlets, manuals, and websites about that already. Personally, I find long checklists most useful after the fact, and flat and forgettable the rest of the time.

This is a book about how the brain works—and the remarkable things human beings can do if they get to know their disaster personalities before they really need them. It is a book populated by stories, people, and science.

For some people, getting to know these characters and how the brain works is enough. It's intellectually compelling to explore this mysterious part of the human condition, and the practical implications for the future flow naturally from there.

But many other people have come to me since the hardcover edition of the book came out and asked me for specific action items. They want more than talk, and I respect them for it. So for those people, here is a collection of things I would do (and have done) that are not to be found on most traditional preparedness lists. Each follows from one basic idea: You matter more than you think.

1. Cultivate Resilience:

It turns out attitude really does make a difference. People who perform effectively in crises and recover well afterward tend to have three underlying advantages:

- They believe they can influence what happens to them.
- They find meaningful purpose in life's turmoil.
- They are convinced they can learn from both good and bad experiences.

We tend to think of a healthy attitude as fixed: You have it or you don't. But the more we learn about the brain, the more we realize that most abilities are like juggling or reading: We have potential, and practice makes us much better. We can build resilience through rehearsal, just as we learn a new language by practicing it over and over again.

When you find yourself feeling overwhelmed by everyday trials, tell yourself you can influence what happens to you. Tell yourself there is meaningful purpose here, and repeat over and over that you can learn from this ordeal. Even if you don't entirely believe it, your brain is listening. Nobody in the first week of a foreign-language class believes comprehension will come, but it happens anyway, eventually, with enough practice.

2. Get to Know Your Neighbors:

If you know that an elderly man lives alone three doors down and a woman with a generator lives around the block, your community will be better equipped to handle most disasters than if you had a bunker full of canned goods.

In most major disasters, as this book illustrates, the people who will save you will not be wearing badges. They will be your neighbors and your coworkers. Towns across the country (such as Ashland, Oregon, and King County, Washington) have mapped their neighborhoods to help identify assets and vulnerabilities. One way to do this is the formal way, through your local Community Emergency Response Team (CERT: citizencorps.gov/cert/).

Or you could buy a case of beer and throw a block party. Pass around a sign-up sheet, have people write down what they might need help with in an emergency and what help they might be able to offer. Make sure everyone has a list of everyone else's phone numbers and e-mail addresses—and an assignment for whom they are supposed to check on the next time the sky opens up or the sun melts the asphalt.

Every year, people are saved from destruction because they knew their neighbors. This is a tradition that has kept our species thriving for many millennia, and it is nothing but foolish to abandon it now.

3. Lower Your Anxiety Level:

People with higher everyday anxiety levels may have a greater tendency to overreact or to misread danger signs, as I explain in chapter 6. If you can learn to control your anxiety, you will benefit in all kinds of ways. Your health should improve and, if you ever find yourself in a life-or-death situation, you have a better chance of being able to control your fear response—and maintain your ability to make decisions and process new information.

Thousands of books have been written on how to lower anxiety. I find that the best place to start is with the activity we do every minute of every day. As I explain in more detail in the chapter on fear, the breath is the only reliable bridge between the conscious mind and the subconscious. So it makes sense to learn how to manipulate it to your advantage. Police officers are now trained to do rhythmic breathing whenever their guns are drawn. They perform better as a result. Yoga or martial arts can achieve the same ends. The best athletes use their breath to relax, focus, and win.

Next time you are immobilized in a traffic jam, practice breathing in for four counts, holding for four counts, and breathing out for four counts. Then repeat. Your driving will improve, and possibly your day.

4. Lose Weight:

I hate to nag, but there is no workaround here. The harsh truth is that obese people move more slowly, are more vulnerable to secondary injuries such as heart attacks, and have a harder time physically recovering from any injuries they do sustain. There is no need to say much more, since there are entire industries devoted to this particularly modern and maddening challenge. But it's worth remembering that on 9/11, people with low physical ability were three times as likely to be hurt while evacuating the towers. Once again, what helps us in regular life helps us in disasters.

5. Calculate Your Risk:

Make a list of your biggest risks. Try to use data, not just emotion. The chapters on Risk and Resilience in this book document how your vulnerabilities vary depending on who you are right now: young, old, male, female, rich, poor. But geography matters too. Check the website for your state or county homeland-security or emergency-management office in order to get a short list of local hazards. If that doesn't work (and it often doesn't, sadly), enter your zip code at floodsmart.gov to get an estimate of your flood risk. Try eqint.cr.usgs.gov/eqprob/2002 to map your earthquake risk. The website for this book (TheUnthinkable.com) lists other tools—on the blog under "Preparedness."

Honestly, the government should make this easier for us. I hope that happens one day. For now, it's still easier than it ever has been. One rule to live by: the most deadly, underappreciated threats in most places are fire, flood, and lightning. Get a smoke detector, replace the batteries every time you change your clocks (or sooner), evacuate well in advance of a major storm, and do not, I repeat do not, drive or walk through water.

Realize that your brain will err on the side of overconfidence when it comes to fire, flood, and lightning—just as it errs on the side of laziness when it comes to getting up at 5:30 in the morning. Both can be overcome with the right motivation and a little knowledge of the consequences.

6. Train Your Brain

By far, the best way to improve performance is to practice. Once you know your real risks, think creatively about how to give yourself or your family a dress rehearsal. The brain loves body memory. It is much better to stop, drop, and roll than to talk about stopping, dropping, and rolling.

For example, we know that fires generally kill more people than all other disasters combined. (If you are poor or African American, your chances of being in a fire are particularly high.) So give your brain something to work with. Make surprise drills an annual tradition in your office or home. Take the stairs down to the ground—don't just stare at the stairwell door.

Create incentives so that people want to do this. This is not hard, but it is still rare. For example, have the boss tell everyone they have to go on a fire drill. That is absolutely essential. Have the boss explain why it matters (because our brains turn to mush in a real fire, and we often lose our eyesight because of smoke). Then announce that the official meeting spot will be the coffee shop two blocks away, where the boss will buy everyone coffee. That way, you boost office morale at the same time. Over doughnuts, tell the story of Rick Rescorla from the Conclusion of this book—or your own tale of walking through hellfire. Storytelling is essential to survival. It's what turns preparation into ritual and victims into saviors.

Appendix 2

Notes

INTRODUCTION: "LIFE BECOMES LIKE MOLTEN METAL"

The Halifax Explosion
See S. H. Prince, "Catastrophe and Social Change."

Material was also drawn from the very helpful archives of Nova Scotia, which can be accessed here: http://www.gov.ns.ca/nsarm/virtual/explosion.asp.

Samuel Prince
See Leonard F. Hatfield, *Sammy the Prince.*

Mayor Ray Nagin
Nagin's quotes come from John Pope's article in the *Times-Picayune.*

The Exploding Streets of Guadalajara
"Ordinary citizens are amazingly capable of avoiding deadly harm," concluded epidemiologist Thomas Glass after completing an extensive National Science Foundation study of ten major disasters, including Guadalajara. "What the lay public does, both individually and collectively, will make the greatest difference in the ultimate outcome."

Survivability of Airplane Accidents
This data comes from the National Transportation Safety Board's *Surviv-ability of Accidents Involving Part 121 U.S. Air Carrier Operations, 1983 Through 2000.*

7/7 Attacks in London
This information comes from the 7 July Review Committee, *Report of the 7 July Review Committee.*

The Conundrum of Modern Civilizations
Here is a good example of what I mean: In May of 2007, a tornado utterly flattened the Kansas town of Greensburg, located smack in the middle of Tornado Alley. Three days later, Major General Tod Bunting, director of emergency management for the state, made the vow that all officials now make after a disaster, mistaking defiance for strength. He promised CNN that the town would be back, that the enemy, whoever that might be, would never win: "You know what? This is America. We build where we want to build. We live where we want to live."

For a thorough description of America's complicated relationship with hazards, see Dennis Mileti, *Disasters by Design.*

The Two Kinds of Evolution
For more on this concept, see Richard Dawkins, *The Selfish Gene.*

More Than 80 Percent of Americans Live in Cities
United Nations Department of Economic and Social Affairs, *World Urban-ization Prospects: The 2005 Revision.*

Hawaiian Tsunami
For more on the Hawaii tsunami, see Brian F. Atwater et al., "Surviving a Tsunami—Lessons from Chile, Hawaii, and Japan," *U.S. Geological Survey,* and Richard Horton, "Threats to Human Survival," *The Lancet.*

Risk of a Disaster
Amanda Ripley, "Why We Don't Prepare for Disaster," *Time.*

Hunter S. Thompson
I am indebted to at least two and maybe three people for this quote. First, my

friend David Carr introduced me to it. The quote is part of his e-mail signature, and I shamelessly lifted it. The quote itself, meanwhile, is widely attributed to Thompson in many different places. But it is also, in other places, described as an Indian proverb. I thank them all.

CHAPTER 1: DELAY

Lethargy in Fire
Guylène Proulx, "Cool Under Fire," *Fire Protection Engineering*.

Laughter During an Emergency Landing
Matthew Kaminski's column appeared in the *Wall Street Journal* on May 19, 2006.

NIST Report on 9/11
The federal government's in-depth investigation into the collapse of the World Trade Center was conducted by the National Institute of Standards and Technology. It is a massive and extremely helpful document. Of the forty-two companion reports, one in particular (NIST NCSTAR 1-7: "Occupant Behavior, Egress, and Emergency Communication") was most relevant to this book. To see the full report, go to http://wtc.nist.gov/pubs/.

Gathering Before Evacuating on 9/11
This survey of 1,444 Trade Center evacuees, funded by the Centers for Disease Control and Prevention and the Association of Schools of Public Health, was conducted by Robyn R. M. Gershon and her team at Columbia University's Mailman School of Public Health. The final quantitative results had not yet been published at the time of this book's printing, but Gershon shared what she'd learned with me in several meetings from 2004 to 2006. You can see many of her findings here: www.mailman.hs.columbia.edu/CPHP/wtc/. Most of the data cited in this book are also included in Gershon's 2007 IRB-Investigator presentation, available on the site.

Fire Marshals in 1993
The quote on training comes from Rita F. Fahy and Guylène Proulx, "Collective Common Sense: A Study of Human Behavior During the World Trade Center Evacuation," *NFPA Journal* (Mar./Apr. 1995): 59–67. The emphasis is mine.

9/11 Commission
The testimony of Alan Reiss can be found here: www.9-11commission
.gov/hearings/hearing11/reiss_statement.pdf. The rest of this invaluable report can be seen here: http://www.9-11commission.gov/. Details on the repeater system start on page 297.

CHAPTER 2: RISK

Hurricane Katrina Evacuation
New Orleans mayor Ray Nagin's quotes come from the Associated Press and
the *New Orleans Times-Picayune,* both dated August 28, 2005.

For a summary of the evacuation's little-known success stories, see Cole-
man Warner, "Contrarians Call Katrina Evacuation a Success," *Newhouse
News Service,* Dec. 28, 2005. The figure about the number of carless households in New Orleans comes from the U.S. Census Bureau, 2004 Community Survey.

For the prescient five-part report on what a major hurricane would do to
New Orleans, see John McQuaid and Mark Schleifstein, "In Harm's Way,"
New Orleans Times-Picayune, June 23, 2002, and the rest of the series, run-
ning through June 27, 2002.

Unintended Consequences of War
For more on this general concept, see Nassim Nicholas Taleb, *The Black
Swan.*

As for the U.S. finding that the Iraq war became a "cause célèbre" for ji-
hadists, you can see declassified portions of the report here: www.dni.gov/
press_releases/Declassified_NIE_Key_Judgments.pdf.

Hurricane Katrina
Knight Ridder's analysis of 486 Katrina victims showed that black victims
outnumbered whites by 51 percent to 44 percent. But in the area overall,
blacks outnumbered whites by 61 percent to 36 percent. The database was
compiled from official government information as well as interviews with survivors of the dead. The database is far from complete. But Knight Ridder
found similar patterns in another analysis comparing the locations where 874
bodies were recovered to U.S. census tract data. For more, see John Simer-
man, Dwight Ott, and Ted Mellnik, "Stats Shake Beliefs About Hurricane;

New Information About Katrina Suggests That Victims Weren't Disproportionately Poor or Black," *Knight Ridder Newspapers*, Dec. 30, 2005.

Max Mayfield's quote comes from a speech I saw him deliver at the National Association of Government Communicators conference in Baltimore on May 25, 2006. The poll of New Orleans residents who did not evacuate is from Mollyann Brodie et al., "Experiences of Hurricane Katrina Evacuees in Houston Shelters: Implications for Future Planning," *Research and Practice* (Mar. 29, 2006).

Competing Causes of Death

For a list of the leading causes of deaths in the United States, see "Deaths: Final Data for 2003," *National Vital Statistics Reports* 54, no. 13 (Apr. 19, 2006); http://www.cdc.gov/nchs/data/nvsr/nvsr54/nvsr54_13.pdf/.

The odds of killing yourself versus being killed by someone else come from David Ropeik and George Gray, *Risk*, Appendix 1.

Kahneman and Tversky

Both men were prolific, but one of their most important papers on risk is Daniel Kahneman and Amos Tversky, "Prospect Theory: An Analysis of Decision Under Risk."

The Donut Quiz

This classic problem has been cited in many studies, including Shane Frederick, "Cognitive Reflection and Decision Making," *Journal of Economic Perspectives* 19, no. 4 (Fall 2005): 25–42.

Increased Driving Fatalities After 9/11

There have been at least two other studies illustrating this phenomenon. I've chosen here to cite the results of the most comprehensive one: Garrick Blalock, Vrinda Kadiyali, and Daniel H. Simon, "Driving Fatalities After 9/11: A Hidden Cost of Terrorism," accepted for publication in *Applied Economics* in 2007. Another study, which did not control for as many factors and looked only at rural interstate highway deaths, found that an estimated fifteen hundred Americans died after 9/11 because they drove instead of flying: Gerd Gigerenzer, "Out of the Frying Pan into the Fire: Behavioral Reactions to Terrorist Attacks," *Risk Analysis* 26, no. 2 (2006).

One other interesting factoid from the third study on this subject: for any trip over thirty-six kilometers (in other words, any trip in which flying is even an option), the air remains safer than the road, according to Michael Sivack and Michael J. Flannagan, "Flying and Driving after the September 11 Attacks," *American Scientist* (Jan./Feb. 2003).

The Personalities of Hazards
Paul Slovic, *The Perception of Risk*.

Fire Deaths
The National Fire Protection Association has a wealth of information on fires—when they happen, why, and what would prevent them from happening. It's all on their website at www.nfpa.org.

Least Hazardous States
This list comes from Dennis Mileti's *Disasters by Design*, which was published in 1999. The list can be expected to change with time.

Three Mile Island
See Robert A. Stallings, "Evacuation Behavior at Three Mile Island."

The Lake Wobegon Effect
The data on Hurricane Floyd drownings come from: "Morbidity and Mortality Associated with Hurricane Floyd—North Carolina, September–October 1999," *Morbidity and Mortality Weekly Report* 49, no. 17 (May 5, 2000): 369–372.

Men are more than twice as likely as women to die during a thunderstorm, according to a study by Thomas J. Songer at the University of Pittsburgh, which is described here: "Seventy Percent of Thunderstorm-Related Deaths Occur in Men," *Public Health* (Fall 2003).

The survey of people living in hurricane zones is here: Robert J. Blendon et al., "High-Risk Area Hurricane Survey."

For more on our tendency toward unrealistic optimism, see Shelley E. Taylor, *Positive Illusions: Creative Self-Deception and the Healthy Mind* 10–11; and Neil Weinstein, "Unrealistic Optimism About Susceptibility to Health Problems: Conclusions from a Community-wide Sample," *Journal of Behavioral Medicine*. The survey measuring predictions of terrorism risk is here: Jennifer S. Lerner, Roxana M. Gonzalez, Deborah A. Small, and Baruch Fischhoff, "Effects of Fear and Anger on Perceived Risks of Terrorism: A National Field Experiment," *Psychological Science* 14, no. 2 (Mar. 2003).

The Connection Between Weather and Stocks
See David Hirshleifer and Tyler Shumway, "Good Day Sunshine: Stock Returns and the Weather."

Our Dependence on Emotions
For the full story of Elliot, see Antonio R. Damasio, *Descartes' Error.*

Crafting Better Warnings
The survey of passengers involved in airplane evacuations comes from: National Transportation Safety Board, *Emergency Evacuation of Commercial Airplanes.* And for more on the suggestions of U.K. civilians, see Lauren J. Thomas, Sophie O'Ferrall, and Antoinette Caird-Daley, *Evacuation Commands for Optimal Passenger Management.*

Dennis Mileti is one of the foremost experts on warnings in the world. He has published hundreds of reports on the subject. For one of his very helpful primers, see Dennis Mileti et al., "Public Hazards Communication and Education: The State of the Art," *Natural Hazards Informer.*

Newspaper accounts of "freak" falling deaths are actually very easy to find. Here are the sources for the two examples I cited: Louise Hosie, "Toddler Dies After Cutting Neck on Vase," *Scottish Press Association*, and "Young Polish Man's Dream of New Life Ends in Tragedy," *Wexford People.*

Gambling and the Brain
To understand more about what happens to your brain in a casino, see Camelia M. Kuhnen and Brian Knutson, "The Neural Basis of Financial Risk Taking," *Neuron.*

Case Studies—Good Warnings and Bad
The story of Vanuatu comes from Costas Synolakis, "Self-Centered West's Narrow Focus Puts Lives at Risk," *The Times Higher Education Supplement.*

The Bangladesh example comes from Philippa Howell, "Indigenous Early Warning Indicators of Cyclones: Potential Application in Coastal Bangladesh," *Disaster Studies Working Paper 6.*

Tilly Smith's quote about the tsunami comes from Duncan Larcombe's article in *The Sun.*

The Personal Strategies of Risk Experts

When I interviewed risk experts, I asked them how their studies had influenced their own behavior. They had different answers, depending upon their lifestyles and the focus of their research. But the one response I heard from at least three different experts was that they do one main thing differently: they don't drive unless they have to.

The quote from Bruce Schneier comes from the May 17, 2007, entry on his blog: www.schneier.com/blog.

Television News

For more on how TV footage of disasters correlates with stress levels, see M. A. Schuster et al., "A National Survey of Stress Reactions After the September 11, 2001, Terrorist Attacks," *New England Journal of Medicine*.

CHAPTER 3: FEAR

The 1980 Hostage Crisis in Colombia

Asencio's story is drawn from my interview with him, as well as news articles from the time and his own book on the subject: Diego and Nancy Asencio with Ron Tobias, *Our Man Is Inside*.

The Brain and Fear

One of the best in-depth descriptions of how the brain processes fear—and all emotions—is *The Emotional Brain* by Joseph LeDoux.

The data about the fear reactions of World War II soldiers is from Samuel Stouffer et al., *The American Soldier: Combat and Its Aftermath, Vol. II*.

The study of 115 law enforcement officers involved in shooting incidents is here: J. Michael Rivard et al., "Acute Dissociative Responses in Law Enforcement Officers Involved in Critical Shooting Incidents: The Clinical and Forensic Implications," *Journal of Forensic Science*.

Self-Talk in Crisis Moments

The story of a soldier's conversation with himself comes from Mark Bowden's book, *Guests of the Ayatollah*.

Perceptual Distortions in Police Shootings

Ninety-five percent of eighty officers involved in shootings reported having experienced some kind of distortion during the incident—from tunnel vision to auditory blunting to slow-motion time—according to David Klinger, "Police Responses to Officer-Involved Shootings," *NIJ Journal*, no. 253 (Jan. 2006).

Interestingly, another study of forty-four officers found that 9 percent actually experienced an out-of-body experience during shooting. See R. M. Solomon and J. M. Horn, "Post-Shooting Traumatic Reactions: A Pilot Study," in *Psychological Services for Law Enforcement*, ed. J. T. Reese and H. A. Goldstein (Washington, D.C.: U.S. Government Printing Office, 1986), 383–394.

The story of the police officer who saw "beer cans" floating past his face comes from Alexis Artwohl, "Perceptual and Memory Distortion During Officer-Involved Shootings," *FBI Law Enforcement Bulletin* (Oct. 2002): 18; www.fbi.gov/publications/leb/2002/oct02leb.pdf/.

Slow-Motion Time

At press time, Eagleman's results (co-authored with his graduate students Chess Stetson and Matthew Fiesta) are under review for publication. He shared the results with me over the phone and via e-mail.

For more on this subject, also see the fascinating work of Peter Hancock, a professor at the University of Central Florida who researches time distortion and other stress effects for the U.S. military; http://www.mit.ucf.edu/timeperception.asp.

Learning to Do Better

For more on how police officers learn to master their fear response, see Alexis Artwohl and Loren W. Christensen, *Deadly Force Encounters*.

The importance of knowledge in reducing injury rates on 9/11 is from Gershon's survey.

For more on Siddle's combat-performance research, see Bruce K. Siddle, *Sharpening the Warrior's Edge*.

Tunnel Vision

To experience a mild version of this phenomenon for yourself, check out the video demos put together by the Visual Cognition Lab at the University of Illinois: http://viscog.beckman.uiuc.edu/djs_lab/demos.html.

The details on the crash of the Eastern Air Lines jet in 1972 come from the official investigation: National Transportation Safety Board, *Eastern Air Lines, Inc., L-1011, N310EA, Miami, Florida, December 29, 1972.*

The story of the crash-landing of United Flight 232 in Sioux City, Iowa, in

1989 comes largely from the recollections of Al Haynes, the plane's captain, which can be found here: www.airdisaster.com/eyewitness/ua232.shtml.

The preliminary results of the Rhode Island cell-phone study come from the following press release: http://www.uri.edu/news/releases/html/02-0610.html.

Learning to Do Better, Part ii

The juggling study is here: Bogdan Draganski et al., "Neuroplasticity: Changes in Grey Matter Induced by Training," *Nature* 427 (Jan. 22, 2004): 311–312.

A description of Darren Laur's knife-attack experiment can be found here: Darren Laur, "The Anatomy of Fear and How It Relates to Survival Skills Training," http://www.lwcbooks.com/articles/anatomy.html.

For the study on the brains of meditators, see Sara W. Lazar et al., "Meditation Experience Is Associated with Increased Cortical Thickness," *NeuroReport*.

On the importance of control, real and imagined, see J. Amat et al., "Medial Prefrontal Cortex Determines How Stressor Controllability Affects Behavior and Dorsal Raphe Nucleus," *Nature Neuroscience* 8, no. 3 (Mar. 2005).

Rosemberg Pabón, aka Commandante Uno

The quotes from Pabón, the hostage-taker-turned-government-functionary, come from the only interview I did not do myself. Sibylla Brodzinsky, a reporter in Bogotá, conducted the interview on my behalf, and I am grateful for her excellent work.

CHAPTER 4: RESILIENCE

Resilience Defined

Over the past five years or so, disaster researchers and trauma psychologists have begun to focus more on the people who recover from disasters—instead of the people who don't. This is a massive and important shift, and it comes, naturally, with jargon. In clinical and research circles, the words *resilience, recovery, resistance,* and *hardiness* are all separate but related concepts. Because this is a book for the layperson, I hope the experts will forgive me for using the word *resilience* to mean, in a way, all of the above. Resilience, in this book, refers to whatever it is that makes some people able to perform extraordinarily well during a disaster—and then recover relatively quickly and fully afterward. For more on resilience, see Al Siebert, *The Survivor Personality*.

Physical Fitness

For more on the effect of obesity in car accidents, see Charles N. Mock et al., "The Relationship Between Body Weight and Risk of Death and Serious Injury in Motor Vehicle Crashes," *Accident Analysis and Prevention* 34, no. 2 (Mar. 2002): 221–228.

The increased odds of people with low physical ability getting injured on 9/11 comes from Gershon's survey of Trade Center evacuees.

Gender

For more on how race and gender subtly shape our risk equation, see Dan M. Kahan et al., "Culture and Identity-Protective Cognition: Explaining the White Male Effect in Risk Perception," *Journal of Empirical Legal Studies*.

The Oxfam study on the female victims of the tsunami is here: Oxfam International, "The Tsunami's Impact on Women," *Oxfam Briefing Note* (Mar. 2005).

The greater likelihood for females to have been injured in the Trade Center comes from Gershon's survey data.

Poverty

The data on African American and American Indian fire fatalities come from U.S. Fire Administration/National Fire Data Center, *Fire in the United States 1992–2001,* 13th edition (Emmitsburg, MD: U.S. Fire Administration, Oct. 2004).

For more on the effect of poverty on disasters worldwide, see James McCarthy et al., eds., "Climate Change 2001: Impacts, Adaptation and Vulnerability," Intergovernmental Panel on Climate Change: Insurance and Other Financial Services (2001), 451–486; and Matthew E. Kahn, "The Death Toll from Natural Disasters: The Role of Income, Geography and Institutions," *Review of Economics and Statistics* 87, no. 2 (May 2005): 271–284.

The comparison between the Northridge and the Pakistani earthquake was made by geophysicist John C. Mutter in the following article: Claudia Dreifus, "Earth Science Meets Social Science in Study of Disasters," *New York Times*, Mar. 14, 2006, Science Desk.

Arrogance

For more on resilience overall and the survival value of self-confidence specifically, see George A. Bonanno, "Loss, Trauma, and Human Resilience: Have We Underestimated the Human Capacity to Thrive After Extremely Aversive Events?" *American Psychologist* 59, no. 1 (Jan. 2004): 20–28.

Military Research

For more on Charles Morgan's study of soldiers at Survival School, see Charles A. Morgan III et al., "Plasma Neuropeptide-Y Concentrations in Humans Exposed to Military Survival Training," *Biological Psychiatry* and Charles A. Morgan III et al., "Relationship Among Plasma Cortisol, Catecholamines, Neuropeptide Y, and Human Performance During Exposure to Uncontrollable Stress," *Psychosomatic Medicine*.

The questionnaire used in Morgan's study was the Clinician-Administered Dissociative States Scale. The three sample questions listed in this book are adapted from this questionnaire. For more on this evaluation tool, see J. D. Bremner et al., "Measurement of Dissociative States with the Clinician-Administered Dissociative States Scale (CADSS)," *Journal of Traumatic Stress* 11 (1998): 125–136.

For Morgan's findings on dissociation in soldiers, see Charles A. Morgan III et al., "Symptoms of Dissociation in Humans Experiencing Acute, Uncontrollable Stress: A Prospective Investigation," *American Journal of Psychiatry*.

As for the Vietnam veteran twins, for Mark Gilbertson's study on the relative size of the brothers' hippocampi, see Mark W. Gilbertson et al., "Smaller Hippocampal Volume Predicts Pathologic Vulnerability to Psychological Trauma," *Nature Neuroscience*.

For Gilbertson's analysis of the twins' overall cognitive performance, see Mark W. Gilbertson et al., "Neurocognitive Function in Monozygotic Twins Discordant for Combat Exposure: Relationship to Posttraumatic Stress Disorder," *Journal of Abnormal Psychology* 115, no. 3 (2006): 484–495.

The ratio of Vietnam vets who have suffered from posttraumatic stress disorder comes from R. A. Kulka et al., *The National Vietnam Veterans Readjustment Study: Tables of Findings and Technical Appendices* (New York: Brunner/Mazel, 1990).

CHAPTER 5: GROUPTHINK

The Beverly Hills Supper Club Fire

The details of the fire come from interviews with survivors, newspaper articles from the time, and the following additional sources: Ron Elliott, *Inside the Beverly Hills Supper Club Fire,* and Richard L. Best, "Tragedy in Kentucky," *Fire Journal.*

Many thanks to Jane Prendergast, a Cincinnati-area reporter who helped connect me with Beverly Hills survivors and who also reported back to me about a thirtieth anniversary memorial service that I could not attend myself.

Milling

Lee Clarke's quote on disaster cohorts comes from Lee Clarke, "Panic: Myth or Reality?" *Contexts.*

For information on milling before hurricanes, see Thomas E. Drabek, "Disaster Warning and Evacuation Responses by Private Business Employees," *Disasters.*

The statistic on 9/11 milling comes from the National Institute of Standards and Technology's final report into the collapse of the Trade Center.

Role Playing in Disasters

See Drue M. Johnston and Norris R. Johnson, "Role Extension in Disaster: Employee Behavior at the Beverly Hills Supper Club Fire," *Sociological Focus.*

The Value of the Group

The miners' study is a good example of how groups stick together during life-or-death situations: Charles Vaught et al., *Behavioral and Organizational Dimensions of Underground Mine Fires* (U.S. Dept. of Health and Human Services, 2000).

For more on monkey groups in Indonesia, see Carel P. van Schaik and Maria A. van Noordwijk, "Evolutionary Effect of the Absence of Felids on the Social Organization of the Macaques on the Island of Simeulue," *Folia Primatologica* 44 (1985): 138–147.

The Richard Dawkins quote comes from his book, *The Selfish Gene,* 4.

For more on the concept of the selfish herd, see W. D. Hamilton, "Geometry for the Selfish Herd," *Journal of Theoretical Biology.*

Fire Dynamics

On its website, the Kansas City Fire Department offers a helpful primer on how fire works: Emergency Services Consulting, "Deployment Analysis," Kansas City Fire Department, www.kcmo.org/fire/deploymentanalysis.pdf.

The Need for Leadership

Ian's quote about the need for leadership during a disaster comes from volume 3 of the report of the 7 July Review Committee into the London transit bombings.

The Cranfield study was conducted by Muir and Cobbett in 1996.

Group Resilience

The tale of Jantang and Langi comes from my interview of Lori Dengler as well as her article on the subject: Brian G. McAdoo, Lori Dengler, Gegar Prasetya, and Vasily Titov, "Smong: How an Oral History Saved Thousands on Indonesia's Simeulue Island During the December 2004 and March 2005 Tsunamis," *Earthquake Spectra*.

For more about how companionship boosts our resilience, even on the cellular level, see Lisa F. Berkman, "The Role of Social Relations in Health Promotion," *Psychosomatic Medicine*.

CHAPTER 6: PANIC

Hajj Deaths

Mortality figures were compiled from newspaper clips. Because the media must rely upon imperfect reporting from the Saudi government, the numbers are far from exact.

Ali Hussain and Belquis Sadiq

Unfortunately, despite my best efforts, I was not able to locate Ali Hussain, whose wife perished in a hajj stampede. The details of her death are drawn from the following articles: Neil Atkinson, "'I Was Down for Only Seconds but When I Got Back Up She Had Gone,'" *Huddersfield Daily Examiner*, Jan. 21, 2006, 5; and Robert Sutcliffe, "Yorkshire Man Relives Horror of Wife's Death in Hajj Stampede," *Yorkshire Post*, Jan. 21, 2006.

The Physics of Crowds

The "undisciplined pilgrims" quote is from Salah Nasrawi, "Dropped Baggage was Catalyst for Stampede That Killed 345 Pilgrims in Hajj Stoning Ritual," Associated Press, Jan. 13, 2006.

For more on crowd physics, see the excellent website developed by crowd expert G. Keith Still, www.crowddynamics.com, as well as the *Physical Review* article by Dirk Helbing and colleagues.

Historical Panic (and the Lack Thereof)

For more on Londoners' reaction to the Blitz, see Mollie Panter-Downes, *London War Notes* (New York: Farrar, Straus and Giroux, 1971).

The Three Mile Island information comes from Robert Stallings's article, "Evacuation Behavior at Three Mile Island."

Quarantelli's article is "The Nature and Conditions of Panic," Nov. 1954.

The details of the Manchester crash come from Air Investigations Accident Branch, Incident Report No 8/88.

The survey of passengers involved in serious evacuations comes from the National Transportation Safety Board's *Emergency Evacuation of Commercial Airplanes*.

Details of the 1991 crash at Los Angeles International Airport come from the National Transportation Safety Board's investigation and survival factors report.

The research study in which money was used to create a stampede during an aircraft evacuation drill was conducted by Helen Muir and her colleagues at the Cranfield Institute of Technology.

The Panic of One

The story of the mysterious death of Scott Stich is compiled from the autopsy report from the Palm Beach County Medical Examiner, as well as his obituary ("Obituary for Mr. Scott Stich") and news articles ("Diver Dies") in the *Sun-Sentinel*.

For more on predictions of panic behavior in individuals, see W. P. Morgan, J. S. Raglin, and P. J. O'Connor, "Trait Anxiety Predicts Panic Behavior in Beginning Scuba Students."

CHAPTER 7: PARALYSIS

The Hypnotized Chicken

For more on the history of animal paralysis, see F. A. Volgyesi, *Hypnosis of Man and Animals* and the work of Gordon G. Gallup and John P. Forsyth.

Livingstone's Lion
See David Livingstone, *Travels and Researches in South Africa.*

Sexual Assault Victims
See the forthcoming article by B. Marx (and Forsyth and Gallup) in *Clinical Psychology: Science and Practice.*

The Sinking of the *MV Estonia*
The details of this section are drawn from articles, interviews, and the official report of the sinking: *Final Report on the Capsizing on 28 September 1994 in the Baltic Sea of the Ro-Ro Passenger Vessel MV Estonia.*

Tenerife Crash
Details of this crash come from newspaper accounts of the time, the official investigation report released by the Subsecretaría de Aviación Civil, Spain, and Daniel Johnson's excellent book, *Just in Case.*

CHAPTER 8: HEROISM

The Body in Extreme Cold
For a good explanation on how the body reacts to cold, see Alan C. Burton, *Man in a Cold Environment.*

For more on this, check out www.coolantarctica.com, a website about Antarctica put together by a marine biologist named Paul Ward who lived there for a time.

The Oliners
For the Oliners' investigations into heroism, see *The Altruistic Personality* and *Do Unto Others.*

Andrew Carnegie and the Heroism Fund
See Joseph Frazier Wall, *Andrew Carnegie.*

Ronald Johnson's study of the Carnegie Heroes comes from *IPT Journal.*

Lenny Skutnik
The *Washington Times* story was written by Cathryn Donohoe.

Columbine High School Massacre

The findings of the Jefferson County Sheriff's investigation into the Columbine shootings come from the official report. It can be ordered from the sheriff's office or found in various places online, including *Salon*: archive.salon.com/news/special/columbine_report/index.html. The relevant section is the "Findings of the Library Team."

A remarkably similar narrative captured the public imagination after 9/11. Todd Beamer, a passenger aboard United Flight 93, was heard to have yelled, "Let's roll!" before he and a group of fellow passengers confronted the terrorists. Soon afterward, the plane crashed in a field in Pennsylvania. (Of the four hijacked planes, it was the only one not to hit a target.) "Let's roll" became a chorus for a stricken nation. Neil Young released "Let's Roll," the song, Todd's widow wrote *Let's Roll!* the bestselling book, and President Bush ended a speech to the nation with the words, "My fellow Americans, let's roll." Later, the 9/11 Commission quietly concluded on page 14 of its report that the more likely statement was, "Roll it," a decidedly less inspiring but perhaps more pragmatic command—possibly in reference to a food cart, which the passengers may or may not have used as a battering ram. As is so often the case in disasters, no one will ever really know for sure.

Paying for Interviews

Legitimate reporters, especially of the print variety, do not pay for interviews. The theory is that paying for information increases the chances of getting bad information. Money distorts the relationship between the reporter and the source—a relationship that is already fraught with complications. Or, as the *New York Times*'s ethics policy explains it, "We do not pay for interviews or unpublished documents: to do so would create an incentive for sources to falsify material and would cast into doubt the genuineness of much that we publish."

Of course, even without payment, all sources have an agenda, even if it is to spread the truth or prevent inaccuracies. But money is particularly toxic, even among people with the best of intentions, as anyone who has done battle over a family estate can tell you. Whether this is a perfect policy, I don't know. Certainly, many reporters have violated it. But I think if you asked most readers whether they wanted journalists to pay for information, they would say no.

For all these reasons, I am profoundly grateful to the many hundreds of people who have allowed me to interview them for this book. They have donated endless hours of time, indulging me in all manner of inane conversations and then taking follow-up calls for months afterward—all for free.

CONCLUSION: MAKING NEW INSTINCTS

Rick Rescorla

The story of Rescorla is based on interviews with his widow and his colleagues, as well as news clippings and the wonderfully written portrait of Rescorla by James B. Stewart, *Heart of a Soldier*.

Robert Edwards's documentary was never completed, but as of the printing of this book, you could watch it here: http://www.atomfilms.com/film/voice_prophet.jsp.

The ratio of Trade Center employees who did not know the roof doors would be locked comes from Gershon's survey.

Major Robert L. Bateman's tribute to Rescorla comes from the magazine *Vietnam*.

Fear of Litigation

The comments from fire-safety officials about New York City's new rules were made at a September 15, 2006, meeting held in New York by Columbia University's Mailman School of Public Health. The meeting was held to discuss the implications and early findings of Robyn Gershon's evacuation study.

Mayor Nagin's concerns about liability come from Bruce Nolan's *Times-Picayune* story on August 28, 2005.

The study of parent-taught driver's education was conducted by V. J. Pezoldt, K. N. Womack, and D. E. Morris at the Texas Transportation Institute.

Room for Improvement

The Temple University study on spatial reasoning was conducted by Melissa Terlecki et al.

Appendix 3

Selected Bibliography

Air Accidents Investigations Branch. *Report on the Accident to Boeing 737-236, G-BGJL at Manchester International Airport on 22 August 1985.* Aircraft Incident Report No. 8/88. London: UK Dept. of Transport, 1988.

Alcock, John. *Animal Behavior.* 7th ed. Sunderland, MA: 2001.

Artwohl, Alexis, and Loren W. Christensen. *Deadly Force Encounters.* Boulder, CO: Paladin Press, 1997.

Asencio, Diego, and Nancy Asencio with Ron Tobias. *Our Man Is Inside.* Boston: Little, Brown and Company, 1983.

Atkinson, Neil. "'I Was Down for Only Seconds but When I Got Back Up She Had Gone.'" *Huddersfield Daily Examiner*, Jan. 21, 2006, 5.

Atwater, Brian F., Marco V. Cisternas, Joanne Bourgeois, Walter C. Dudley, James W. Hendley II, and Peter H. Stauffer. "Surviving a Tsunami—Lessons from Chile, Hawaii, and Japan." U.S. Geological Survey Circular 1187, Version 1.1 (2005).

Bateman, Major Robert L. "Rick Rescorla: Ia Drang Hero." *Vietnam*, Jun. 2002.

Berkman, Lisa F. "The Role of Social Relations in Health Promotion." *Psychosomatic Medicine* 57 (1995): 245–254.

Best, Richard L. "Tragedy in Kentucky," *Fire Journal* (Jan. 1978).

Blanke, Olaf et al. "Out of Body Experience and Autoscopy of Neurological Origin." *Brain* 127, no. 2 (2004).

Blendon, Robert J. et al. "High-Risk Area Hurricane Survey." Harvard

School of Public Health Project on the Public and Biological Security, 2006; http://www.hsph.harvard.edu/hurricane/topline.doc/.

Bowden, Mark. *Guests of the Ayatollah*. New York: Grove Press, 2006.

Brooks, Charles. *Disaster at Lisbon: The Great Earthquake of 1755*. Long Beach: Shangton Longley Press, 1994.

Bryan, John L. "Behavioral Response to Fire and Smoke." *The SFPE Handbook of Fire Protection Engineering*. 3rd ed. Quincy, MA: National Fire Protection Association, 2002.

Burton, Alan C. *Man in a Cold Environment*. New York: Hafner, 1955.

Cirillo, Jim. *Guns, Bullets, and Gunfights: Lessons and Tales from a Modern-Day Gunfighter*. Boulder, CO: Paladin Press, 1996.

Clarke, Lee. "Panic: Myth or Reality?" *Contexts* 1, no. 3 (Fall 2002).

Damasio, Antonio R. *Descartes' Error*. New York: Putnam, 1994.

Davis, Lynn E. et al. *Individual Preparedness and Response to Chemical, Radiological, Nuclear and Biological Terrorist Attacks: A Quick Guide*. Santa Monica, CA: RAND, 2003; www.rand.org/pubs/monograph_reports/MR1731.1/.

Dawkins, Richard. *The Selfish Gene*. Oxford: Oxford University Press, 1989.

"Diver Dies," *Sun-Sentinel*, Jun. 1, 1993, 3B, Palm Beach Edition.

Donohoe, Cathryn. "Anniversary of Sorrow." *The Washington Times*, Jan. 13, 1992, A1.

Downey, Cheryl. "Vacation Turned to Tragedy in World's Deadliest Air Crash." *Orange County Register*, Mar. 22, 1987, A1, Evening Edition.

Drabek, Thomas E. "Disaster Warning and Evacuation Responses by Private Business Employees." *Disasters* 25, no. 1 (2001): 76–94.

Elliott, Ron. *Inside the Beverly Hills Supper Club Fire*. Paducah, KY: Turner Publishing Co., 1996.

Federation of American Scientists. *Analysis of Ready.gov*. Washington, D.C.: updated regularly. Accessed for this book in August 2007 at www.fas.org/reallyready/analysis.html.

Final Report on the Capsizing on 28 September 1994 in the Baltic Sea of the Ro-Ro Passenger Vessel MV Estonia. Helsinki: The Joint Accident Investigation Commission of Estonia, Finland and Sweden and Edita Ltd., Dec. 1997.

Gershon, Robyn R. M. "A Roadmap for the Protection of Disaster Research Participants: Findings from the WTC Evacuation Study." Paper presented at Columbia University's monthly Institutional Review Board investigator meeting, New York, NY, March 20, 2007.

Gershon, Robyn R. M., Kristine A. Qureshi, Marcie S. Rubinand, and Victoria H. Raveis. *World Trade Center Evacuation Study*. [Quantitative results not yet published at time of book's printing, but findings can be viewed here: www.mailman.hs.columbia.edu/CPHP/wtc/.]

Gigerenzer, Gerd. "Out of the Frying Pan and into the Fire: Behavioral Reactions to Terrorist Attacks." *Risk Analysis* 26, no. 2 (2006).

Gilbertson, Mark W. et al. "Smaller Hippocampal Volume Predicts Pathological Vulnerability to Psychological Trauma." *Nature Neuroscience* 5, no. 11 (Nov. 2002): 1242–1247.

Glass, Thomas A. "Understanding Public Response to Disasters." *Public Health Reports* 116, Suppl. 2 (2001): 69–73.

Gonzales, Laurence. *Deep Survival*. New York: W. W. Norton, 2003.

Grossman, Dave. *On Combat*. Millstadt, IL: PPCT Research Publications, 2004.

Hallett-Hughes, Lucy. *Heroes: A History of Hero Worship*. New York: Knopf, 2004.

Hamilton, W. D. "Geometry for the Selfish Herd." *Journal of Theoretical Biology* 31 (1971): 295–311.

Hariri, Ahmad et al. "Serotonin Transporter Genetic Variation and the Response of the Human Amygdala." *Science* 297, no. 5580 (Jul. 19, 2002).

Hatfield, Leonard F. *Sammy the Prince: The Story of Samuel Henry Prince*. Hantsport, Nova Scotia: Lancelot Press, 1990.

Helbing, Dirk, Anders Johannson, and Habib Zein Al-Abideen. "The Dynamics of Crowd Disasters: An Empirical Study." *Physical Review* E75 (2007).

Hershfield, Valerie. "The Worst Part Was the Fear of the Unknown." *National Fire Protection Association Journal* (Mar./Apr. 1995): 64–67.

Hirshleifer, David, and Tyler Shumway. "Good Day Sunshine: Stock Returns and the Weather." Dice Center Working Paper No. 2001-3 (2001); http://papers.ssrn.com/id=265674/.

Horton, Richard. "Threats to Human Survival." *The Lancet* 365 (Jan. 15, 2005).

Hosie, Louise. "Toddler Dies After Cutting Neck on Vase." *Scottish Press Association*, Feb. 19, 2007, Home News Section.

Howell, Philippa. "Indigenous Early Warning Indicators of Cyclones: Potential Application in Coastal Bangladesh." *Disaster Studies Working Paper 6*, Benfield Hazard Research Centre, Jul. 2003.

Jefferson County Sheriff's Office. *Columbine High School Shootings, April 20, 1999: The Jefferson County Sheriff's Office Report*. Boulder, CO: Quality Data Systems, May 15, 2000.

Johnson, Daniel A. *Just in Case: A Passenger's Guide to Airplane Safety and Survival*. New York: Plenum Press, 1984.

Johnson, Ronald C. "Attributes of Persons Performing Acts of Heroism and of the Recipients of These Acts," *IPT Journal* 12 (2002).

Johnston, Drue M., and Norris R. Johnson. "Role Extension in Disaster: Employee Behavior at the Beverly Hills Supper Club Fire." *Sociological Focus* 22, no. 1 (1988): 39–51.

Kahan, Dan M. "Culture and Identity-Protective Cognition: Explaining the White-Male Effect in Risk Perception." *Journal of Empirical Legal Studies* 4, no. 3 (2007): 465–505.

Kahneman, Daniel, and Amos Tversky. "Prospect Theory: An Analysis of Decision Under Risk." *Econometrica* 47, no. 2 (Mar. 1979): 263–292.

Kaminski, Matthew. "Brace! Brace! Over the Atlantic, a Bit of Panic." *Wall Street Journal,* May 19, 2006.

Kates, R. W. "Hazard and Choice Perception in Flood Plain Management." Research Paper No. 78. University of Chicago, Department of Geography, 1962.

Kauffman, Captain R. H. "Warning: Hotels Could Be Hazardous to Your Health." LA County Fire Dept., n.d.

Kuhnen, Camelia M., and Brian Knutson. "The Neural Basis of Financial Risk Taking." *Neuron* 47 (2005): 763–770.

Larcombe, Duncan. "Mummy, We Must Get Off Beach . . . Now." *The Sun,* Jan. 1, 2005.

Lazar, Sara W. et al. "Meditation Experience Is Associated with Increased Cortical Thickness." *NeuroReport* 16, no. 17 (Nov. 28, 2005).

LeDoux, Joseph. *The Emotional Brain*. New York: Simon & Schuster, 1996.

Livingstone, David. *Travels and Researches in South Africa*. Whitefish, MT: Kessinger Publishing, 2004.

Marincioni, Fausto. "A Cross-Cultural Analysis of Natural Disaster Response: The Northwest Italy Floods of 1994 Compared to the U.S. Midwest Floods of 1993." *International Journal of Mass Emergencies and Disasters* 19, no. 2 (Aug. 2001): 209–239.

Marx, B. et al. "Tonic Immobility as an Evolved Predator Defence: Implications for Sexual Assault Survivors." *Clinical Psychology: Science and Practice* (forthcoming).

McAdoo, Brian G., Lori Dengler, Gegar Prasetya, and Vasily Titov. "Smong: How an Oral History Saved Thousands on Indonesia's Simeulue Island During the December 2004 and March 2005 Tsunamis." *Earthquake Spectra* 22, no. S3 (2006): S661–S669.

McQuaid, John, and Mark Schleifstein. "In Harm's Way." *New Orleans Times-Picayune,* Jun. 23–27, 2002.

Mileti, Dennis. *Disasters by Design: A Reassessment of Natural Hazards in the United States.* New York: Joseph Henry Press, 1999.

Mileti, Dennis, Thomas Drabek, and J. Eugene Haas. *Human Systems in Extreme Environments: A Sociological Perspective.* Program on Technology, Environment and Man. Monograph #21. Institute of Behavioral Science, University of Colorado, 1975.

Mileti, Dennis et al. "Public Hazards Communication and Education: The State of the Art." *Natural Hazards Informer* 2 (2004).

Miller, Ian. "Human Behaviour Contributing to Unintentional Residential Fire Deaths 1997–2003." New Zealand Fire Service Commission Research Report Number 47, 2005.

Mills, Eleanor. "The Drowned and the Saved," *The Observer,* Jan. 28, 1996, 9.

Morgan, Charles A. III et al. "Plasma Neuropeptide-Y Concentrations in Humans Exposed to Military Survival Training." *Biological Psychiatry* 47 (2000): 902–909.

Morgan, Charles A. III et al. "Relationship among Plasma Cortisol, Catecholamines, Neuropeptide Y, and Human Performance During Exposure to Uncontrollable Stress." *Psychosomatic Medicine* 63 (2001): 412–422.

Morgan, Charles A. III et al. "Symptoms of Dissociation in Humans Experiencing Acute, Uncontrollable Stress: A Prospective Investigation." *American Journal of Psychiatry* 158, no. 8 (Aug. 2001): 1239–1247.

Morgan, William P. "Anxiety and Panic in Recreational Scuba Divers," *Sports Medicine* 20, no. 6 (1995): 398–421.

Morgan, W. P., J. S. Raglin, and P. J. O'Connor. "Trait Anxiety Predicts Panic Behavior in Beginning Scuba Students." *International Journal of Sports Medicine* 25 (2004): 314–322.

Muir, Helen, and Ann Cobbett. *Influence of Cabin Behaviour in Emergency*

Evacuations at Floor Level Exits. CAA Paper 95006. London: Civil Aviation Authority, 1996.

Muir, Helen, Claire Marrison, and Alyson Evans. *Aircraft Evacuations: The Effect of Passenger Motivation and Cabin Configuration Adjacent to the Exit*. CAA Paper 89019. London: Civil Aviation Authority, Nov. 1989.

National Institute of Standards and Technology. *Final Reports of the Federal Building and Fire Investigation of the World Trade Center Disaster*, Washington, D.C.: U.S. Department of Commerce, Sept. 2005.

National Transportation Safety Board. *Runway Collision of US Air Flight 1493, Boeing 737 and Skywest Flight 5569 Fairchild Metroliner, Los Angeles International Airport, Los Angeles, California, February 1, 1991*. Aircraft Accident Report NTSB/AAR-91/08. Washington, D.C.: NTSB, 1991.

National Transportation Safety Board. *Runway Collision of US Air Flight 1493, Boeing 737 and Skywest Flight 5569 Fairchild Metroliner, Los Angeles International Airport, Los Angeles, California, February 1, 1991*. Survival Factors Group Chairman's Factual Report of Investigation. Washington, D.C.: NTSB, Apr. 12, 1991.

National Transportation Safety Board. *Eastern Air Lines, Inc., L-1011, N310EA, Miami, Florida, December 29, 1972*. Aircraft Accident Report NTSB-AAR-73-14. Washington, D.C.: NTSB, 1973.

National Transportation Safety Board. *Emergency Evacuation of Commercial Airplanes*. Safety Study NTSB/SS-00/01. Washington, D.C.: NTSB, 2000.

National Transportation Safety Board. *Survivability of Accidents Involving Part 121 U.S. Air Carrier Operations, 1983 Through 2000*. Safety Report NTSB/SR-01/01. Washington, D.C.: NTSB, 2001.

Nolan, Bruce. "Katrina Takes Aim." *New Orleans Times-Picayune*, Aug. 28, 2005, 1.

"Obituary for Mr. Scott Stich." *Sun-Sentinel*, Jun. 3, 1993, 6B, Final Edition.

Oliner, Samuel P. *Do Unto Others*. Cambridge, MA: Westview Press, 2003.

Oliner, Samuel P., and Pearl M. Oliner. *The Altruistic Personality*. New York: The Free Press, 1988.

Palm Beach County Medical Examiner. *Autopsy Report for Mr. Scott Stich*. ME Case No. 93–0467. West Palm Beach, FL: Medical Examiner Office, Jun. 15, 1993.

Pezoldt, V. J., K. N. Womack, and D. E. Morris. *Parent-Taught Driver Education in Texas: A Comparative Evaluation*. College Station, TX:

National Highway Traffic Safety Administration, 2007.

Pope, John. "Evoking King, Nagin Calls N.O. 'Chocolate' City." *New Orleans Times-Picayune,* Jan. 17, 2006, 1.

Prince, S. H. "Catastrophe and Social Change." PhD diss., Columbia University, 1920.

Proulx, Guylène. "Cool Under Fire." *Fire Protection Engineering* 16 (2002): 23–24; http://www.fpemag.com/_pdf/archives/FPE_FALL_2002.pdf

Proulx, Guylène, Rita F. Fahy, and Amber Walker. *Analysis of First-Person Accounts from Survivors of the World Trade Center Evacuation on September 11, 2001.* National Research Council of Canada Report, Oct. 2004.

Quarantelli, Enrico L. "The Nature and Conditions of Panic." *American Journal of Sociology* 60, no. 3 (Nov. 1954): 267–275.

Ripley, Amanda. "Why We Don't Prepare for Disaster." *Time*, Aug. 28, 2006, 31.

Rivard, J. Michael et al. "Acute Dissociative Responses in Law Enforcement Officers Involved in Critical Shooting Incidents: The Clinical and Forensic Implications." *Journal of Forensic Science* 47, no. 5 (Sept. 2002): 1093–1100.

Ropeik, David, and George Gray. *Risk: A Practical Guide for Deciding What's Really Safe and What's Really Dangerous in the World Around You.* Boston: Houghton Mifflin, 2002.

Schuster, M. A. et al. "A National Survey of Stress Reactions After the September 11, 2001, Terrorist Attacks." *New England Journal of Medicine* 345 (2001): 1507–1512.

The 7 July Review Committee. *Report of the 7 July Review Committee.* London: Greater London Authority, Jun. 2006.

Siddle, Bruce K. *Sharpening the Warrior's Edge.* Belleville: PPCT Research Publications, 2005.

Siebert, Al. *The Survivor Personality.* New York: Perigee, 1996.

Slovic, Paul. *The Perception of Risk.* London: Earthscan Publications, 2000.

Stallings, Robert A. "Evacuation Behavior at Three Mile Island." *International Journal of Mass Emergencies and Disasters* 2, no. 1 (1984).

Stewart, James B. *Heart of a Soldier.* New York: Simon & Schuster, 2002.

Stouffer, Samuel et al. *The American Soldier: Combat and Its Aftermath.* Princeton, NJ: Princeton University Press, 1949.

Subsecretaría de Aviación Civil, Spain. *KLM, B-747, PH-BUF and Pan Am, B-747, N736, Collision at Tenerife Airport, Spain, on 27 March 1977.* Joint Report, English version. Madrid: Oct. 1978.

Synolakis, Costas. "Self-Centered West's Narrow Focus Puts Lives at Risk." *The Times Higher Education Supplement*, Jan. 14, 2005, 16.

Taleb, Nassim Nicholas. *The Black Swan*. New York: Random House, 2007.

Taylor, Shelley E. *Positive Illusions: Creative Self-Deception and the Healthy Mind*. New York: Basic Books, 1989.

Terlecki, Melissa S., Nora S. Newcombe, and Michelle Little. "Durable and Generalized Effects of Spatial Experience on Mental Rotation: Gender Differences in Growth Patterns." *Applied Cognitive Psychology* (forthcoming).

Thomas, Lauren J., Sophie O'Ferrall, and Antoinette Caird-Daley. *Evacuation Commands for Optimal Passenger Management*. ATSB Report B2004/0239. Canberra City: Australian Transport Safety Bureau, 2006.

United Nations Department of Economic and Social Affairs. *World Urbanization Prospects: The 2005 Revision*. New York: United Nations, 2006.

Vaught, Charles et al. *Behavioral and Organizational Dimensions of Underground Mine Fires*. U.S. Dept. of Health and Human Services, 2000.

Volgyesi, F. A. *Hypnosis of Man and Animals*. Baltimore: Williams & Wilkins, 1966.

Wall, Joseph Frazier. *Andrew Carnegie*. Pittsburgh: University of Pittsburgh Press, 1989.

Weinstein, Neil. "Unrealistic Optimism About Susceptibility to Health Problems: Conclusions from a Community-wide Sample." *Journal of Behavioral Medicine* 10, no. 5 (1987).

"When You Suddenly Become a Celebrity." *The Washingtonian*, Sept. 1984, 148–149.

"Young Polish Man's Dream of New Life Ends in Tragedy." *Wexford People*, Feb. 15, 2007, General News Section.

Index